The Decline and Fall of the Roman Church

THE
DECLINE
AND FALL
OF THE
ROMAN
CHURCH

MALACHI MARTIN

Secker & Warburg
London

Library of Congress Cataloging in Publication Data

First published in England in 1982 by
Martin Secker & Warburg Limited
54 Poland Street, London W1V 3DF

Copyright © 1981 by Malachi Martin Enterprises, Ltd.

ISBN: 0-436-27336-5

Printed in the United States of America

For Tia and Alexandra

Contents

The Decline and Fall of the Roman Church

The Breakdown

The most surprising and the most puzzling development in the last twenty years has been the sudden and undoubted decline of the Church of Rome in its ecclesiastical organization and ideological unity. The sheer suddenness of this development makes the decline catastrophic. And catastrophe may be exceeded by demoralizing horror, as near-future television viewers sit in their living rooms and helplessly watch the public assassination of a pope, and contemplate the once majestic dome of St. Peter's shattered and ruined by the well-placed explosives of international demolition experts.

As things now stand, there appears to be no reasonable hope that this decline can be arrested, and no reasonable expectation that the present organizational structure of this venerable Church can outlive our century. What form Roman Catholicism will take—its religious spirit and faith will not die, nor will a successor to St. Peter's throne ever lack—is one of the tantalizing enigmas we moderns will not live to see solved.

The relevant statistics and other details are horrendous for the traditional Roman Catholic mind. When plotted on a graph covering the years 1965-80, the number of priests, nuns, religious brothers, monks, junior and senior high school students, private college students, baptisms, conversions, inter-Catholic marriages, communions, confessions, confirmations—every significant statistic available—describes a plummeting, nonstop, downward drop. Added to these key factors are the figures of those

Roman Catholics who totally reject Roman teaching about divorce, contraception, abortion, homosexuality, and Communism.

There are, furthermore, some "invisible" but nonetheless potent factors. For instance, it is now impossible to reckon how many validly ordained priests are available. For, certainly, many bishops ordaining candidates for the priesthood have no intention of creating priests with the sacramental powers to offer the sacrifice of the Mass and to absolve penitents of sins, and many candidates do not have the intention of receiving such powers. Without such powers, there is no priesthood, no Mass, no absolution in confession. Such lack of validity, although unvalued outside the church, means the death of the church for the Roman Catholic mind.

The preceding figures may be appalling, but they are not so indicative as the overall fracture of the vast Roman Catholic body. The approximately 740 million Roman Catholics in the world represent the biggest, the richest, the best educated, the most influential single sector of the world's religious population. Their church is headed by the oldest and one of the most prestigious chancelleries in the world—the Vatican. Yet, on the issues of war and peace, hunger and plenty, depression and progress, this powerful Catholic body is of no appreciable weight and wields no specifically Roman Catholic influence. In fact, the Roman Catholic body is split down the middle between Communist and capitalist causes. And this is more surprising than the sharp decline in worship and internal loyalty, because a relatively short time ago the Roman Catholic Church was a power to be reckoned with in the international political and ideological field.

This decline, although apparent only in the last twenty years, has been a very long time in the making. In hindsight, we today can say that one could have predicted it some four hundred years ago. For by then, the Roman institution had tried a thousand-year-long experiment. And the experiment had finally failed because the institution was found wanting. It had attempted total invasion of the political and social as well as the cultural fields of human endeavor. And, in the doing, it had abandoned specifically Roman Catholic as well as general Christian principles. It had accepted purely secular categories.

A small and little noticed incident in late 1979 underscored this failure of the Roman institution. On November 3, sixty-three American hostages were taken at the Teheran Embassy by the revolutionary cadres of the Ayatollah Khomeini. John Paul II instructed his Teheran representative, Archbishop Annibale Bugnini, to intercede in his name with the Ayatollah for the release of the hostages. But it was all to no avail.

"I am surprised," the Ayatollah admonished Bugnini, "that only now does the great Pope want to see hostages freed . . . the great Pope did not intervene for us when the Shah oppressed our people . . . you Christians do not behave like Christ . . . we expected you to do what Jesus would have done . . . for he would certainly have protested against the Shah's oppression . . . why has the great Pope and his Christians behaved like that . . . ?"

Of course, while Khomeini was pointing the finger at the abuse of Vatican power, he did not address one crucial underlying question: Should *any* religious institution, whether the Roman Church or Islam, wield any secular power at all? The Ayatollah dare not raise the question, because for him, secular and spiritual power are identical, separate manifestations of the single seamless power of Allah. This had never been the case in the early Christian church.

For the first 250 years of the church's existence, there was no doubt in churchmen's minds about the answer to the question that the Ayatollah asked. The power of the church, they knew, was solely and purely spiritual. They remembered the word that had been most frequently on the lips of Jesus in order to describe the new state of affairs he was inaugurating: the "Kingdom of God," the "Kingdom of Heaven." And they drew their understanding of what Jesus had meant from a recorded exchange between him and the Roman governor, Pontius Pilate, who had condemned him to die.

"Are you then a king?" Pilate had asked.

"I am. But my kingdom is not of this world. If it were like any other kingdom in this world, my servants would certainly have sought to free me. . . ."

Between the death of Simon Peter the Apostle in A.D. 67, and the year 312, there were thirty-one popes, successors to Peter as bishops of Rome.

13

Not one of the first eighteen popes died in his bed. All perished violently. While he lived, each of the first thirty-one popes wielded the authority of that spiritual kingdom, and taught what his predecessor had taught before him: Abide in the kingdom of God's spirit. Wait for the return of Jesus, the final end of this visible world, and the ultimate triumph of God's rule.

In the year 312, the Roman emperor, Constantine, became a Christian and, ten years later, established Christianity as the religion of the empire. For most of the following 1,650 years, Christianity was the most important political and social factor in Europe. During most of that time, the Roman pope was the most important personage in Europe and the Western world.

By the early Renaissance, the church that Jesus had started was incarnated in a highly specified institution: a hierarchic church, centralized in its government, absolute in its authority and its claims on all authority, with few elective and mostly appointive offices, and reflecting the traits of a kingdom as men had always known a kingdom to be: "a political and social order anchored in preset ideals and ideas, a hierarchical pattern of structures by which it is sustained, the sublimation of social and other group interests, organic growth, a reliance on tradition in order to safeguard and hallow its symbols, vigorous defense against threats from outside, and protection of peace within, both materially and in terms of ideas." So Eric M. de Saventhem recently defined "kingdom." That is how the Christian church evolved in Rome.

But from the time the popes entered the temporal arena, heavy and irremovable chains were forged around their churchly kingdom. They threw their friendship and their influence and their spiritual power to one side or another, and the chains started to form and to choke. In time the popes became some of the greatest power-brokers among men; and, until our day, they have never abdicated that role. Not really; indeed, far from it. It became almost an article of faith that the popes had to be engaged in public affairs—*"gli affari publici,"* as the phrase of the Italianate bureaucracy of the church put it—and that these affairs should be their everyday concern. Even when specifically Christian values were at stake, the popes had to take into consideration diplomatic niceties, club obligations, political alliances, cultural affiliations, territorial claims, financial interests, personal ambitions, family motives, and dynastic aspirations.

The lives of past popes sometimes illustrate how low the weight of those chains could bring churchmen who preached the supreme law of love and the highest moral ideals. But, in cameo after cameo, history also reveals that various popes had opportunities to rid the church of its temporal power and wealth, to stand naked of all human and secular protection, to rely only on the promise made by Jesus that his church would never fail, and to employ the only power Jesus authorized them—the power of the spirit. Usually, such opportunities arose as a disastrous result of pontiffs playing power politics just like secular leaders. On each such occasion, however, we find that the Roman leaders refused the invitation, retreating in horror and confusion from the edge of the precipice. The worst of them fought—and to a large extent succeeded—in reacquiring whatever power they had lost. The best of them—a Pius IX or a Pius XII, for instance—never wholly surrendered the use of power. And the general practice of popes over the centuries has been to try to regain whatever lost power they could.

Yet always within the church—right from the day the bargain was first struck with the Roman emperors in the year 312—there has been a lingering, if usually submerged, desire to sever that fateful linkage with power by those who saw it as fatally compromising the church's spiritual mission. The great Florentine poet Dante Alighieri in *The Inferno* concentrated the issue in a few short lines about Pope Silvester I, "the first rich father," who made the agreement with Emperor Constantine that in an instant changed the church from being the prey of civil authority into its moral and spiritual prop:

> *Ahi! Costatin! Di quanto mal fu matre*
> *Non la tua conversion, ma quella dote*
> *Che da te presse il primo rico patre!*
> Alas! Constantine! What evil you bore into the world!

15

Not by your conversion, but by that dowry
Which the first rich father took from you!

For Dante, as for other laymen and clerics down the centuries, in play-ing the lion, the lamb would always and only make an ass of itself.

RAGS
TO
RICHES

Pontian Who Waited for Jesus

If you want to know what the church of Jesus was once like—and could become again—and what once preoccupied all the attention of Peter's successors, look at a man called Pontian.

Two hundred years after Jesus announced his church and named Peter as its leader, the Christians of Rome, as they had been from their beginnings, were hoping and anxiously waiting for Jesus to reappear, triumph over their enemies, and bless them with eternal happiness. They hoped firmly in that triumph and that blessing, which they now felt were long past due.

For Peter had told them, "The end of the world is at hand . . . set your hopes on the moment when Jesus appears." They also remembered that, when Peter was about to die, he had appointed a slave, Linus, as his successor so that, he told the Christians, "You will be reminded of what I preach." And when Linus came to die, he appointed a man called Cletus with the consent of the whole group. So it went. There was always one man endowed with Peter's central job as pope—the word is a translation into English of the Italian "papa," which is an abbreviation of *pater patruum*, meaning "father of fathers" or "principal father."

Somewhere between Clement's successor, Evaristus, and a pope called Hyginus (the eighth successor of Peter), the whole group of Roman Christians did the appointing of their head—probably because the incumbent leader, or pope, had been taken away to be killed without warning. When that happened, as it often did, the Christians called on their remembrance of what the early followers of Jesus had done when Judas Iscariot left them: they gathered together, prayed a little, then held a one-man one-vote election to replace the suicide, accepting the outcome as the decision of Jesus, because he had told them through Peter, "Whatever you allow on earth will be what Heaven allows." So the election process in the Roman group was equally simple, and had only two conditions: only Roman Christians—men *and* women, by the way—could vote, and only a citizen of Rome could be chosen. This simple election process was followed in the early centuries whenever a dying pope did not nominate his successor.

Once a new successor to Peter had been chosen by appointment or election, the news went out by word of mouth or smuggled letter: "Clement is dead. Evaristus is our choice." . . . "Sixtus is dead. Telesphorus is our choice." . . . So it always went. The other Christian communities around the Mediterranean had to know because all of them looked to Peter's group as keepers of that special power Jesus had promised Peter when he spoke to him near Hermon in the Holy Land. Their only hope lay in that power. No other power was available to them. So in the year 230, the word went out: "Urban is dead. Pontian is our choice."

From the start, Pontian had his hands full. Personally, of course, as a Christian his outlook was bleak. At any moment of day or night, he could be killed on the spot; Roman law permitted this. Or he could be arrested, imprisoned, then killed in prison or paraded in the Roman stadium to be eaten by animals to the delight of as many as 80,000 screaming fans, or be sent to work and to die in Roman mines somewhere around the Mediterranean. But outside of certain short periods, it had been like that ever since he was born into a family of slaves. Trained as a shorthand secretary, given his freedom by a grateful master, converted to Christianity in his teens, ordained priest at the age of twenty, he worked under four popes (Victor, Zephyrinus, Callistus, and Urban), each one of whom he saw cut down and killed. Yet Pontian's chief headache came not from the ever-present threat of sudden and violent death, but from another Christian called Hippolytus.

Two more different men there could not be. Pontian was big, bulky,

slow, sure, prudent, not well educated, rather unimaginative, but certainly a compassionate man grounded in Christian belief, and—like many
pious people—of an obstinate, unbreakable will. Hippolytus, three years
older than Pontian, was a Greek born in Alexandria, Egypt, educated in
Athens and Rome, small in size, fierce and combative in manner, with a
nimble imagination and subtle mind, widely read, multilingual, with little understanding for the weaknesses of less-endowed people, and carried
forward by a deep sense of his own mission. Hippolytus was made by
nature to be distrusted by a man like Pontian. Pontian was made to be
despised by a man like Hippolytus. A clash between them was almost
inevitable. And when it took place, it reminds us in many ways of the
clash between Pope Paul VI and the traditionalist French Archbishop
Marcel Lefebvre in the twentieth century, who denounced Paul as corrupt and unworthy, just as the Rome of Pontian's time was eerily similar
to the Rome of Paul VI and today.

In Pontian's time, the old Roman world was dying and with it the ideal
of the *Pax Romana*, the Roman peace created by the universally applied
Roman law. Paul VI was one of the first to point out that the end of the
twentieth century would see the old world of monolithic Roman Catholicism disappearing while its solid moorings within a capitalist Western
Europe were being cut. Pontian's Roman world, like the late twentieth-
century Roman Catholic world, was dying in a welter of new creeds,
ready-made messiahs, exotic urges, economic crises, civil disturbances,
and political revolutions, and in a maelstrom of conflicting theories and
utterly new alternatives for Christians.

We wonder today at the mixture of ideas, philosophies, crazes, and
movements led by quite extraordinary figures, which envelops our world.
But the world of Pontian and his Rome was just as confusing. From
Egypt, Syria, Persia, Palestine, Mesopotamia, Greece, Gaul, Britain,
Germany, and Africa—from all the farflung colonies of Rome, and
beyond—there poured into Rome a flood of fortune-seeking, quick-think-
ing, exotic astrologists, herbologists, magicians, literateurs, musicians,
theologians, theosophists, physicians. Public and secret cults, new doctrines, groupies of all kinds mushroomed—and died—almost literally
overnight.

21

The established religion of ancient Rome and the new Christian religion were both affected. The old Roman gods were soon jostling for room in the Pantheon with a motley crowd of new figures: Jupiter and Hera and Apollo with Phrygian faun-gods, Nilotic cat-goddesses, Gnostic beings, sub-Saharan leopard-powers, Indian elephant-demons, Celtic seahorse-fairies, Germanic bird-gods, and Asiatic she-devils waving a thousand arms and legs. The old civic religion of Rome was bastardized. Schools, public disputations, study groups, pamphlets, plays, poems, books, histories, sects, lectures, mystics, warlocks, alchemists, transformed the old solid order into a viscous mass ever in ferment, ever ebullient, ever diffusing.

Runaway inflation, government price-fixing, unfavorable export-import balances, heavy taxes, unemployment, increased crime, all exacerbated the conditions of living. The Christians of Pontian's time could not escape being affected by it all. It was in the air.

Even in that small cosmos of Rome, and when Christians did not number more that 70,000 in the whole world, Christianity was racked by the conflicting theories and theologies of self-appointed messiahs, just as today the ancient teaching of Rome is being dissected and transformed by the "new" theologians, by renewal groups, and simply by the changes in society. Just as today, there seemed to be no answers in Pontian's time, only the clashes of extraordinarily active minds and charismatic personalities: Valentinian, the high priest of cosmic consciousness, Hegisippus (the first of the Jews for Jesus), Marcion the ferocious Unitarian, the cynical Semitic scholar Tatian, Justin the Greek philosopher, Aristides the humanist Athenian, Tertullian the Charismatic, the Bible-quoting Origen, Irenaeus the polemicist, and scores of others, all disputing and praying and squabbling and anathematizing each other, but all standing in a common danger of death because they were Christian. Hans Küng, Malcolm Boyd, Andrew Greeley, Billy Graham, Marcel Lefebvre, Teilhard de Chardin would all have been at home in that stewpot of ancient Christianity.

The old-timers of Pontian's time—led by Hippolytus—were stern in morality, unbending in logic, and intolerant of any opposition. They fought any change or any immersion in the new modes of thought and living. A second, progressive group lapped up the new theories. They saw nothing wrong in likening Jesus to some African or Egyptian godlet, and they translated the Gospel message into social grouping, sexual liberty, or esoteric philosophy.

In between stood popes like Pontian and his immediate predecessors, Callistus and Urban and Victor. They would not permit any deviation from basic belief in Jesus as sole savior and in his church as the sole means of salvation. But they continually adapted the church and Jesus' salvation to changing circumstances.

It was about one of these supposed adaptations that Pontian and Hippolytus clashed. It started before Pontian became pope. Originally, anyone guilty of sins like denying the faith, fornication, or adultery had been expelled forever from the church on the ground that, as Peter had said, Jesus would soon come again and the body of the church must be kept entirely pure in expectation of this. But Callistus, as well as popes before him, decided that these sins did *not* warrant perpetual exclusion. After all, more than two hundred years had passed; the return of Jesus might not be as imminent as all that. There was *time* to repent. Moreover, by his own example, Jesus had shown that he desired the salvation of all sinners—even Christians who had sinned. So Pope Callistus decided.

"Blasphemy!" thundered Hippolytus. "Once you're out, you're out!"

When Callistus decreed absolution for repentant prostitutes and adulterers, Hippolytus wrote sarcastically in a pamphlet: "Where is he going to hang up the decree? On the doorposts of brothels?" Hippolytus and his followers were so sure that Callistus was corrupt and wrong that they declared Callistus no longer to be pope, and chose Hippolytus as the new pope. Hippolytus thus became the first of a line of people whom the church later called anti-popes—men who, the church decided, had not been validly elected.

The mass of Christians, however, still accepted Callistus, and when Callistus was killed in a streetscuffle between Christians and pagans, and his successor, Urban I, was quickly arrested and killed by the Roman authorities, Pontian was chosen pope. Hippolytus went after Pontian hammer and tongs just as he had attacked and vilified Callistus. Pontian's answer would doubtless have been simple and something like: "To Peter,

23

Jesus said: 'You are Peter. On you I build my church.' How can you, Hippolytus, claim to be faithful to the church of Jesus when you attack the rock on which Jesus built it?"

This acrid dispute was abruptly halted by an event familiar to all Christians of that era: sudden persecution by the Roman authorities. On September 27, 235, an edict came from the new emperor, Maximinus: Arrest all the Christian leaders—priests, deacons, scholars, bishops, all! Burn all their buildings. Close all their cemeteries. Confiscate their personal wealth. (During periods of guarded toleration, Christians were permitted to bury their dead in certain specified places, and even to live in society, but not to own property.)

Maximinus, nicknamed "Thrax" (meaning a man from Thrace, as well as something else quite obscene), was a huge, uneducated shepherd who had hacked his way to the top from being a sergeant in the Roman army. His motives for moving against Christians were multiple. He needed soldiers, and the Christians refused to fight with him. Individual Christians had a certain amount of wealth; he needed all he could get. He also needed scapegoats because his murder of the previous emperor, Alexander, and Alexander's mother Mamea, had caused a tremendous furor. Maximinus needed to blame someone, and the Christians were ready at hand.

Pontian was picked up by Maximinus's guards on that September 27, 235, and thrown into the Mamertine Prison. The next day, the sixty-seven-year-old Pontian abdicated in favor of a man called Anterus, who automatically became pope according to accepted custom. In the meanwhile, the seventy-year-old Hippolytus, as a long-standing and prominent Christian, was also arrested, on September 29, and immediately shipped off to the lead mines on Sardinia. Back in Rome, Pontian was tortured for about ten days in the hope that he would inform on other Christian leaders (he did not), and then he too was condemned to the Sardinian mines, where he arrived about October 12. It was Pontian's first (and last) sea trip. Besides hunger and thirst, he had to contend with the wounds of his tortures, a grueling seasickness, the humiliation of his chains, and the almost animal desperation of his fellow convicts. But Sardinia was the end.

All things considered, in the year 235 there was no more unhealthy, more inhospitable, more alien, more joyless, more lethal, and therefore more likely place for a pope and his anti-pope to have a face-to-face confrontation and reconciliation than the island of Sardinia. Sardinia was two-thirds rolling plateaus with a tabular skyline punctuated by one main 6,017-foot mountain, Gennargentu. To the north, the northeast, and the northwest of this mountain there was fertile land, rich vegetation, and bearable conditions. But southwestward from Gennargentu lay a sinister arch, triangular in shape, sixty miles at its widest between the gulfs of Oristano and Cagliari.

Here it was a different story. As the only genuine lowland in Sardinia, it was hot and humid in the summer, cold and windy in the winter. It was treeless, its basalt plain unsuitable for pasture or agriculture, but rich in lead mines. It was precisely and only into this area that Christians were allowed to come from Rome. In fact, they had no choice: the Roman authorities transported them here as criminals and felons condemned "*in metallum* (to the mines)," much as the British transported their undesirables to Australia and the French theirs to Devil's Island.

There were three kinds of human beings in Sardinia at this time. There were the Roman garrisons at Caralis (modern Cagliari) and Othoca (modern Oristano) with their families and slaves. There were, also, the natives—a mixture of Phoenician, Asiatic, Greek, Berber, and Philistine, who skulked in the hills and lived to kill or be killed by the Romans. And, then, there were the prison gangs, criminals and political prisoners sentenced to hard labor in the mines. In Roman street slang, to tell someone to go *in metallu* was the equivalent to our "Go to hell!" The minimum sentence was ten years, and only the rare few served out their time. Still fewer escaped. Neither Pontian nor Hippolytus was to last long. From the beginning, they were both marked men.

When Pontian and his fellow-convicts arrived at Othoca in the early morning, they were herded ashore and force-marched to the mining area just outside the village of Metalla. The land all around was bare, dotted with hundreds of stone towers, dolmens, and rough obelisks (menhirs), the relics of an earlier culture. The nearest cities, Sulcis and Neapolis, were thirty miles away on either side of Metalla.

Here they were all—men and women—properly inducted as slave miners: the left eye was gouged out with a dagger and the socket cauterized with molten iron; the joints of the left foot were burnt; and one nerve at the back of the right knee was sliced. All males under thirty years were castrated. Then, when all had been branded with a number on the forehead, each one was manacled in the slave-miners' fashion: iron rings were soldered around the ankles and linked together by a six-inch chain; then a tight chain was placed around the waist (prisoners lost weight rapidly, so the chain had to catch at the hip-bones); this chain was attached by a third chain to the ankle-chain in such a way that the prisoner could never straighten up again. He had to bend down anyway for twenty out of the twenty-four hours per day. No locks were used; all chains were soldered permanently.

Immediately on being chained and branded, each prisoner was tied to one of the rough obelisks and given sixty strokes of the lash, then handed a pick and shovel, and sent to work in the mine. The system always worked the way it was supposed to work. By that first nightfall, the weaker had died, and only the stronger survived. Of each new slave contingent, two-thirds usually made it to the first evening.

Henceforward, they neither shaved, washed, cut their hair or finger and toenails, were not supplied with more clothes, got one meal of coarse bread and water per day, worked four five-hour shifts, had a daily assigned work load, and slept on the ground in their own filth. Prisoners generally lasted a surprising six to fourteen months, after which they died from disease (arthritis, tuberculosis, heartfailure were the common killers), exhaustion, malnutrition, beatings, or infection of some kind. Some were killed by fellow-convicts. Others committed suicide (usually by stuffing their nostrils and throat with earth during the four one-hour rest periods allowed). Some went mad with superstitious fear when thrust by their guards into the "houses of witches," as the caves where they slept were called. These were artificial grottoes and shrines dug out of the rock by an earlier Sardinian people and adorned with crude male and female forms. The guards were Roman mercenaries, mainly Asiatics, who spoke no Latin, no Greek, no Aramaic, no Gaulish, no German nor any language generally known in the empire. Communication between masters and slaves was one-way, and only by blows. Mad or ailing or crippled or malingering prisoners were killed without hesitation. It was a perfect system for brutalizing and dehumanizing. And it was a costless, profitable labor force to boot: the lead supplies kept coming.

It was only at night that Pontian and Hippolytus could have gotten together (and their first meeting would have been a surprise to both, because each thought the other dead). It must have taken place between Pontian's arrival in October and the following January when both were killed. But it is likely, virtually certain, that they did meet, because Hippolytus's reconciliation with Pontian was later confirmed when the church declared that Hippolytus was a saint.

Evidently Pontian was able to persuade Hippolytus that Pontian, as Peter's successor, did have the authority to decide who should be readmitted to the Christian fellowship, and that Hippolytus would have to tolerate it even if he didn't like it.

Late in January of 236, the grapevine probably informed the two men that they were both to be killed. Incoming Christian slaves told them that Pope Anterus had been martyred and buried already in the cemetery of Callistus. On his death, the priests and people assembled to elect his successor. An ordinary laboring man, a Roman freedman from Ostia, Fabian by name, happened to be in Rome collecting manure for his master. He went, as was his Christian right, to the electing assembly. When he entered there, everyone saw a white dove alight on his head. Taking this as a sign of God's will, they forthwith confirmed Fabian as pope. Fabian was a layman, so they ordained him priest and consecrated him bishop.

A few days later Pontian and Hippolytus were killed. It would have happened like this: the soldiers would have separated them from the file of prisoners and flung them to the ground. Then they would have been thrashed with a stock, and a guard, with one stroke of his short broadsword, would have practically severed the head of each from his shoulders. The stroke came always at the left side in order to cut the jugular vein. The dogs would have crowded around delightedly, pawing at the dying men's faces and necks as they lapped up the warm blood. If either of them had shaken, or had a spasm, the dogs would have bitten and

27

worried them until they were still. When all the slaves were at work, a burial detail would have come, shoved their carcasses onto a flat board, carried them over to the cesspool, and tossed them in.

About ten days later, in early February, three Romans arrive with the morning transports. They are freedmen, insolent with the pride of the typical Roman citizen. They treat the mine officials with the same attitude of disdain that any decent Roman treats civil servants exiled to work for the government in godforsaken places like Sardinia. They are actually crypto-Christians and come provided with forged papers purporting to be orders from the governor of Rome to deliver the remains of prisoners Pontian and Hippolytus into the custody of the bearers of these letters. The seal and the signature on the documents seem official. Anyway, who cares? The remains are fished out of the cesspool, washed, wrapped in canvas, and loaded on the evening boat. By February end, the remains of Hippolytus are buried in a Roman cemetery for martyrs. Pontian's remains are buried with those of other popes in the cemetery of Callistus on the Appian Way.

The life, the pontificate, and death of Pontian were concluded (as Pontian would no doubt have died believing) in Peter's tradition. He had reconciled one individual, Hippolytus (and with him, all Hippolytus's followers), to Christian unity. He would have seen this as an exercise of Peter's spiritual power and authority: to allow and to forbid in the dimension of spirit. And, all in all, Pontian had been preoccupied with the one area that he and all Christians saw as officially and uniquely his: the integrity of the church and the spiritual good of his fellow-men.

The First
Rich Father

Hippolytus would not have believed it. Pontian might have. Exactly one hundred years and fourteen popes after those two men were killed and thrown into a Sardinian cesspool, the thirty-third pope since Peter, Silvester I, died. Died old. Died peacefully. Died in a real bed, and a comfortable bed, too, placed in an upper room of the huge Roman Lateran Palace. And, sure enough, around that palace were Roman guards standing watch. Beside each one, the traditional emblem of the Roman army, the Roman eagle—but now topped by a new sign: an X and a P, the first two letters of the Greek name XPISTOS, Christ.

Around Silvester himself were brightly clothed clerics, bishops and priests, and when he died his body was washed reverently, dressed in ceremonial robes, placed in an expensive casket, carried in solemn procession through the streets of Rome, and buried with all honor and ceremony in the presence of Roman magistrates, generals, nobles, officers, soldiers, important officials, and the mass of the Roman people.

No torture now. No rude mercenaries. No dogs. No wooden slabs. No cesspool burials. A far cry from all that, and the first remote steps have been taken in the vast change that will lead to the world we live in. Had Silvester died more or less as Pontian had, we would probably have inherited a world as different from our actual one as Sunset Boulevard is from Jokhang Plaza in Lhasa, Tibet.

These changes are not only in Rome. Travel through the entire Roman

Empire of that time—all of Italy, France, Portugal, most of Spain, Belgium, half of England, part of Germany, all of Yugoslavia and Greece and Turkey, Palestine, North Africa. Everywhere on the Roman roads, you meet Christian clerics traveling under armed escort and treated with respect. In fact, although it is still very much a pagan world, you find clerics everywhere, bishops and priests and deacons, in honored positions, with churches, schools, shrines, and houses of their own. In cities and towns, there are even streets named after Christian martyrs. Major urban centers still have amphitheaters but nobody is fed to lions any longer— least of all Christians. In bookstores, you can buy Christian books. In local courts of justice, felons are still executed but never crucified according to the old Roman custom: now they are beheaded, burned, stabbed, or garroted. Crucifixion is the way Jesus died, and it is now forbidden that anyone else die the same way. And the most radical change is the honor, civil and national, given to clerics and their ceremonies.

What on earth had happened? Hadn't it been the idea that nothing would reconcile Christians to the world around them until Jesus returned and gave them the triumph and the blessing? And the Roman authorities? What had happened to them? Not even twenty-five years before Silvester's comfortable death, those same authorities were still burning Christians, feeding them to wild animals, hunting them down like mad dogs. What on *earth* had happened?

A mere handful of mortal men were the principal actors in the extraordinary drama that changed the Christian church almost beyond recognition: two popes, one emperor, one religious zealot, and a few Jewish Christians from the mother church in Jerusalem. The popes were Miltiades, who feared the change, and Silvester, who envisioned a new order. The emperor was Constantine, who saw the sign of the cross in the sky and ever after rode under that banner. And the religious fanatic was Donatus.

Every Christian church that exists today, from the ancient communions of Roman Catholicism and Eastern Orthodoxy to the most recent ones, was made possible by what these men did. Furthermore, what they did, however modified over the centuries by other popes, other fanatics, other emperors, endured and in fact is the very heart of the present crisis in Roman Catholicism—a crisis that will soon decide the fate of the church and the fate of all Christianity.

Four scenes comprise the drama:

1. A Generous Offer

It is October 28 in the year 312. The pope, the undersized Miltiades with his chocolate-brown face and coal-black eyes, emerges timidly from the back of a small private house in an obscure street of the popular Trastevere district of Rome. With him is his chief priest, Silvester, fifty-nine. Outside in the bright sunshine stands the six-foot Emperor Constantine with pale, square face, blue eyes, and bull neck, his horse by his side, his guards around him with drawn swords. Emperor, guards, horses, all are stained with blood, dust, and sweat. They have just fought and won a key battle at one of Rome's principal bridges, the Milvian. The victory assures Constantine's crown. And Constantine's first action, even before taking possession of the city, is to persuade Christians he knows to take him to this obscure little man, the head of Rome's Christians, their bishop.

Miltiades, sixty-two, is of Greek and Berber parentage, culturally limited, fluent only in street Latin and a North African Greek dialect. He has spent all his adult years in mortal danger of arrest and execution. Knowledgeable only in Christian theology, he has absolutely nothing in common with the thirty-one-year-old Constantine, the warrior-king of German race, a pagan who has already traveled and fought all over the known world from the Scottish borders to the Rhine in Germany and as far east as the Black Sea. Constantine has lived at the imperial court, speaks Latin, Greek, Pict, Gaulish, Frankish, and at least one Asiatic dialect. He has always been fighting battles or administering imperial governments. He is now, by the might of his own hand, emperor of the West. The most powerful man in Miltiades's world.

Even Miltiades's "cockney" Latin would have been difficult for Constantine, with its slurred consonants, wide vowels, and African idioms. And Constantine's court Latin—clipped, correct, lapidary—would have baffled Miltiades.

31

But the fundamental barrier separating the two men is Miltiades's Christian attitudes. For Miltiades, this world and its power are the enemy, to be shunned. Poverty, suffering, martyrdom—that is the Christian's portion, to be embraced. So Miltiades is wary. What can the emperor want from him? Again, the conversations were not recorded, but soon the positions were known.

Silvester, a Roman who speaks educated Latin, interprets between the two men.

Constantine wastes no words. He is a decisive man and he has made a decision. He has just won a great victory, and he attributes it to Christ's intervention. So he has immediately determined to utterly reverse the empire's policy toward Christianity and Christians. All this he quickly announces. Then he has some questions: Where are the bones of Peter and Paul? The nails that crucified Christ? The cross itself? Who will succeed Miltiades as bishop of Rome?

The bones of the apostles, Miltiades answers, are in the old cemetery on the Vatican Hill at a certain well-known spot.

The nails, the three of them, were brought to Italy by Peter, Miltiades goes on. They were kept in the upper back room of a house in the town of Herculaneum until the eruption of Vesuvius in A.D. 79; then they were brought to Rome and kept in the house of Peter. Yes, the nails could be here tomorrow for the emperor. Miltiades doesn't like any of this, but sees no way to evade it. As to the cross of Jesus, no one knows where it is. And he himself will appoint his successor, if there is need for one (that is, if Christ has not come again) and he is able to, Miltiades concludes; otherwise the Christians of Rome will choose someone.

Constantine explains himself more fully. On the previous evening when preparing his troops for battle, he saw a sign: the cross of Jesus superimposed over the evening sun. And a mysterious voice, much like the voice Paul heard on the road to Damascus, spoke to the emperor saying: "In this sign you will conquer." That was last night. This morning, he went into battle with that sign roughly painted on shields and horses' heads. He won the battle of the Milvian Bridge by the power of that sign, he is convinced. He won it as an apostle of Jesus. And now he wants to put one of the nails from that cross of Jesus on his crown to signify that he is going to rule the empire in the name of Jesus. Another nail he will make into the bit for his horse. In Christ's name, he will ride that horse into battle against all enemies of Christ and of Christ's representative, the bishop of Rome. "I am now the servant of the highest divinity," Constantine concludes in his stilted Latin.

To the old pope he says: "In the future, we as the apostle of Christ will help choose the bishop of Rome." Then he leaves.

The following day at dawn, Constantine is back, accompanied by his wife of four years, Fausta, and by his mother, Helena, a Christian who had told her son of the new church and had opened his mind to its possibilities. Pope Miltiades and Silvester ride with them to the Vatican Hill, past the stadium of Caligula and the temples of Apollo and Cybele.

Near the top is a Roman cemetery, and at one spot in that cemetery there is a little stone or *tropeum,* the trophy or "memory" of Peter, marking where the apostle was killed and later buried. The remains of the Apostle Paul had been brought here from the place on the road to Ostia where he had been killed, about a mile from the city, and also buried alongside those of Peter. Here Constantine kneels and prays. Then he rises and walks around the cemetery, measuring off the area in paces. He stops at a small mausoleum and peers in, then beckons to Silvester and Miltiades to look at the ceiling mosaic; it is a picture of Helios, the Roman sun-god, in a white chariot drawn by five white horses, as a representation of Jesus, the sun of salvation. The walls of the mausoleum are covered with mosaics depicting Jesus as the Good Shepherd and as the Fisherman of Souls.

Then he tells them of his plans to build a basilica dedicated to Peter on that very spot. The bones of the Apostle Paul must be removed from here and placed at the spot where he was killed. Over them he will build another basilica.

Miltiades nods, but he is too dazed to answer. The idea of a Christian basilica is too much for him. All his life, he has only known the little churches and chapels, the "dominica" houses of the Lord—really little back rooms. For Miltiades a basilica has always been a pagan building in whose central portion, the apse, there was the *Augusteum,* a place filled with the statues of the emperors who were worshiped as divinities by the Romans. For Miltiades, a Christian basilica is a square circle, and he

33

will never change, never accept the emperor turning everything upside down and making the world a pleasant and easy place for Christians.

But Silvester has another view: perhaps this Constantine could serve in Jesus' plan of universal salvation.

From the Vatican Hill, the party proceeds over to the Lateran Hill. All the palaces and houses here once belonged to the great ancient Roman family of Laterani. Now, one palace, the largest, is the property of Constantine's queen, Fausta—part of her dowry as daughter of the Emperor Maximilian. The ceremony between Constantine and Miltiades here is simple. Constantine throws open the main doors, and states sonorously: "Henceforth, this is the House of Miltiades and of every successor of the blessed apostle, Peter."

Then they return to Miltiades's house, where the nails from the cross of Jesus are awaiting them. Constantine takes two. The third will remain with Miltiades.

There are a few more words between the emperor and the pope. Then Constantine rides off. He has battles to fight and an empire to consolidate. His parting words are for Silvester: "The Godhead," he says, "wills us two to do great things in the name of Christ. Be here when we return."

By January of 314, only fifteen months later, the frail Miltiades is dead. He dies without ever having changed his mind. Lands and buildings given to the church by Constantine he could accept. But he could not accept a Christianity sanctioned and propagated by civil and military power.

Silvester, however, by now has seen a new form for the Church: it could spread by means of Roman roads, Roman arms, Roman law, Roman power. The world would belong to Jesus entirely. Thus the triumph and the blessing could be prepared. Besides, Silvester remembers, no one knows when Jesus will reappear. Therefore, why not make straight the way of the Lord?

2. The Dowry—and Its Curse

A month after Miltiades's death, Constantine returns to Rome and assembles all Christians—priests, deacons, people. He tells them simply:

"We have chosen to approve of Silvester as successor to Miltiades and to Peter the Apostle, as representative of Jesus the Christ." The assembly of Christians confirms the emperor's choice.

After his coronation—Silvester is the first pope to be crowned like a temporal prince—Silvester sits down in the Lateran Palace with Constantine. It is the first and last time the two men will talk together at any length. They have decisions to make.

Constantine makes a full confession of his whole life, asking for Silvester's advice and the forgiveness of Christ for his sins.

Silvester takes the first step toward a genuinely universal church. He accepts an alliance between church and empire, so that the church can spread everywhere.

The 232 successors to Silvester will never modify or deviate from that fateful step. From that day to this their spiritual power will be entangled in temporal alliances. Essentially, obstinately, blindly, they will stand in Silvester's shoes down to the late twentieth century. We have accounts—although only secondhand—of the conversation between pope and emperor, but those accounts seem to agree on essentials.

Constantine pours out his worries: spiritually, he feels filthy and diseased—"like a leper." For men of his time, the epitome of untouchable uncleanliness was leprosy. From his birth in A.D. 280 until that October evening last year, the emperor states, he never knew Christ Jesus. Now he has been privileged to become the apostle of Christ. What do I do as emperor? Do I dismantle the old religion of Rome? Do I destroy what is Roman? I believe in the sign of Jesus, his cross. Should I receive baptism now? Shall I be immortal like Alexander the Great? What do I do? Tradition tells that Constantine cried tears, saying: "Father Silvester, I am not even of Roman blood. My father was a German, a simple potter. My mother was a saloon girl. I am a barbarian. What is to become of me? And, if I am baptized now, I know I will sin again. So I want to wait until death comes."

By the time of this conversation, Silvester's understanding had clarified. As he now saw it, Christ's triumph and blessing do not have to be put off until Jesus reappears. The triumph does not consist of continual persecution and death. It is a public and established Christianity honored with primacy and authority and dignity. The blessing is nothing so dra-

35

stic as the return of Jesus to destroy the Roman world and lead the elect into heaven. No. It is, rather a universal and worldwide reign of Jesus through the successors of Peter under the protection of the Roman emperor. The church can be both in the world and of it. It can *be* in the world, and yet be apart from it spiritually.

In that light, obviously, Jesus has converted Constantine so that Constantine can in turn convert the whole empire, that is, the whole world. Once this conversion is complete, Jesus will reappear and establish the Messianic age on earth. It all seemed so simple, so right. Poor Silvester!

In his certainty, Silvester's answers to Constantine's urgent questions are precise and clear.

The emperor is neither German nor Greek nor Roman, Silvester tells him, because in Christ Jesus, as the Apostle Paul says, there is no longer any distinction between races: all are sons and daughters of the father in Heaven. And it is as such that he, Constantine, will reign over a new world. He is the chosen apostle of Jesus. Baptism now? Wait until death comes, if he prefers. This is Silvester's advice. As for the future: Go out, he tells the emperor, and spread the Gospel to the East where Jesus was born and died, and even further, as far as India and China. Spread Rome and Roman rule, so that the baptism of Jesus flows on Roman aqueducts to the four quarters of the earth. Let the bishop of Rome reign as his pontiff. Together they can establish a blessing for all humans.

These are the answers Constantine needs. His irresolution is wiped out. He is healed of his weakness.

They take practical decisions. The two basilicas will be built, one for Peter and the other for Paul. Constantine will also have a basilica and a baptistry built on Lateran Hill beside the Palace of the Popes. He further decides that the Stadium of Caligula and the Temple of Apollo standing on Vatican Hill will be leveled, their stone and marble to be used for the new basilica of Peter. He has only one detailed command about that basilica. It must have three windows in its facade, one each in honor of the Father, of the Son, and of the Holy Spirit. Above the windows, there must be a mosiac representing Jesus, the Virgin Mary, and St. Peter.

Actually Silvester and Constantine will see only the beginning of the basilicas of the apostles. But they have the satisfaction of seeing the beautification of Peter's "memorial" on Vatican Hill. Before he leaves Rome this time, Constantine has it encased in blue-veined marble and covered by a canopy of stone supported by four white spiral columns. After his death, when the basilica of St. Peter is completed, the memorial will be in the exact center of a square between the apse of the basilica and a triumphal arch. In modern St. Peter's, built in the sixteenth century to replace Constantine's basilica, the memorial lies beneath the main altar.

The emperor's decisions also concern other things. All slaves can be legally freed within the sanctuary of any Christian church. Land grants will be made to the church. Indeed, he offers Silvester the imperial villa at Alba Longa outside Rome. Silvester refuses it. But later popes will absorb it, build the papal summer home there, and rename it Castel Gandolfo.

All anti-church laws will be revoked. Constantine abolishes crucifixion as the supreme capital punishment—no criminal should die in the same way as Jesus the Christ died for men's sins. Sunday will be a public holiday in honor of Jesus' resurrection. Throughout the West, Constantine decides, he will use the bishops of the church just as former Roman emperors used the pontiffs of the old Roman College of Pontiffs, with the pope being supreme pontiff. All local bishops will have civil jurisdiction. Pope Silvester and his successors will have supreme civil jurisdiction over all localities in the western half of the Roman Empire. (Later, successive popes will try to extend their domination over the eastern half as well, including Constantine's new capital of Constantinople, thus forcing the first great split in Christianity. But neither Constantine nor Silvester can foresee this. They are looking merely at immediate problems.) These two men, the pope and the emperor, have now set the stage for the next 1,600 years. The Church of Rome will always be allied with some temporal power. At one stage, it will even claim to be the source of all worldly power—political, civil, military, diplomatic, financial, cultural. And it will make that claim stick for quite some time. But what a price it will pay!

Yet this is how Silvester now understands what Jesus said to Peter on that long-distant day near Mount Hermon: "I give to you the keys of the kingdom of Heaven. Whatever you allow on earth will be what Heaven allows. Whatever you forbid on earth will be what Heaven forbids."

Still more profound is the effect Silvester's decision will have on the internal structure of the church. For, under this new conception, that structure will take on all the trappings and manners of political and economic power centered in Rome as a capital. In fact, from this moment on, the spiritual power of Peter is enslaved in the pomp of empire. Far from liberating the church, Silvester's decision has trapped it—even though the cage is studded with jewels and lined with ermine, and the bars are made of gold.

None of this is obvious to Silvester or Constantine on this day, however. Constantine leaves their meeting carrying "the healing of Peter," as he told his retinue. "I walked in a leper. The successor of the apostle made me clean." Constantine is talking about a healing in spirit, of course, but his gratitude is so palpable that Christians of the time even invented the myth of Constantine's physical leprosy and of his having been healed by Silvester's "touch."

Later, they were to go much further. Five hundred years after Constantine, when Roman churchmen were battling their Eastern brethren over civil jurisdictions, they actually forged an infamous document, *The Donation of Constantine,* according to which the grateful emperor had given the Roman pontiff jurisdiction forever over the lands of the East as well as the West. Another thousand years had to pass before Roman pontiffs conceded that the document was a fake.

3. The Fanatic's Attack

A black Numidian named Donatus now takes center stage. His scene is bloody, but it affects all the plans of Silvester and Constantine and therefore the Christian church down to our own day. If, indeed, Donatus had won the fight, Constantine's plan would have failed, Silvester would have remained an obscure cleric, and both our world and the church would be totally different.

Pope Miltiades and his predecessors rejected the notion that the church should be allied with political and military power—above all, with the

Roman emperor. Many, in fact, were still of the mind of Hippolytus, the old anti-pope: whoever sinned against the faith (by renouncing it when faced with the alternative of death, for example), should not be forgiven. The church was to be spotless and pure in waiting for Jesus, who was due to reappear at any moment. Donatus embodied all these attitudes.

He was an African, of mixed Bantu and Semitic blood, bishop of a small town called Casae Nigrae ("Black Houses") that stood on the fringes of the Sahara. Contemporaries described Donatus as "the terrible," much as Ivan of Russia was later on to acquire the same epithet. With his flowing black beard, his deep booming voice, his harsh doctrines, his total commitment to a pure church, his downright solution for all opposition ("Kill them!"), Donatus was the ready-made fanatic. He was the Ayatollah Khomeini of his time.

He came to the fore in the first instance by his violent action during the early years of the fourth century. Emperor Diocletian had instituted a widespread and thorough persecution of Christians during which many Christians (priests and bishops as well as layfolk) had sworn in front of Roman officials, with a copy of the Gospels on the ground in front of them, that they abjured Jesus, his church, his teaching, and the whole Christian religion. As a reward, they were allowed to go about their business in peace. When Constantine became emperor, he ended all that persecution, and the crypto-Christians and the renegade Christians came out into the open again in droves to ask forgiveness and to rejoin the church.

In Numidia, Donatus is adamant. The renegades can never be saved, he says. They have damned themselves by their betrayal. Besides, there would be no point in any of those renegade priests and bishops administering the sacraments because their treachery has invalidated their powers. Jesus is about to reappear, Donatus declares, and only the sinless can be saved. Once you have sinned, you are damned. Always. The doctrine was more Calvinist than anything John Calvin ever proclaimed more than a thousand years later.

And Donatus does not stop there. He has even larger aims. He organizes his own peasant militia into warring bands of guerrillas whom the Romans fear and call *circumcelliones* (a word with about the same connotation as mau-mau). He refuses to accept the idea that the emperor and

39

his authorities can become Christians. They cannot be saved, he preaches. In addition, he rejects allegiance to the emperor and preaches social revolution: the people of God are to rise up and seize all the lands and wealth so as to prepare for the coming Kingdom of Jesus.

Donatus's first violent action is far outside Numidia, in the town of Carthage (in modern Tunisia). It concerns the appointment of a new bishop. Pope Silvester has appointed a man called Caecilianus, who during the Diocletian persecution had abjured the faith. Donatus with his armed warriors on horses and camels rides to the palace of the bishop of Numidia and at swordpoint extracts from that primate a document deposing the pope's choice and installing Donatus's creature, a certain Majorinus.

With this document in hand, Donatus rides to Carthage. Surrounded by his warriors screaming and brandishing their banners and swords and lances, Donatus breaks into an assembly of seventy African bishops. His warriors ring the assembly, pointing their lances and swords at the bishops' throats. Then Donatus harangues the assembly. The Pope's candidate is deposed and excommunicated, he tells them, and Majorinus is to be appointed. One old bishop rashly points out that this doesn't look good because Majorinus is merely the foot-servant of a certain Lucilla, Donatus's rich lady friend. Donatus has the old man cut down in front of the others as an example, then resumes his harangue: "The Lord is about to reappear. The church is to be pure and spotless. And in the name of the apostles, I am the arm of the Lord until he comes back among us," were his concluding words. The bishops thereupon declare Caecilianus deposed and Majorinus to be the new bishop of Carthage.

Then Donatus goes on to explain the "correct" doctrine. Christ's church is an organization for a chosen few, all vivified by the Holy Spirit at baptism. The organization is utterly opposed to the pagan world which is heading for final doom. All that Christians should hope for is a martyr's crown. Sin and riches are identical. To be rich, to be powerful, is to be in sin. The Roman world is Mammon and to be shunned. So far, this does not differ substantially from the teachings of Paul and Peter three hundred years before, nor of Clement and Pontian and Miltiades. But Donatus now goes one step further.

40

The Roman world, he declares, *cannot be made good* (this means that Jesus has failed to save a significant portion of human beings) and therefore must be destroyed. Hence Donatus's revolution, including massacres and tortures and destruction of property. Worse: On his own authority and under the guidance of the Holy Spirit, he says, only those in communion with him, Donatus, can administer the sacraments validly.

It was here that Donatus separated himself completely from the doctrine of Jesus, and of his apostles and church. At heart, Donatus was not quarreling over doctrine but, like the Ayatollah, grabbing for power. Numidia, Egypt, and North Africa composed a rich and prosperous territory. Donatus wanted it, and religion was a means to achieve it, although for many of his followers, fidelity to the old hard-line teaching of Hippolytus was all that mattered. But the sincerely religious were here enveloped in the ambitions of the sincerely worldly.

Donatus and his Donatism, although condemned by Pope Silvester and two councils of bishops and persecuted by Constantine and his officials, remained a running sore in the side of the Roman Empire and a cancer in the African church for three whole centuries after Silvester and Constantine were dead. But they never held sway in the whole body of the church.

If Donatus had prevailed, the church would have been forever recognized as just another pipsqueak backwater religious-political revolutionary satrapy, its spiritual power submerged in its politics and indistinguishable from them. For Donatus preached the old Jewish idea of a temporal kingdom, just as the Ayatollah proclaims in behalf of Islam.

The Roman popes, no matter how subordinate they became to political power, no matter how greatly corrupted by it, always saw their spiritual power as distinct from the political and never wholly identified the two. This was the narrow but all-important hair-difference between Donatus and the bishop of Rome.

4. The Blood Relatives of Jesus

In defeating Donatus, Silvester rejected only one extreme that could have spelled early death for Christianity. There was another that in its own attractive way could have been just as lethal. This was the policy of the Jewish Christians, who occupied the oldest Christian churches in the Middle East and whose leaders were always from the family of Jesus himself. Like all Christians, including the Donatists, they expected an imminent return of Jesus. Unlike the Donatists, and now the Romans, they shunned all worldly power and revolution, and were for the most part dirt-farmers and petty merchants, hugging close to their obscurity even though their first bishop was James, first cousin of Jesus.

Yet the issue that arose between Silvester and the Jewish Christians was nothing less than the whole nature of the church. A meeting between Silvester and the Jewish Christian leaders took place in the year 318. The emperor provided sea transport for eight rough-and-ready men as far as Ostia, the port of Rome. From there they rode on donkeys into the imperial city and up to the Lateran Palace, where Pope Silvester now lived in grandeur. In their rough woollen clothes and leather boots and hats, and with their earthy smell, they contrasted sharply with Silvester's retinue of smartly clad and pomaded bishops and officials. They refused to sit. Silvester spoke with them in Greek—he could not understand their Aramaic; they had little or no Latin. The vital interview was not, so far as we know, recorded, but the issues were very well known, and it is probable that Joses, the oldest of the Christian Jews, spoke on behalf of the *desposyni* and the rest.

That most hallowed name, *desposyni,* had been respected by all believers in the first century and a half of Christian history. The word literally meant, in Greek, "belonging to the Lord." It was reserved uniquely for Jesus' blood relatives. Every part of the ancient Jewish Christian church had always been governed by a *desposynos,* and each of them carried one of the names traditional in Jesus' family—Zachary, Joseph, John, James, Joses, Simeon, Matthias, and so on. But no one was ever called Jesus. Neither Silvester nor any of the thirty-two popes before him, nor those succeeding him, ever emphasized that there were at least three well-known and authentic lines of legitimate blood descendants from Jesus' own family. One from Joachim and Anna, Jesus' maternal grandparents. One from Elizabeth, first cousin of Jesus' mother, Mary, and Elizabeth's husband, Zachary. And one from Cleophas and his wife, who also was a first cousin of Mary.

There were, of course, numerous blood descendants of Joseph, Mary's husband, but only those persons in bloodline with Jesus through his mother qualified as *desposyni*. All of them had clung to Jesus and to his mother, and when both these had gone, to the first Christian community, in Jerusalem from the beginning and, later, throughout the Middle East.

The Jewish Christians had been the subject of the first crisis in the church. They had been split by factions from the start; and at the first council, in A.D., 49. Peter and Paul had broken with them, insisting that non-Jewish converts need not be circumcised to become Christians, and that *only* Jewish converts need be bound by the Torah, the law of Moses. The decision was momentous, allowing Christianity to spread beyond Judaism, but it left the Jewish Christians in a sort of religious no-man's-land.

Ever since the Emperor Hadrian had conquered Jerusalem in the year 135, all Jews, and that included Jewish Christians, had been forbidden to enter Jerusalem under pain of instant death. That ban had not yet been lifted, at the time of Silvester's meeting with the Jewish Christians.

Silvester knew their history well. Jewish Christians had composed the only church ever in Jerusalem until the year 135. They left it only once in 102 years following Jesus' death, just before the city's capture by the Emperor Titus. Led by their bishop, Simeon, son of Cleophas, who was Jesus' uncle by marriage, they had fled to Perea (in modern Jordan). In A.D. 72 they had returned to Jerusalem and had remained there until Hadrian's ban. After that, Jewish Christian churches were set up all over Palestine, Syria, and Mesopotamia, but they were always hated by the local synagogues as apostates of Judaism, and always in quarrel with Greek Christians who refused to be circumcised and observe the Torah— things the Jewish Christians insisted on.

They therefore asked Silvester to revoke his confirmation of Greek Christian bishops in Jerusalem, in Antioch, in Ephesus, in Alexandria, and to name instead *desposynos* bishops.

In addition, they asked that the Christian practice of sending cash contributions to the *desposynos* church in Jerusalem as the mother church of Christianity, which had been suspended since the time of Hadrian, be resumed.

43

Silvester curtly and decisively dismissed the claims of the Jewish Christians. He told them the the mother church was now in Rome, with the bones of the Apostle Peter, and he insisted that they accept Greek bishops to lead them.

It was the last known discussion between the Jewish Christians of the old mother church and the non-Jewish Christians of the new mother church. By his adaptation, Silvester, backed by Constantine, had decided that the message of Jesus was to be couched in Western terms by Western minds on an imperial model.

The Jewish Christians had no place in such a church structure. They managed to survive until the first decades of the fifth century. Then, one by one, they disappear. A few individuals reconcile themselves with the Roman Church—always as individuals, never communities or whole Jewish Christian churches. Another few pass into the anonymity of the new Eastern rites—Syriac, Assyrian, Greek, Armenian. But most of them die—by the sword (Roman garrisons hunted them as outlaws), by starvation (they were deprived of their small farms and could not or would not adapt themselves to life in the big cities), by the attrition of zero birthrate. By the time that the first biography of Jesus (apart from the Gospels) is published in Chinese and in China at the beginning of the seventh century, there are no more surviving Jewish Christians. The *desposyni* have ceased to exist. Everywhere, the Roman pope commands respect and exercises authority.

5. The Gift of Hope

It would be easy to condemn Silvester for rejecting the Jewish Christians, and to say that he helped destroy the Donatists only because they had attacked the Roman Empire, which had romanced the church and become its patron. But it would not be entirely fair to do so, because neither Donatists nor Jewish Christians could offer the one commodity vitally needed in the world of Silvester and Constantine. This commodity was hope.

The capital event in Rome and throughout the empire in Europe, Asia, and Africa in those years, happened in spirit among the populations which Rome had just recently dominated. By the mid-300s, within twenty years of Silvester's death, the Roman legions were defending Constantinople, which Constantine had only just finished building. The mortar was still wet. Within another hundred years, the last Roman legions on the Thames, on the Rhine, on the Seine, and on the Ebro had been sucked back to Constantinople by the vortex of war for survival against barbarian invaders. What then began to fail the city of Rome and the Europe which Rome had forged was not primarily military force or the primacy of law. It was the old Roman hope.

For a time, Roman power had promised the men and women of its empire that they could hope to be human, that is, distinguished from barbarians and slaves, and enjoy something of the peace, the freedom, and the confidence which the gods and heroes of Rome were believed to enjoy.

For the classical form of Roman civilization had an anthropology all its own, as definite and as dogmatic as the anthropology which jumped from the brains of nineteenth and twentieth-century scientists. It was not as "scientific" as pure Darwinism, but just as groundlessly dogmatic, just as full of myth and unscientific presumption, and its backbone was hope.

By accepting Roman law, worshiping Roman gods, wearing Roman clothes, accepting Roman citizenship, bearing Roman arms, using Roman utensils, thinking and living "the Roman way," adopting Roman culture as expressed in aqueduct, viaduct, circus, theater, medicine, schools, literature, language, birth and marriage and death customs, any man or woman could hope to have significance, to have meaning—even if that significance and meaning ceased with the grave and became merely part of communal memory and ancestral legacy. The hope was to be able to say, as St. Paul blurted out defiantly and confidently at his Jewish accusers in court: *"Civis Romanus sum* (I am a Roman citizen)." But by the end of the fourth century that old Roman hope had failed, and with it went the anthropology on which great achievements had been founded.

Constantine's dynasty lasted sixty years, during most of which time he was busy repelling Goths, Franks, and Alemanni from the borders of the empire. (All the effort he put into building Constantinople didn't help much.) After his death in 337, his three sons succeeded him. The last of

45

these, Costantius, died in 361. By the time of Emperor Gratian's death (383), the Balkans had been ceded to the Goths. By 405, the Romans had evacuated Britain. Soon Spain fell to the Vandals. In August of 410, Rome itself was plundered by the Goths under Alaric. Hope was extinguished.

But as the old Roman Empire was declining, in remote parts of Palestine and North Africa, in back streets and cellars of the main cities of Europe, a new message of hope began to flourish among the riffraff, the obscure, and the powerless. As far as human judgment and every Roman standard went, the message was rank nonsense—"foolishness" and "inanity" and "childish folly" are the terms Paul heard on the lips of his pagan contemporaries in the last third of the first century. To begin with, the instrument of this new hope—a felon's cross—was foolish. We still have the mocking graffito scratched by Roman soldiers on the paving stones of their barracks courtyard: a donkey crucified on a cross with the words "Alexander's god!" Obviously a Christian soldier being twitted by his pagan buddies.

But the appearance of foolishness went even further. Christians did not merely say that God had died because of human sins, nor even that God had died and risen from the dead because of human sins. The message went much further—too far for human credulity. The entire human universe had been transformed, the message ran. Time, which had been a tyrant, now was become a period of salvation. Space was now filled with the presence of God. Death, still the final pain of the living and the ultimate disfigurement of the human body, was no longer a mystery or the privileged purlieu of a handful of gods, godlets, and heroes. And within time and space, each human had become new in an unheard-of fashion.

The newness itself was the most outlandish part of the messsage. But for the ever-increasing number of believers it was the center of an unbreakable hope. Jesus, who had died on that cross, was present in each believer and in his world. Through identity with that presence, each human being became part of God during mortal life. And this Jesus had a personal representative, his vicar, living in one place, who had the spiri-

46

tual authority to transmit the forgiveness of Jesus, the law of Jesus, and the love of Jesus.

If men and women subjected everything, every activity and phase of their lives, to the law of Jesus—birth, marriage, commerce, politics, war, disease, wealth, sickness, poverty, fields, trees, cities, houses, instruments, and utensils, their very bodies—all, then the entire universe would be renovated and a millennial existence would be ushered in. In the meanwhile, Christians could be washed clean of sin. They could be united with Jesus by partaking in the Eucharist. Their marriage as well as their dying could be sanctified by special rites.

As long as Christians remained "in the catacombs," a persecuted or at best a barely tolerated minority in the obscure strata of society, the achievement of this new universe and its millennial age was put off until Jesus reappeared again with all his divine power. Thus Christians had an undying hatred of and revulsion from the "world," the secular structure around them, with its wealth, its pomp, its economic sinews, and its military solutions for problems. But the first promise of Christianity to Constantine on the eve of battle at the Milvian Bridge, just as to the populations bereft of Roman hope, came entwined around the cross of Jesus. It was: "In this sign you will conquer." And the first message of the bishop of Rome and his missionaries from the fourth century onward was: "In this sign, there is salvation, a new salvation, and a fresh hope for us all." Once Constantine's favor placed Christians in a privileged position, the Christian focus narrowed from remote eternity to passing time and measurable space.

If either Donatists or Jewish Christians had had their way, the appeal of Christianity as a universal way of life would have been restricted to a small number of Jews or an impotent and doomed minority in the great urban centers. The Roman world would have gone on disintegrating. There would have been no cement to bind the peoples of Europe together, and no hope that they could survive with meaning. No learning would have been preserved. No engineering techniques, no art, no history would have lived on. There could have been no Middle Ages science and philosophy and exploration, nor any European Renaissance, nor any later

47

birth of science and technology. Europe would have shared the immobile and static state of the Near East under the Ottoman Turks, of India under the Mongols, and of China under successive dynasties. There could have been no United States of America, because what made democracy possible would never have been born.

However mixed their motives, Silvester and Constantine rejected Donatists and Jewish Christians, and so the new message of hope could spread. Within four centuries that new hope of salvation had been elaborated into a new anthropology which nothing was able to stop.

It encountered only one serious enemy in its early years: the Emperor Julian who briefly mustered against this new creed all that Constantine had mustered in its favor. Julian, a scholar turned general and pamphleteer, reared as a Christian, converted to the old pagan religion of Rome, ferociously attached to the ancient gods and goddesses, almost succeeded in his attempt to out-Constantine Constantine.

Apart from his literary output in religious tracts, lampoons, laws, letters, speeches, and disputes (in the three volumes of his extant works, his *On the Gods and the World* is still of vital interest to us moderns), he reorganized the pagan priestly orders in the empire. And he set out to restore the old religion by force of arms. But not by force alone. "We must compete with the new irreligion [Christianity] on its own level. . . ." he wrote. "What has most contributed to their [Christians'] success is their charity toward strangers, the care they take of cemeteries, and their claimed seriousness about human life." So, to give an example of his tactics, Julian gave one pagan high priest an annual endowment of 30,000 bushels of wheat and 60,000 pints of wine—all to be given to the poor, as the Christians did.

But it all came to nothing. True, Constantine had used every one of these means to propagate Christianity. He even bought up whole towns and cities to ensure they accepted the new belief. He waged wars on its behalf. He endowed it heavily. He organized international meetings where, to quote a contemporary, he appeared "like an Angel of the Lord" with lances to prove his point but with his burning belief to enthuse all present. But Constantine had one other element in his favor. Julian was not up against merely the purchasing power of imperial wealth nor its armed might. Something had happened in spirit to human beings. Something new had entered the human ambient. Nothing Julian had, nothing he did or could do, none of his undoubted gifts—his flamboyance, his taut skill in administration, the unnerving confidence he communicated to his followers, his deadly concern for the gods and their cults, his brilliant strategy—nothing could change the course of events. And Christian legend-makers wrapped up the truth about his failure and its true causes in the words of a Syrian priest, called Ephraim, the greatest poet among the anthologists. Ephraim, they recounted, came out of the town of Nisibin and gazed on the dying body of the Emperor Julian lying in the dust at Kermanshah behind the Sierra of the Zagros Mountains, where he had been defeated in battle in 363. "Is this the one who forgot that he is dust," Ephraim is said to have spat out, "and contended with God himself?"

Whether Ephraim said it or not, the fact is that the old Roman hope had been laid to rest by the barbarians even before the extraordinary bargain between Constantine and Silvester created an environment in which a new hope would grow. Against that mushrooming force, Julian never really stood a chance.

Between the hands of Silvester and Constantine, the spiritual power promised to Peter by Jesus near Hermon was concentrated exclusively within one culture (Roman), one ethnic group (white men), in one geographical area (Western Europe), and within one political governing structure (imperial Rome). It was an accomplished fact by the time Silvester and Constantine came to die within a year of each other, Silvester in Rome, Constantine in faraway Nicomedia (Ismir, in modern Turkey).

It is a somber January evening in 336 when the eighty-one-year-old Silvester suffers his first and last heart attack. By this time he is the supreme religious and civil power in the central metropolis of the whole world, in this Rome with its one and a half million people, its 1,792 palaces, its 46,602 dwellings, its 21 miles of huge, weather-beaten walls, its glory and wealth and prestige. The Roman tradition Silvester has received from Peter through Clement, Pontian, Miltiades, and all the other popes is now clad in imperial raiment.

49

Outwardly, the city is still pagan. Even on Vatican Hill at the end of this fourth century, when the basilica to St. Peter has been built, the ceremonies of the Sacred Bull will still be practiced in the shadow of that basilica. The city streets still show 324 government-registered pagan street-shrines to Jupiter, Minerva, Mithra, and other pagan deities. But, already in Silvester's time, Christian churches, meetinghouses, and basilicas dot the city—St. Pudentiana's, St. Maria's, St. Alexius's, St. Prisca's, the Lateran Basilica. Helena, the mother of Constantine, went to Palestine and said that she had found the cross on which Jesus had died, which she later gave to Silvester. She built churches over the sites of Jesus's birth and where, Christians believe, he ascended into Heaven.

Far more radical and power-giving is the new papal organization. Rome is now divided into seven ecclesiastical districts, each one in the charge of a Vatican official. The church as a whole is divided, has been divided by Constantine, into three Apostolic Patriarchates—Rome, Alexandria, and Antioch. Later, there will be the non-Apostolic Patriarchates of Jerusalem and Constantinople. The bishop of Rome has full jurisdiction over Rome, Italy, the Balkans, Africa, Sicily, France, Germany, Britain. And, with that spiritual jurisdiction, he wields already preponderant political, civil, even military power. His prestige is worldwide. The church's missionary efforts use all the imperial facilities: roads, stations, convoys, guards, garrisons, lawyers, judges, courts, forts, public buildings, treasuries Already, the bishop of Rome possesses by legal title huge estates outside the city, in Campagna, over at Ostia (the port of Rome), eastward on the Adriatic coast, and down in Calabria and Sicily. All this has come under Pope Silvester's rule.

As he lay dying, perhaps Silvester's chief regret would have been having so churlishly dismissed the blood relatives of Jesus. Some of those Jewish Christian *desposyni* must have borne facial characteristics that Jesus himself would have had.

Silvester died, having been Pope for 21 years, 10 months and 12 days. His feast day as a saint is still celebrated on December 31 of each year, and his significance for the church remains huge. For he colored the Roman tradition, not with the red of Christ's blood, but with the purple of Constantine's court. And the resulting Roman mentality will not even begin to lose that powerful tint until the last third of the twentieth century, over 1,600 years later, when the cardinal-electors gather in conclave to elect a successor to Pope Paul VI.

When Constantine came to die on May 22, 337, he immediately asked for and received baptism. He also had a deep regret. Not for the men he killed or caused to be killed in the seventy-three battles he fought and won; nor the execution of his own Queen Fausta for perjury; nor his execution of Christian heretics—the Donatists, the Arians, the Ebionites. He had much to be proud of: his regal residence of Constantinople, the "New Rome" on the Golden Horn of the Bosphorus, with its basilicas, statuary monuments, quays, baths, streets, marketplaces, walls, treasury, army, and wealth. Over in eternal Rome stood his sixty-five-foot triumphal arch of white marble and bright festive colors. And Romans gazed daily on his colossal statue in the Forum (the head alone three feet in diameter) bearing the sign of the cross and the inscription which says: "Under this sign, I have liberated Rome." His was the supreme power in the world he knew, from the Irish Sea to Iran, from the Baltic to the Sahara.

As he started to die in earnest, he had the two nails of Christ's cross brought to him—the horse's bit and the crown—together with the first crude cross he fashioned just before battle at the Milvian Bridge. A few minutes after his baptism, his spirit was clearly refreshed and a great gentleness set in on this rough-hewn emperor of millions. When asked to pass judgment on the life or death of a convicted felon (he reserved the right of judgment until he died), he answered with typical breveity: "You ask a judgment from me who now awaits the judgment of Christ?" And he told those around him that he had waited too long for the baptism of Jesus.

He was silent after that, like the true soldier facing certain death. And those around him said afterward that he seemed to regret he triumph he had afforded Christianity and the sword by which he had given the blessing to the Roman pontiff and his church. They heard him say before he died: "Not the sword! . . . Not the sword! . . . Knowledge! . . ." Was Constantine regretting it all? The wealth he had conferred on the church, the power he had put at the Roman pontiff's disposal? Dante, in

51

the thirteenth century, would write sarcastically about him at the end of his *Inferno*; and, for certain, many miseries were bought by the wealth and the power of Constantine's gifts to the pontiff. But perhaps the emperor was saying in a soldier's unpoetic, unrefined way what the sophisticated St. Augustine of Hippo put in undying words one hundred years later: "Too late have I known thee, O beauty ever ancient, ever new!"

The Curse
of Constantine

Constantine sowed his newfound religion, Christianity, with the seeds of its own disintegration. What he had established, east and west, as solid foundations were to turn into the direct causes of betrayal and fragmentation. Like a fateful heirloom, Constantine's bequest became a curse, bedeviling each successive generation and leading first to fratricide and finally to suicide.

Constantine first established the bishop of Rome in full power in Western Europe. The popes received from him considerable real estate, extensive judicial authority, much liquid wealth, control over the armed forces, and political dominance. The Roman Church and Christianity thereby acquired inestimable status in the eyes of the public and very privileged access to the great emperor himself. In short, because of Constantine, the Bishop of Rome became a monarch and his church a monarchy.

To crown his efforts, Constantine organized a general ecumenical council of Christian bishops in the year 325 at Nicaea (in modern Turkey). The council was called "ecumenical" because it concerned the whole *oikumene*—the whole inhabited world (as Christians then understood it). There the formal beliefs of Christians were hammered out in concrete formulas known ever since as the Nicene Creed. Further, in one of its decrees or canons, the council recognized four main centers of Christianity: Rome, Alexandria (in Syria), Antioch (in Syria), and Jeru-

53

salem. Each of these places was called a patriarchate, the bishop of Rome being the patriarch of the west and taking precedence over the other three. Constantine's reason for this precedence: "Because the Apostles Peter and Paul had lived and died in Rome" (and the pope of Rome was Peter's successor).

Already, while the Council of Nicaea was in session, Constantine had chosen a site on the Bosphorus as the new capital of his empire. It was a small Greek city called Byzantion; its position was strategically important. Finished in 330, it would be in Constantine's mind the "New Rome," and its bishop would soon be called patriarch of the East.

But the emperor, although he moved to Constantinople and lived there, did not make his new patriarch there a king. Instead, like King David of Israel over one thousand years before, in the East, Constantine separated the "state," represented by himself, from the "church," as represented by the patriarch, although the two spheres were viewed as the two elements of a single organism. And, like David, Constantine considered himself as divinely appointed to assure the material well-being of the church and to safeguard the purity of its beliefs. This relationship between Byzantine emperor and patriarch lasted for over eleven hundred years and eighty emperors until Constantinople and its empire died in 1453.

Over in "old Rome," however, its bishop, the pope, continued as veritable monarch, his power over Western Europe increasing with every century. Even so, relations between the patriarchs, east and west, were not at first unfriendly, or were at least correct. When Pope Mark was elected in January 336 to succeed Silvester I, he wrote news of his election to the patriarch of Constantinople as well as to the other patriarchs, in Alexandria, Antioch, and Jerusalem. The patriarch of Constantinople inscribed Mark's name in the official lists of the patriarchates, the Dyptychs. Similarly, when a new patriarch was appointed in Constantinople or in the other patriarchates, he wrote official news of it to Rome as well as to the others. In Constantine's mind, this pentarchy of patriarchates was the grid on which the Christian world would rest and flourish. The emperor would protect all and foment all. In all minds, Rome had precedence of honor and, bluntly said, a final decisive vote in matters of faith and morals. Rome had the prestige.

But all this was too military, too neat. Within fifty years of Constantine's death, a second ecumenical council met in Constantinople in 381. This council refurbished the Nicene Creed and, significantly, in its Canon III stated that "the Bishop of Constantinople shall have precedence in honor after the Bishop of Rome because Constantinople is the New Rome." The then bishop of Rome, Damasus I, never accepted Canon III. Nor did any of his successors. If there was a "New Rome," that meant the finish of the "old Rome." That they could never accept. (Only over eight hundred years later, in 1215, would a Roman pope accept Canon III, and that was only because the patriarch and emperor had been driven out temporarily and the pope had installed a Roman archbishop as patriarch of Constantinople.)

Already in 381, the pope in Rome recognized the growing threat of Constantinople. And already there were profound differences between the two churches growing out of the pope's role as temporal ruler. In time, popes would claim absolute, complete, and supreme imperial power over all men. In time, a council of stern bishops would declare the pope to be above and beyond the reach of any mere council of bishops.

But the patriarch of Constantinople governed through his college of fellow patriarchs from Alexandria, Antioch, and Jerusalem. In time, each of the Eastern patriarchs would head a nationalist church, as additional patriarchs were established in Bulgaria, Cyprus, and elsewhere. And each one would be identified with the interests of the local ruler and his own nation, but acknowledge the precedence of Constantinople's patriarch in "honor." In time, the monarchic regime of the popes would clash with the collegial regime of the East as the Romans claimed overall authority rooted in the Apostle Peter. The Easterners would retort with a claim of unique orthodoxy of belief. Roman authority and Eastern Orthodoxy would become bitter and irreconcilable enemies, but by that time, the two parts of Christianity would have long separated in language, culture, methods of worship, laws of conduct, and political allegiance.

One element in the curse of Constantine provided both sides with a hypocritically religious reason for their break, which actually was a function of politics and economics. The verbal excuse for the split was the so-called *filioque* clause.

From their beginnings, Christians believed in one God. Unlike Jews

55

and Muslims, however, they said there were three persons in that one God. They called them: the Father, the Son (Christ), and the Holy Spirit. Further, they said each of the persons was God. This is the Christian Trinity of three persons in one God. In discussing the origin of the Son and the Holy Spirit, Christians said the Son originated from (but was not created by) the Father, and that the Holy Spirit originated from (or proceeded from) Father and Son as one principle.

In the Latin, or Roman Church, in response to particular questions that had been leveled, this belief was couched in words that defined the Holy Spirit as "proceeding from the Father *and from the Son.*" (In Latin "and from the Son" is expressed in the one word, *filioque.*)

In the Eastern, or Greek, Church. they preferred to say that the Holy Spirit proceeded from the Father *through* the Son: *dia tou uiou.*

It may seem a ridiculously petty point to modern minds. It was not so for the reverend gentlemen who disputed the issue. It is sure that Roman belief and Eastern belief agree that the Son originates in the Father, and that the Holy Spirit originates in Father and Son. The only argument was how best to express it.

But it was petty men, motivated by greed for money and power, who used this theological quibble literally to break the Christian church in half.

The first really great challenge to general Christian belief came from a bishop called Arius. He maintained that the Son was a *creation* of the Father, and therefore was not God. When Constantine assembled Christian bishops at the town of Nicaea in 325, they explicitly rejected Arius's view by declaring it a fundamental of faith that the Son was God and proceeded from the Father in an uncreated, mysterious way. They did not speak of the origin of the Holy Spirit because that was not under dispute; so all Christians still held that the Holy Spirit originated, or proceeded, *dia tou uiou*, through the Son.

Also, the Council of Nicaea declared that there would be no further tinkering with the wording of Christian belief.

But the church in the West *did* later make an addition. At the council of bishops at Toledo, Spain, in 589, they added the *filioque* clause to repel claims that the Son was not God because he did not participate in origi-

56

nating the Holy Spirit. "The Holy Spirit," the bishops laid down, "proceeded from the Father and *from* the Son." *Filioque.* From then on, the use of this formula spread to France, Belgium, Germany, Italy, England, Ireland, and North Africa. The Eastern Church kept using the word "through," and the Latins kept on using the word "from." Both believed the same thing, although the emphasis was different.

In the eighteenth century, Jonathan Swift savagely ridiculed the whole dispute by comparing it, in his *Gulliver's Travels*, to people quarreling over whether to break eggs at the little end or the big end. But this big-end versus little-end dispute could have gone on indefinitely, and benignly, except for arrogance, jealousy, and cupidity that came from being politically and militarily supreme.

Rome's first step along that road began with changes in the method of electing popes. Within a few short years of Constantine's conversion, the election of a pope had become an occasion for bitter, sometimes violent clashes. Electioneering time usually began after the death of a pope. Sometimes, his last days and dying hours were filled with factional disputes, the nobles and the Roman Senate against the bishops and priests, the deacons and subdeacons and the people against the bishops, various ambitious papal candidates with their followings of family, kinsmen, and friends, one against each other. Vicious enmities were created. Blood was shed. Lives were taken. At the election of Pope Damasus I in A.D. 366, thirty-seven corpses littered the environs of the Liberian Basilica after a fracas between the followers of Damasus and his archrival, Ursinus.

Now a pope was only sometimes appointed by his predecessor. Sometimes a dying pope was forced to nominate his successor in the presence of witnesses, or an already dead pope was quoted by several candidates, each in his own favor. However it was accomplished, the semifinal step in the election of a pope was taken when the clergy and laity of the Roman Church assembled and, by voting, chose a candidate. Rarely did they confirm the appointee of a dead pope. The chosen candidate's name was then forwarded to the emperor for ratification. Often, when the Roman community of Christians assembled for an election, they found the emperor's nominee facing them. They merely had to acclaim that nominee as their pope.

57

In any case, from the year 314 onward until the invention of the conclave system as the official method of election, there were 147 popes. The vast majority of these were elected at the beck and call of Roman emperor, Gothic king, Frankish king, Roman family or faction, German tribesman, German emperor, or local Italian petty tyrant. The Roman assembly of Christians continued to hold elections, but in each case their chosen candidate had to be ratified or confirmed by some temporal prince or ruler.

As the Roman emperors collapsed in the West under barbarian pressure, the emperors of the East stepped into the power vacuum and, during two long periods, the pope acclaimed in Rome had to be approved in Constantinople.

The fourteen popes from Silvester I (314–335) to Simplicius (468–483) were either chosen by the Roman assembly and ratified by the emperors in Constantinople or directly imposed by those emperors. One of the last popes to be approved by Constantinople was the first pope to be given the title "Great."

In addition to emperors and the popes themselves, one group of men became in time the very hinges upon which the election of the popes turned: the cardinals.

The name cardinal and the functions of a cardinal grew out of the earliest form of clerical organization in the Christian church, beginning with the appointment of seven deacons by Peter the Apostle. Peter ordered his immediate successor in Rome, Pope Linus, to ordain twenty-five priests in order to serve the various churches already existent there before the end of the first century A.D. Not before the year 100 did parishes as we know them exist, except in Rome and Alexandria. Instead, grouped around each church or in a single village or town there was what was called the presbytery (from a Greek word meaning "priest"), an assembly of priests and deacons. The presbytery assisted the bishop of the local church.

In Rome, by A.D.107, Pope Evaristus had established seven major administrative regions—deaconries—in Rome. They constituted his "presbytery." One hundred years later, Pope Callistus reduced them to six. As the church increased in numbers and complexity, these had become inner-city bishoprics: the pope was bishop of the whole city, and he had these six bishops to help minister to all the people.

By now, a big distinction had been made between clergy working in isolated churches in the countryside, and the clergy attached to the big city churches. Christianity began as and always has remained an urban-based religion. Country churches were regarded as mere adjuncts, sometimes served part-time by monks or priests and deacons from the city.

The Roman city clergy came to be called cardinals because they were the centers of support for the church—the word "cardinal" comes from the Latin *cardo*, meaning "hinge" or "support." The city clergy—bishops, priests, deacons—were "incardinated" to, the hinges of, the city churches. They were "cardinals"—cardinal-bishops, cardinal-priests, cardinal-deacons.

In 366, Pope Julius II fixed the number of such Roman cardinal-clergy at twenty-eight—seven for each of the four patriarchal churches in Rome: St. Peter's, St. Paul's, St. Lawrence's, St. Mary Major's. And this rule remained in vigor for almost a thousand years.

As the wealth and political power of the Roman popes increased, so did the position and influence of the cardinals. In Roman parlance, there was now a *collegium*, a collection, a "college" of cardinals. Those cardinals stationed at the Vatican brought wealth and prestige with them from their families, or they acquired them once they took office, from its emoluments. Outside Rome, it was the same story. Landed property, liquid wealth, military force, family connections, and sometimes the mere acquisition of what were called prince-bishoprics, conferred princely power, and with it always came an association with the political and economic fortunes of the lands they inhabited. Over and above all that, cardinals in their own lands also were representatives of the man who was to become the principal ruler in the whole of Europe, and effectively the Western world—the pope in Rome. The first to stake such a claim was Pope Leo I.

THE
NEW
ANTHROPOLOGY

Staking the
Great Claim

In the oppressive summer heat of AD. 452, a meeting on the south bank of the River Po in northern Italy decides the fate of Europe for the next 1,500 years. Attila, king of the Huns and emperor of all the Scythians, meets with Leo I, "Leo the Great," bishop of Rome. Immediately at stake is the city of Rome, its life or death. Beyond that, the continuance of a Western civilization.

Leo, seated on a mule, approaches the southern bank. Bearded, grim, he is wearing the white robes of a bishop; on his head a simple miter; in his hands a staff. Before him walks a black-garbed cleric carrying a cross flanked by two others with incense-burners. Behind him walk two lines of brown-and-white clad monks singing psalms. It is late afternoon. This is Leo's supreme gamble, the gamble of a great belief backed by great courage.

Leo, of Tuscan blood, a native of Rome, has come with the consent of the Roman emperor, Valentinian, as a last hope. Valentinian, himself under siege over in Constantinople, cannot defend Rome. "Do what you can. God help you all," was Valentinian's order.

Everything in Leo's life has prepared for this moment. Born in 396 of an old Latin family. Educated in Rome, Milan, and Constantinople. Fluent in Latin and Greek. A priest at twenty-two. A bishop at thirty-five. Pope at forty-four. Since the age of 23, absorbed in affairs of state involving the Roman Empire, the church, and the new peoples rushing

63

down on the empire from the cold north. Leo is slightly over medium height, with the rounded shoulders of the cleric, brown-haired, black-eyed, with a high forehead, an aquiline nose, a well-set mouth. They say about Leo: What men most like about him are his words, and what men most respect are his eyes. Those black Tuscan eyes stare fixedly at you, never wavering, looking inside you, seeing beyond you.

Leo has strongly and repeatedly asserted the primacy of Rome's bishop over all other Christian bishops. Not too much new there except perhaps the two adverbs. But more than that, he has declared the authority of the Roman bishop over all temporal rulers as well. And that is staking out a huge new claim. Leo has asserted that Christian faith and practice mean not merely a hope of immortality in the next life, but order and wisdom in this life.

Eventually, Leo's claim will become so central to papal policy that to most mortal eyes the temporal concern will almost eclipse the spiritual. But no sooner has he made it than it faces a mortal threat. Can Leo, by the force of his faith, save Rome from a bloodbath? He is unarmed. Rome is without armies. Can Leo's unaided belief save it from this Asiatic?

The Northern bank of the Po is lined with Huns: small men with, to Europeans, oddly formed skulls, narrow waists, broad shoulders, long arms, large chests, faces flat, beardless, yellow; each one a bundle of fur bristling with bows, arrows, daggers, astride small skittish long-haired horses; each one's lance carries a rotting human head. The sky behind them is red with their flaming banners. Attila rests on his horse surrounded by his bodyguard, watching the Romans approach. At a signal, they stop, except for Leo, who continues alone. He urges his mule into the thin sluggish water. Attila's bodyguard finger their bows and lances, looking for the slightest sign of trouble.

Attila moves forward into the river from the northern bank. Both men are watching each other; Leo is now still, Attila advancing slowly. The distance narrows. Leo now sees Attila as an oldish man, with bent back, slanting eyes, rolling restlessly hither and thither, a lined face, narrow-lipped mouth. He sees Attila's worn tunic embroidered with precious stones, the black fur cap pulled down over the eyebrows, the curving longbow and colored quiver of arrows, the battle-ax slung in the belt.

Attila has a forceful, quiet, and primitive dignity. The distance narrows. Their eyes meet. Attila barks a sudden question:

"Your name?"

"Leo."

This question and answer are just about all that history has preserved with any surety of the words which passed between Attila and Leo. Onlookers hear Attila's question pronounced in heavy nasalized Latin. They see his eyes glitter in challenge. Leo's head comes up, his eyes staring into Attila's. Men see his right hand raised for a moment in the Christian Latin salute: the palm turned toward Attila, index and forefinger held erect and together, the third finger bent and apart, thumb and little finger joined. He speaks. Attila listens, then rides closer to the cleric, and together they regain the southern bank. The rest of the conversation has escaped us. For these moments, Leo is alone with Attila and with history.

From this distance in time, Leo's visit to Attila looks so simple. In reality, it was as if President Lyndon Johnson had walked on foot through the DMZ between North and South Vietnam in search of President Ho Chi Minh during the Tet festival of January 1968, or as if Pius XII, accompanied by cross-bearer and incense-burners and ten chanting cardinals, had personally confronted Adolf Hitler in the Reichskanzellerei off the Wilhelmstrasse in Berlin at the opening of spring 1942. By human calculations, it was a piece of madness.

The Huns had appeared like scavenging hawks and carrion birds from nowhere: first on the borders of China, then on the Caspian Sea, then in the Balkans and throughout Europe. They were always rushing headlong, driving to the horizon, the men on small sturdy horses, the women and children in chariots, ever flying away from the edges of the great desert where, men said, they had been born of demons. But the Huns were running from demons: the sand and the wind. Their gods lived above the clouds, and an ancient legend exhorted the Huns to search for their land.

Time and time again, they found a new pastureland, settled there, only to find the lithe, tawny toils of the sand monster descending on them in howling billowing storms, driving them onward. Blasting desolation pur-

65

sued them from Asia, slithering and searching the earth mercilessly for them. The Hun always sensed the demons at his back hunting him, now eastward to China, now westward to Europe, wherever he sought the land of his dreams. The Huns read the future in ruffled sand dunes as the Romans had in the entrails of hens and cocks. They felt the will of the Bird-King in hot grains stinging their eyes. Thus, by 374, they had crossed the Volga and advanced to the Danube.

They had no constructive laws, and intended to build nothing. They killed unmercifully, burned endlessly, raped as a matter of course, took no prisoners, kept few slaves, had an insatiable greed for riches, hated all that was stable, nourished themselves on goat's cheese and raw meat carried between their thighs and their horses' flanks, and drank millet and barley wine. Their religion was animistic and simple: in air and water and earth and fire there lurked demons and gods to be satiated with blood.

Attila, the son of Mundzuk, traced his lineage back through thirty-five generations to Schongar, the Bird-King, who ruled all flying things. Born in 395, of mixed Mongol and Hun ancestry, somewhere along the plains of the Danube. A daring horseman by the age of six, soon hunting, killing. A hostage in Roman imperial hands at the age of twelve, because his uncle Rua, ruler of the empire that stretched from the Alps to the Caspian Sea, wanted to gain time and lull the emperor of Constantinople into a false sense of security. Back among his own people before his twentieth year. A onetime ambassador to the imperial court of Constantinople. Widely traveled through Europe and Asia. Almost unique among his people in his knowledge of Greek and Latin in addition to Hunic. By 434, at the age of thirty-nine, king of all the Huns. By 445, having killed his brother Bleda, he is emperor of all the Scythians and heir to an empire stretching from the Alps and the Baltic in the West to the Volga and the Caspian sea in the East, an area roughly covering present Soviet Eastern Europe and southwestern Russia of today. Before his mysterious death in 453, he had expanded this empire to the Great Wall of China; thrashed Greeks and Latins in Turkey, Greece, Germany, France, and Italy; extorted peace money amounting perhaps to over $2 million from two unwilling empires, and an annual tribute of 2,100 pounds of gold from them; assembled a gargantuan treasure by plunder; earned the name of "God's Scourge' (the grass never grew again where his horse had trod, men said); and threatened both Constantinople and Rome.

We do not know the correct form of his name. Western ears picked it up as Attila, Atli, or Etzel. It was the Hunnic name for the Volga. Even the name of his race is obscure: Chinese chronicles refer to it as *hioung nu*; Latins heard the brief nasal grunt *hioung* and they Latinized it as *hunnus*. We know Attila was as bloodthirsty, as greedy, as ruthless, and as unscrupulous as any Latin or Greek emperor before or after him. We know one trait of his character which may be the key to his destiny: his superstitiousness, shared by all the Huns. Having overrun Rheims with blood and fire and cruelty, this irresistible band was put to flight by some loud sound emanating from the cathedral. At another time, Attila would not offend the bishop of Troyes because the latter's name was Lupus: the wolf was a deathly totemic symbol for the Huns, and "wolf" was the meaning of this bishop's name.

Attila had an autocratic personality. Told by an envoy of the Emperor Theodosius that the latter prayed for his welfare, Attila answered: "May it be unto the Romans as they wish it to me!" Asked by another delegation, come to discuss peace and war, whether they should return with a final answer to his demands, he retorted with one laconic Latin syllable: "No." Offered 35C pounds of gold (approximately $2 million today) by the Romans as a peace price at a truce meeting on the banks of the Morava River in 434, he casually answered; "Make it 700," and got it. To an imperial legate starting his speech with the words: "My Lord, the Emperor, has lived up to his promises and . . . " Attila shrieked: "That is a lie!" Told that Orleans could not resist beyond the 23rd of June, he replied: "On that day I shall arrive." On the eve of his onslaught against Rome and Constantinople, he sent couriers to both cities bearing the identical message: "My master, who is also yours, orders you to prepare his palace for him!"

Attila had an ambition based on his descent from the Bird-King, enlivened by the perpetual flight of Huns from the demons of wind and sand,

67

and fed by his burning hatred of Rome. All Hun warriors employed by Rome as mercenaries would return to their people, he vowed. Rome and Constantinople would be destroyed. The Great Wall would be demolished, the Chinese Empire seized. India and Persia would be overrun. The Bird-King would reign from the China Sea to the Atlantic. The Huns would find the land of their seeking and settle down in towns and cities of stone and wood. They would live on the spoils of nations, dominate all in the name of their ancient gods, and impose the law of the Huns on all men. But he had sworn a special oath to destroy Rome. It was the object of his living hate. His night bodyguard, Edecon, often heard Attila grind out the name of Rome hoarsely in his dreams.

It was this man and his hordes who had appeared on the banks of the Rhine in 451. In quick succession he had taken Worms, Windisch, Spires, Mayence, Basle, Strasbourg, Colmar, Besançon, Troyes, Arras, Metz, Rheims, Laon, St. Quentin. At Orleans he had been stopped and driven back. He lost a battle at the Catalaunian Fields near Châlons. He had returned to Etzelburg, his stronghold, and reorganized his forces. In a quick change of methods, he had replaced the fur clothing of his warriors with armor. He had employed Roman tacticians and trainers. The rough flying hordes were drilled and disciplined in military formation and tactics. Huns learned the use of seige weapons: scaling-ladders, ballistae, catapults, onagri. He decided to march on Rome. He invaded Italy. By 452, he had taken Aquileia, Padua, Verona, Bergamo, Brescia, Cremona, and Mantua. He was now camped north of the Po and was prepared for the last leg of his southward conquest to Rome. No army capable of stopping him stood between him and Rome. The only things in front of him were a round-shouldered bishop on a mule and a choir of baldheaded clerics.

Attila threatened not merely the ancient imperial city. At stake was the loose coagulation of nations, now settled throughout Europe, which formed the basis of her future civilization and the greatness which the Occident would achieve over 1,500 years. The Visigoths in Spain and southern France, the Franks in Northern France, the Lombards in northern Italy, the Saxons and Thuringians in Germany, they and the indigenous populations would have fallen under the blight of Hun rule, thus nullifying all the West possessed of her past.

There was more at stake: Christianity had become a center of unity and a hearth of rekindled hopes for the already disintegrating Roman Empire. The Christian faith had happened, and it presented the alternative of hope both to the dead works of effete religions and to the mortal necessity of death. Rome and the eastern Mediterranean is strewn with broken funerary inscriptions representing every cult known to the men of Leo's time: Mithra, Serapis, Isis, Osiris, Zoroaster, Greek mysteries, Oriental rites, the Roman gods, and the Greek pantheon. Yet the universal message carried by all was set forth succinctly and poignantly by Horace in his famous lines to Torquatus. Turning his eyes from the contemplation of spring, he looked at the human condition and wrote to his friend:

> Do not hope for immortality,
> This is the message of the passing year,
> And the hour which snatches our happy days.
>
> Swift months renew the heavens and the earth.
> But we, when we die,
> Just as when our father Aeneas died,
> Just as when divine Tullus and Ancus died,
> We are but dust and shadows.
>
> Torquatus, when once you die,
> And the underworld has claimed you,
> Nothing, not your family,
> Not your accomplishments,
> Not your piety,
> Nothing will restore you to life.

In contrast, the Christian faith offered a hope and a guarantee of eternal life after death. The epitaph of one Petrolanus, found on the Aventine

69

overlooking the Vatican Hill, sums up that hope and that faith in five simple words: "*Petrolanus, Deum videre cupiens, vidit* (Petrolanus, who desired to see God, now sees him)."

At the time of Leo, Christianity had just begun to insert itself throughout Europe as the way of life. Radiating from Italy, it had spread long lines of communication through Gaul, Belgium, England, Ireland, Germany, Spain, and Eastern Europe. Within 300 years, it would dominate the entire continent. Under the tutelage of Christianity, Medieval and Renaissance Europe, with all its faults and successes, evolved into modern Europe. All this would have been impossible if the Hunnic Empire had engulfed Europe. That it did not is due to Leo.

Leo's conversation with Attila lasts just a few minutes. Did Attila superstitiously fear the priest in Leo? The totemic symbolism of Leo's name ("lion")? Had he already made up his mind to retreat because of famine, disease, and discontent in his own ranks? Did Leo threaten the punishment of Heaven and Hell? We do not know. We only know that suddenly Attila turns his horse, recrosses the river, enters his camp at a gallop, shouting hoarse orders. Tents are lowered and folded. Chariots are harnessed. Horse lines are emptied. Toward nightfall, the clatter of hooves begins to die away. By morning, the camp of the Huns is deserted.

Christianity promises men hope and life; on that basis, it claims to dominate *all* of man's life. That day, on the banks of the Po, it confirmed hope and delivered life. It would go on to exercise its claim for over a milennium.

All the evidence we have tells us that Attila was a merciless, egotistical, ungovernable, self-willed, ambitious, cunning barbarian with whom ordinary appeals for pity or reasonableness would have absolutely no avail. Leo never wrote of what he said to the Hun. Yet no one can doubt that the decision Attila made at the Po was due in large part to Leo's belief in his mission, and he was able to communicate this to Attila. Up to Leo's time, Christianity had dwelt in the shadow of the empire. Its kingdom "was not of this world." Only slightly more than a hundred years before that, it had been liberated from the catacombs.

Leo saw all human history on two levels. What happened in the visible world was a mere reflection of the invisible and supernatural world of spirit from which salvation and prosperity came to men through Christ's church. He made his two-level vision of history quite clear in sermons preached to the Roman populace after the Vandals had come to loot but, by his persuasion, spared the people and the city of Rome as a whole, in 455. That was three years after his epochal meeting with Attila:

> Who has liberated it [Rome], preserved it from massacre? . . . Ascribe our liberation, not, as the godless do, to the influence of the stars but to the ineffable mercy of the Almighty who has softened the rage of the barbarians. . . . The glory of Peter and Paul is so great that you have become a holy people, a chosen people, a priestly and royal nation, and, thanks to the presence of the Holy See of the Blessed Peter, you have become lords of the world, and by holy religion you are able to extend your dominion further than by earthly might.

Leo was the first leader of Western Christianity who presented his religious beliefs as a total explanation of man and his environment. Fifty years before, Augustine had divided this world into "two cities": the City of God and the City of Mammon. According to Augustine, reconciliation between the two was impossible. Now Leo proposed baldly that Christianity's authority extended to both worlds.

In confronting Attila with this assertion (as it seems likely he did) or merely in confronting Attila, Leo risked his own life and the survival of Christianity, in order to stake the great claim of Christianity. If he had failed, Christianity may never have stepped onto the empty throne of the Roman Empire. Because he was willing to die, he lived and Christianity lived to shape Europe for more than a thousand years.

By the time Leo I became pope, the growing separation between Eastern Orthodoxy (under the patriarchs of Constantinople, Alexandria, Antioch, Jerusalem, Cyprus) and the Roman Church under the popes had become obvious and troublesome. Very few in the West could speak or read Greek. Still fewer in the East could read or speak Latin. The Romans (Latins) fasted on Saturdays; the Easterners thought this weird and wrong. The Latins believed that only unleavened bread (*azymes*) could be used in celebrating the sacred mystery of Christianity, the Mass. The Easterners believed you could and should use leavened bread. And there were other differences.

Leo drew a sharper line of disagreement with the Easterners. In 449, he published his *Tomos*, a document setting forth the basic beliefs of Christianity. It was accepted everywhere, east and west. But a difference must be noted. Western churches accepted it merely because Leo, all-powerful ruler, proclaimed it. The Easterners accepted it merely because, as the patriarch of Constantinople wrote back, Leo was simply echoing what the five Eastern patriarchates had always taught. The point was not lost on Leo, and when the Council of Chalcedon in 451 reaffirmed the patriarch of Constantinople as second in honor only to the pope of Rome, Leo immediately replied that the bishop of Rome was not merely first in honor but first in authority and orthodoxy. *Every* bishop and patriarch was second to the bishop of Rome, said Leo. And make no mistake about it!

Attila died violently in 453 by an unknown hand; in 461, Leo died peacefully in his bed. His legacy: a Christian church indistinguishable from the Roman Empire, a Christian church that *was*, for good and for evil, the Roman Empire.

On Septenber 4, 476, the last Roman emperor of the West was deposed and pensioned off into obscurity by a strange, barbaric figure, a German called Odovacer (or Odoacer) of the tribe of Scirri who lived beyond the Danube. Odovacer ruled Italy and appointed two popes (Felix III, Gelasius I) before he was killed by the Ostrogoth, Theodoric, in 493. Theodoric now controlled the election of popes. With the exception of Pope Anastasius II (496–498), the next four popes (Symmachus, Hormisdas, John I, Felix IV) were all either ratified or appointed by Theodoric. On his death, his daughter Amalasuntha was responsible for the first German pope, Boniface II. Then Theodoric's son, Theodatus, made Popes John II, Agapitus, and Silverius.

In the meantime, papal election rules were being refined. By the beginning of the fifth century, the election process by assembly was becoming too bloody in its results and too disturbing in its duration. The politics of empire and kingdom and of the city were being injected into an issue which already included family interests, clerical ambitions, doctrinal differences, and individual greed. At the Roman Synod of 499 (where twenty-five of the clergy signed in as cardinal-priests), Pope Symmachus endeavored to get rid of the political influences by excluding the Senate and ordinary layfolk: "Without a firm indication by a preceding pope about his successor," Symmachus laid down, "only the clergy of Rome may elect the new pope, and that by a simple majority."

But the law of Symmachus remained a dead letter. We find in the sixth century that, according to the official Roman election formula, the election of the pope was carried out by "all the priests and leaders of the Church and the whole clergy and the nobles, and the entire body of the armed forces, together with citizens in good standing and the whole body of the ordinary people in this city which has endured so long."

As part of the electoral body, the clergy's title was *venerabilis* (venerable), the army's *felicissimus* (most triumphant), and the people's *sanctus* (holy). Their usual place of election was the old Roman Forum at one spot called The Three Fates. And this was the mode of papal election, whether this vast, self-consciously preeminent elective body ratified an already chosen candidate of a preceeding pope or that of an emperor or some other prince or ruler; or whether it chose a candidate and sent his name for ratification to the particular military ruler who happened to dominate Rome at that time. But no outside power ever questioned the right and obligation of the Roman assembly to choose a candidate. This was one reason why the Romans called Pope Gregory I the "Great." Gregory insisted that the Roman spirit was the spirit of Christ and should be the spirit of the whole church.

Gregory the Great and His Empire of the Spirit

As they climb the stairs behind their leader to enter St. Andrew's Monastery in Rome, all sixty followers tailor their gait to match his slow, laborious progress. He moves with the aid of a cane. His finger joints are swollen with arthritis, his body bent and cadaverous. His face is drawn and white, but still lit by the sparkling intelligence of two blue eyes.

It is late February in the year 604, 269 years after the death of Pope Silvester. During those two and three-quarter centuries, great waves of change have swept across the vast breadth of the Roman Empire; but in that welter of political, economic, military, religious, and social upheaval two salient facts emerge: the temporal empire temporarily buttressed by the military might of Constantine now has finally and utterly collapsed: inevitably, inexorably, it has been replaced by the only unifying authority still vital and even growing in the furthest extremities of its once all-powerful body.

That authority is the Roman Church, and the author of that gigantic achievement of succession is this now broken and dying man so painfully making his way into St. Andrew's Monastery. For this is Pope Gregory the Great, sixty-fourth in the line stretching back to the Apostle Peter. Only three of the 265 popes will have the epithet "Great" traditionally attached to their names: Gregory is one of them. Even in letters written on the day he dies—March 4, less than two weeks from now—they will call him that.

Governor of Rome at thirty, a monk at thirty-four, papal envoy to the emperor of Constantinople at thirty-nine, abbot at forty-six, pope at fifty, Gregory and Gregory alone by the force of his genius, his personal devising, is responsible for the fundamental mind-set of the 199 popes who will succeed him down to the middle of the twentieth century. He determined the theology, the piety, the moral outlook and practice, and the intellectual attitude of some billions of human beings who have lived since his day.

He is just over sixty-four, but ever since the rigorous fasts and hardships of his years as a monk, Gregory's health has been precarious and is now irretrievable. In his prime, men noted, Gregory's appearance was magnificent: tall for a Roman of his era (over five foot five inches), blue-eyed, brown-haired, high and broad in forehead, with an aquiline nose, full red lips, prominent bearded chin, exquisite tapering hands. Now an accumulation of miseries weighs him down: a few old wounds from early youth, the dysentery that attacked him on a long sea journey to Constantinople in 579, the rheumatism he contracted in the Roman plague of 589, the visible aftereffects of his second heart attack two weeks previous to this day. He is limping, cautiously negotiating the steps up to the doors, his cane ringing sharply on the marble, his wheezing breath audible to all. Gregory knows he is only days from death, and he wishes to hold a "meeting of the world," a *statio orbis*, here in the monastery built on the site of his birthplace on the Coelian Hill. Here his life began. Here his service of God began. Here will be his last public act as pope.

Once in the vestibule of the monastery, Gregory turns to the right and proceeds down the corridor as far as the doors of his special chapel. Inside he stops, breathing heavily and waiting for the people to gather around him. One by one they file in. Some gaily dressed Roman men and women. Five Byzantine Greeks. A dozen tall, blond Britons in short tunics and black cloaks; these are of the tribe of Angles. (When Gregory saw them first and was told their name, he made the famous pun: "*Angli quasi Angeli!* Angles who look like Angels!"): they are Gregory's favorite clerical students and the nucleus of his choir. A company of ten Franks, Gregory's bodyguard. And a mixed group of Spanish, French, Germans, Corsicans, Sardinians, Sicilians, clerics and lay people. There are some

Irish monks, one Lombard from Turin, one Indian, and two black men from North Africa. Gregory's whole world.

Today's ceremony is traditionally simple and of ancient significance. The participants are drawn from all parts of the world; as representatives of all other men and women, they are standing here today in the presence of the personal representative of Jesus. For the believer, the whole world is standing together at this moment of worship. This is the *statio orbis*, the standing-to-attention of the whole earth. Behind this ceremony lies the old belief that, just as once in the dawn of God's creation the children of God, angels and humans, stood up and laughed with joy and love for their creator, so in the Kingdom of Jesus on earth all humans together with the guardian angels of the human universe will stand together and rejoice in Jesus.

No one speaks for a short while. They wait for Gregory. Like him, they lift their eyes to gaze at the three rectangular frescoes running around the semicircular walls of the sanctuary. Gregory himself has had these frescoes put there to commemorate the events of his pontificate. On the left panel, they see a long procession of Romans led by Gregory. On the center one, there is a panorama of Rome as city and as center of the world. To the right, the artist has depicted the pope as representative of Jesus among men.

A few present glance at the old man bent on his stick, loving him, fearing him. "The day I do not give bread to the poor is a lost day," he told them once. "You sent me a miserable horse and five good asses," Gregory wrote to one of his stewards. "The horse I cannot ride because he is wretched. The asses I will not ride, because they are asses and I am pope. I as pope am the servant of the servants of God"—the title used ever since by every pope. "I will not yield to any creature on this earth. I am the successor of Peter," he wrote to the emperor. The Romans love Gregory's mixture of imperiousness and solicitude.

The Romans are the first to speak today. "Holy Father, we thank the Lord Jesus for your hand in saving us from the plague . . ." All eyes are on the procession in the left fresco. That was fourteen years ago in March of 590. The plague had decimated the Roman population for nine months. Gregory in his sermon of August 29, 590, tells us that more than

77

17,000 died of it. Gregory, not yet pope, organized a penitential procession of all Romans, walking at their head, carrying a portrait of the Virgin. Church historians record that the Archangel Michael appeared above the procession on the Bridge to St. Peter's (it will be known later as the Bridge of the Angel). By December, the plague is gone . . ."And when the unmentionable race [Romans never pronounce the name "Lombards" if they can help it] wanted to devour the city of God, you saved us . . ." Indeed, Gregory had. Not by force of arms. "I am become the paymaster of the Lombards," Gregory complained later. He bought off the Lombard leader, Agilulf, with papal gold. "But how could I, pastor of men, do nothing, when daily thousands of Romans chained together like dogs were led off bleeding to be sold as slaves in France and Germany?" he wrote later. In fourteen years, Gregory contained the Lombards and made Rome stronger and more defensible.

As his beloved Romans wind up, Gregory laughs with pleasure. He remembers how he thrashed them with his tongue in their darkest hour: "All the glory of earthly dignity has expired within this city," he shouted at them in his first sermon as pope. "The world grows old and hoary, and through a sea of troubles hastens to approaching death." That first sermon was in September 590, a funeral oration over the grave of ancient Rome. "Now is the city deserted . . . destroyed . . . weighed down with a groaning." Before any other Roman realized it, Gregory saw clearly: ancient Rome with her empire was gone forever. Contemptuous of Greco-Roman literature and art, indifferent to the beauty of antiquity, Gregory refused to learn to speak or even read Greek. He set out to create a new empire with new strength, fresh beauty. He refused to act as a temporal ruler even when requested by the warlike Lombards and Franks. Gregory has his foothold only in the spiritual realm.

We do not know whether Gregory's rejection of Greek language and culture grew out of a policy of asserting Roman domination over Constantinople. We do know that in 595, Constantinople's patriarch, John the Faster, wrote sententiously to Gregory, calling himself "the ecumenical patriarch," that is, chief priest of the whole world, including Rome. That was too much for Gregory.

"Antichrist must surely be at hand," he wrote back tartly to Patriarch

John. Like Leo the Great, Gregory embraced the title that Pope Celestine (422–432) had promoted for the popes when he declared that the bishop of Rome was *pater patruum*, meaning bishop of all bishops.

Gregory knew all this, as well as the refusal of Leo the Great to accept Constantinople as "the New Rome," "the Second Rome," and its patriarch as second only to the bishop of Rome. Gregory also fully affirmed Pope Gelasius's assertion that popes were independent of emperors of Constantinople and of any "college of bishops," specifically, the one that governed the Eastern Church.

The fact of the matter was that by the year 420 the emperors in Constantinople no longer wielded any real power. Western Europe, Italy and Rome in particular, were now overrun by barbarian tribes, Goths, Ostrogoths, Visigoths, Vandals, Franks, Celts, Huns, Burgundians. Rome had been pillaged and sacked twice in a space of forty-nine years of the fifth century. The only figurehead and leader that survived it all was the pope. Constantinople had ceased to matter for the moment. It would matter again for a short space of time during the reign of Emperor Justinian, but then it ceased to matter altogether.

The Irish monks are next. Gregory likes them because they never ask questions, are blindly loyal. They and the Italian Benedictines have been his chief instruments in creating the common mentality of his new empire. Through them, Gregory has revived the old dream; and he now remembers as they speak: ". . . the Holy Virgin, the martyrs, the angels, you taught us to revere. . . . You showed us that around and through the stuff and matter of this world there breathes the Spirit . . . by whom we live . . . by whom we can do all things . . . and in whom the earth and heavens will be cleansed of its demons and false gods and renewed—to be just as it was before Adam and Eve sinned and fell. . . . "

Now, one by one, the various nationalities represented take up their refrains. The Corsicans: ". . . you saved us from slavery and rebuilt our churches." Sardinians: ". . . wheat you gave our families and holy baptism to our children." Africans: "School and hospitals and good bishops came from your hand to us." Germans: ". . . a different Rome, not oppressor but liberator, you showed our race." Franks: ". . . our king, our princes, our people have prospered with your blessing." The Lombards: ". . . you removed the stain of sins and gave us peace." The Spanish: ". . . by your grace and power we are in peace." The Britons: "Our land is now a blessed province of this Rome, this city of God." The Indians: "We have found the truth for all men with you." The Sicilians: "Six monasteries for our bishops and prosperity over our island, this you did for us." The Greeks: ". . . worthy priest of John and Paul and Jesus, you have the light of God."

Gregory sees them all now in retrospect—Queen Theodilind of the Lombards, King Recoard of the Spanish Visigoths, King Adelbertand and Queen Adelburgh of Britain baptized by the monk, Augustine, whom Gregory sent to England. Gregory through Augustine reclaimed Britain for Rome as a spiritual province almost two hundred years after the last Roman legionnaries had left. And there is a long line of Sicilian dukes, Calabrian princes, Byzantine emperors—Justin, Tiberius, Maurice, Phocas, and others. Gregory winces at the memory of Emperor Phocas. He had compromised on that one, he remembers with pain. Phocas with his queen, Leontia Augusta, had captured Emperor Maurice and his five sons. With Maurice looking on helplessly, Phocas had beheaded each son, then put out Maurice's eyes and, after torture, disemboweled him. Gregory, knowing all this, still had prayed, tongue in cheek: "Grant, God, life to Phocas and to Leontia Augusta." But thereby Gregory had maintained the pope's position as head of all the church—Byzantine as well as Roman, the East as well as the West—but for how long?

Ah! Well. Rome was now mistress of a new empire. Gregory listens. The Britons are now singing the closing hymn, pouring out in clear strong voices the sonorities and shadings of Gregory's new church music in pianissimo measures and passages of organ fullness and tonal virility, while the thin-voiced Lombards accompany them with their peculiar melodies full of sentimental phrasings and expressive devices as luscious and sensuous in their rapid enumeration as the cattle the Lombards prize so much . . . "*Roma superat, Christus regnat* (Rome commands, Christ rules)." This was Gregory's achievement. He had formed the heartland of Christianity in Italy, and clustered around it the provinces of Spain, France, Germany, Sicily, Britain, Ireland, Greece, and the whole Greek empire, Africa, even parts of the outer world beyond the Red Sea. Gregory had built a new hierarchy on the ruins of the old Roman government and encouraged the first nuclei of nations which became the future states of Western Europe. On that central fresco panel it was all clear as a Roman mandala: the nations are concentric circles grouped around the innermost circle of Rome. The City.

The last solemn moment of the ceremony has come. Gregory looks up at the third panel: St. Peter on his throne. Behind him, Jesus with crown and scepter. In front of Peter, Gregory's parents, Gordian and Silvia. And with them, Gregory as pope. Around this group, a multitude of white, brown, yellow, and black men and women and children, emperors, slaves, clerics, and lay people.

Now, Gregory's sixty guests are running through the last phrases of the Profession of Faith: ". . . [Jesus] rose on the third day . . . will come to judge the living and the dead . . . and the Holy Spirit." These are the consecrated words drawn up by the first great council of the church 279 years ago before, on June 19, 325, at Nicaea. Gregory bows his head as the unanimous shout rings through the chapel and cloister. "Alleluia! The Lord is Risen! Alleluia!" Then: "Life to our Lord, the Pope!" Gregory responds: "Your bishop and your servant." Then he turns and limps out. A few people remain to look at a fresh portrait of Gregory in the apse of the chapel. It is a stucco circle. There is a square frame of light color behind the pope's head, awaiting the addition of the halo—the sign of sanctity. Only when the subject is dead, will Gregory's portrait be completed with that sign of approbation.

After Gregory, the Roman Church and the Western world entered what historians have conventionally called the Dark Ages, which in many respects certainly were very dark. But in reading the cameos that follow, keep in mind the astonishing test to which Rome and its church were exposed during this extraordinary period:

Suddenly—and almost without warning—a whole series of violent storms swept across the empire and down over Rome. Like hurricanes, these storms had names: Vandals, Goths, Lombards, Franks. In sum, perhaps ten million of them, barbarians all, all armed to the teeth, virtually all illiterate (Charlemagne himself could neither read nor write,

81

and spoke only rudimentary war-camp Latin in addition to his native Frankish), and all determined to glut themselves on the wealth of the empire.

It is as though within a decade, say, the population of the United States were to be *doubled* by a wholly unexpected influx of an entirely alien people ignorant of our language, laws, and customs, yet powerful enough to take our wealth, our women, and our land as they pleased.

Obviously the Church of Rome bent under these storms. Obviously it could not wish these invaders away. Obviously it had to accommodate them, not only within the empire but within the church—and ultimately within its hierarchy, even in the papacy. Obviously it had a monumental problem of digestion, and obviously a series of rather severe bellyaches.

The miracle is that—despite the blood and the corruption—Rome eventually swallowed the barbarians and not the other way around. It took a thousand years, but it happened; and, on the dungheap, Western civilization flowered.

Shortly after Gregory died, there was further legislation about papal elections. At the beginning of the seventh century, Pope Deusdedit had to lay down a new law in order to exclude deals and bargains made before the death or during the dying hours of a pope and of any diocesan bishop. "Nobody," Deusdedit ruled in the autumn of 615, "may presume, while the Pontiff [of Rome] or the bishop of his own city is alive, to create votes for himself. Three days must elapse after the burial of the Pontiff or the bishop. Then, when all the clergy are assembled together with the people, they may hold an election and choose whomever they prefer as their spiritual leader."

Gregory himself had been made pope with the approval of the emperor in Constantinople. Six popes before Gregory and twenty-six after him needed Constantinople's approval and ratification. The need for ratification of a Roman election often left the Roman See without a pope for months, sometimes for up to two years. In the case of Benedict II, communication across land and water was completely blocked by war, so that Benedict II proceeded to rule as pope with the presumed ratification of Constantinople. But Constantinople's control of the eastern Mediterranean and Eastern Europe finally became so weak that one emperor, Constantine Pogonatus, notified the Romans in 684 that they no longer need bother him about ratification. But later emperors, like Justinian II, insisted on their right. However, Gregory II was the last pope to request Constantinople's approval.

Immediately on the death of Gregory II, the elections of popes became the work of Roman and Italian factions. Eight popes, from Gregory III (731–741) to Leo III (795–816), were chosen by contentious disputes among a Frankish faction (supported by the Franks in France), various clerical parties, some factions among the noble families in and around Rome—Lombards, Goths, and Italians—and the Roman army.

In 759, Pope Paul I gave a new status to the long-established group of twenty-seven Roman cardinal-priests: he placed them and seven cardinal-deacons and one archdeacon specifically in charge of overseeing the election of popes, and of helping in definite sectors of Church government. The reaction was violent in the Roman noble families and in the armed forces, both of whom wished to retain their influence in the election. By now, in Rome, there were papal families (families of past popes). Nepotism was beginning to reign in the papal court. But no matter the mechanism, the steady progress of the popes to attain and retain power continued. Some like Stephen IV had to deal with domestic enemies: some like Leo III had to deal with power on an international plane.

Enter the Snake

The Palace of the Popes stands on the Lateran Hill in Rome, its porticos and facades glistening in the yellow Roman sun. Cavalry and infantry detachments of the Roman army, flags flying, weapons drawn, completely encircle the palace. No one can get in or out: this is the reckoning day when debts are to be paid.

The palace itself is a sprawling mass of single buildings—chapels, baptistry, papal house, archives, treasure room, dining halls, kitchens, pantries, storerooms, servants' quarters, guards' barracks, stables, baths, clustering like beehives around the great basilica of St. John that Fausta, wife of Constantine the Great, gave as residence to Pope Silvester some 450 years ago. Each of the sixty-one popes following Silvester has added something to the original. And here all popes will live and govern until the fourteenth century.

On this morning of August 12 in the year 769, the palace is shrouded in a solemn silence broken only by the faint echoes of music and chanting from the Vatican Hill across the Tiber where Pope Stephen IV is finishing High Mass in St. Peter's Basilica. Within the palace, awaiting his arrival, are 150 cardinals, archbishops, bishops, and their theologians. This is a Lateran synod. They stand around the papal throne in the famous dining hall of Zacharius surrounded by the high vaulted walls on which colored mosaics depict every land and every ocean of the world. In brilliant greens, yellows, whites, purples, blues, oranges, reds, golds, this

85

is the whole universe confided to the guidance and care of Peter's ninety-fifth successor and Jesus' personal representative among humans.

By 8:15, Pope Stephen is at the huge doors of the main tower in the Lateran Palace. Before him, chanting clerics. Around him, the bearded warriors of the north, Franks all of them, his personal bodyguard. Within five minutes, he is standing near his throne at the head of the dining hall; all the cardinals and bishops are waiting to sit down; the Franks, with their backs to the mosaic-covered walls and their hands on their long swords, close the circle around the whole assembly. All eyes are fixed on the mobile face of Pope Stephen. Stephen, son of Olivus, is a narrow-shouldered, sallow-faced, flat-footed Sicilian, four feet ten inches in height, balding, thin-lipped, round-chinned, every line around his mouth telling of wile and ruthlessness, his black eyes dancing vivaciously with stratagem and ruse.

In the 165 years since the death of Gregory the Great—who by any measuring rod one could apply was indeed truly great—the new empire of the spirit that he founded has come to, well, to Stephen the snake. Someone has to wield the power, but this is what the power can do:

Now almost sixty, Stephen has survived—and conquered. Nothing has ever distracted Stephen. He drinks and eats little, thinks women are "vessels of Satan," has an unshakeable belief in the protection of Jesus over the papacy, and would go to any length to obtain his purposes. He will at one point forbid a royal marriage, condemning the idea as "diabolical" and the proposed union as merely "concubinage." In simple fact, the marriage would have interfered with his politics. So when he wrote his warning letter to the Frankish prince in question, he first laid the unfinished letter on the tomb of St. Peter and received Holy Communion over it. Then he finished the letter saying: "If anyone does do otherwise than help us, then by the authority of Peter, Prince of the Apostles, he will be condemned to burn in Hell-fire with Satan and his godless crew." The prince renounced the marriage.

Pope Stephen sits down. The cardinals and bishops sit down. Before nodding to the master of ceremonies, Stephen glances around. Standing beside him are those who put him on this throne, Secretary of State Christophorus and his son Sergius. They will have to do—for now. Then,

Duke Desiderius, Lombard king of Pavia—a useful ally, although he had tried to have Stephen killed only a few mornings ago on July 28. Duke Theodocius, Lombard king of Spoleto: too fawning, too greedy. All Lombards smelt. Gratiosus, papal archivist, turncoat, assassin, specialist in carving prisoners' eyes out of their sockets without killing. Stephen gives the signal.

The first item of business is a man. Jailers bring him in loaded with chains and dump him unceremoniously at Stephen's feet. This is Constantine, a nobleman. His kneecaps have been broken, his body whipped, his eyes carved out. All by gracious permission of Stephen.

The papal prosecutor reads the indictment: ". . . *And that on Saturday, July 28, the prisoner did consent to be made Bishop of Rome and successor to St. Peter, by force of arms and in contravention of the Holy Laws of Mother Church. . . .*"

On July 27, in the evening, just sixteen days previously, Stephen himself as a simple cardinal had sat alone with the dying Pope Paul I, and he heard the turmoil of arms and the cries of dying men in the streets outside as Constantine's brothers, Duke Antonio of Nepi (nicknamed Toto), Passivus, and Paschalis, acclaimed Constantine as pope.

Stephen also heard the agonizing words of the dying Paul: "Jesus, I deserve this! Forgive me!" Paul, twelve years before, had set about getting himself elected pope even before the then pope was dead. "Forgive me," Paul kept whimpering until he died the next day. By that time, Constantine, a layman, had been made pope. Stephen himself was of another faction and had to flee for safety, first to the chapel of St. Petronilla, then to an obscure church in Trastevere. Secretary of State Christophorus and son Sergius took refuge at the high altar in St. Peter's where Toto's sword and Gratiosus's carving dagger could not reach them. On July 29, the bishop of Praeneste, with Toto's sword at his throat, had conferred the sacred orders of subdeacon, deacon, and priesthood on Constantine. On July 30, Constantine had been consecrated pope in St. Peter's.

"*The Holy Synod, therefore, condemns Constantine to perpetual prison for his blasphemy and invalidates the ordination of all bishops and priests during his pontificate.*" The prosecutor now addresses Constantine. "*Do you regret your blasphemous acceptance of this Holy Office?*"

"The Romans put me there by force," Constantine mumbles in his pain. "Holy Father! Have pity!"

Stephen stiffens and leans forward in cold fury. "Why did you accept the Papacy?" he shouts. Constantine had indeed written to Pepin, king of the Franks, asserting that he was the validly elected pope. "Why?"

"Other laymen, Sergius of Ravenna, Stephen of Naples, Fabian of Rome. They were laymen, they accepted. . ."

"All according to the canons and our traditions." (Stephen did not speak. He spat out words like fishbones from between his teeth.) "But you by force of arms."

"You, Holy Father," rejoins Constantine, "you were put on the throne by force of arms. . ."

Pope Stephen has had enough. "What do you think?" he asks the assembly. As if to answer him, the cardinals and bishops in the front rows rush on Constantine, beating him, kicking him, spitting on him, shouting "Usurper! Blasphemer! Antichrist!"

Yet Constantine was entirely correct. Secretary of State Christophorus and son Sergius had fled Rome and gone to the two Lombard kings, Desiderius and Theodocius. A Lombard army led by a gigantic Lombard, Rachimpert, and a Lombard priest named Waldipert had been guided by Sergius and invaded Rome on the night of July 30. The following morning, they had hacked their way to the Lateran Palace, killed Constantine's brothers together with about 1,500 others and captured Constantine, who had hidden himself in a little chapel of St. Caesarius in the palace. Then Christophorus had summoned all the Romans to the Forum; and there Stephen had been elected (canonically and unanimously, he would claim, and the church down through the ages would officially accept).

On August 6, a week ago, at Stephen's consecration as pope, Christophorus had said to him: "We have created a pope free of Lombards and devoted to the Franks." Did that "we" smack too much of mastery? Was it too possessive? Within a year, Pope Stephen will have used Duke Desiderius to get Christophorus, Sergius, and Gratiosus imprisoned, first their eyes cut out, then their lives ended. He then will turn on Desiderius and by December of 771 will encompass his ruin and death. Stephen doesn't forget.

He returns his attention to the synod. The bleeding, unconscious Constantine has been removed to his perpetual imprisonment. The next issue concerns the Lombard priest, Waldipert, and a Roman monk, Philip. Their crime is even more abominable, as the prosecutor outlines it.

On July 31, after Constantine and his faction had been defeated and he, Stephen, had been elected, Waldipert (under instructions from Duke Desiderius, as Stephen well knows, but recognizes as impolitic to mention now) had assembled the Lombard faction in Rome, gone to the monastery of St. Vitus on the Esquiline Hill, extracted a simple monk called Philip, and had him acclaimed pope in the Lateran Palace, the Lombards shouting in their execrable Latin: "Philip! Pope! St. Peter has chosen him!" And this in the tail-end confusion of battle when nobody knew what was happening. Philip foolishly accepted, sat on the papal throne, gave the papal blessing, was consecrated bishop the same day, and that evening gave a huge banquet as pope for the nobles and officers of the Roman army. But, late at night, hearing that Secretary of State Christophorus was looking for him with sword in hand, Waldipert had fled, and was found clinging to a statue of St. Cosmas in the Pantheon. Gratiosus had put his eyes out, of course.

The synod now condemns him to a slow death by being cut to pieces a little bit each day until he expires. Philip, the foolish monk, will be flogged and incarcerated forever in a small cell in his monastery which, the decree said, *"he should never leave again except for burial."*

When these affairs are decided, the synod enacts Stephen's new rules for future elections of popes, makes decrees about the ordination of bishops and priests, and decides that images and statues of saints may be used in churches. Stephen forbade any participation by the people. "Only clergy may vote in the election. The people may acclaim the chosen candidate" (*not* confirm him).

Stephen ruled further: "No layman and no other man except a clerical member of the Roman Church who has attained the grade of deacon or priest can be pope." In practice, this meant that only a Roman cardinal, bishop, priest, or deacon could be pope. Stephen was explicit: after the election of one man and before he was proclaimed and crowned as pope, the Roman army was to come in full force and regalia, together with all the Roman people. Non-Romans were forbidden to enter the city during the election. Together, the army and the people were to salute the pope-elect. Then he was to be carried in triumph and enthroned and consecrated in the Lateran Basilica.

When the business of the synod is finished, all the participants march in procession from the Lateran to St. Peter's where all decisions are read aloud to the people in the name of Jesus, in the name of St. Peter, and in the name of Pope Stephen IV.

On his own deathbed, less than three years later, January 24, 772, Stephen kept repeating the two names: "Paul . . . Constantine . . . Constantine . . . Paul . . ." He was praying to the saints, the Romans say.

Leo III:
Renewing Old Ties

The time: just after 6 A.M. when the sky is still dark. The day: Christmas Day in the year 800. The place: the old Basilica of St. Peter's on Vatican Hill. The ceremony: a High Mass to be celebrated by the pope for a specially honored guest. The pope: Leo III. The guest: Charles, better known as Charlemagne, king of the Franks. Around the ninety-six columns supporting the Basilica roof, the Romans are packed in silence. The choir hymns triumphantly in the style of Gregory the Great, in long rising and falling cadences about the baby who is king, the Virgin who is his mother, God who is his father, and the peace this baby brings to all men of good will on earth.

This basilica was built by the Emperor Constantine over 500 years ago to enshrine the tomb of St. Peter. (It will be torn down after another 800 years and replaced with a more grandiose one.) At the back of the sanctuary, there is a locked door flanked by porphyry columns and surmounted by a triumphal arch. It guards the steps that lead down to the crypt where the dust and bones of Peter and his successors lie. One thousand candles have been lit. Standing at the left side of the altar are all the cardinals and bishops of Rome, Charlemagne's bishops, Charlemagne's daughters and sons, and the Roman nobility with their ladies. Leo, with the gaunt look of one who has not quite recovered from a recent whipping, sits on his throne placed on the right of the altar.

It is only twenty-eight years since the death of Stephen IV, less than two hundred years since Gregory the Great created his new empire of the spirit out of the rotting cadaver of the old Roman Empire. So quickly, the snake of power has entered and corrupted the empire of the spirit. It is all over, Leo knows. Unless . . .

Leo is waiting for the king. He is small in stature, tonsured (shaven head, except for a small rim of hair running around his temples), with heavy curved eyebrows, humped Roman nose, and jutting chin; his hands rest palms downward on his thighs. It is the eyes and mouth that strike a wry note. Both eyes are red and swollen (he has the use of only one). The lower lip hangs loose; and you can see Leo's tongue lolling around his mouth restlessly. Just eight months ago, on April 25, his Roman enemies, clerical and lay, had knocked him from his horse, then tried to squeeze his eyes out of their sockets in the Byzantine fashion and to cut out his tongue. They had no intention of killing him (that would have been a sacrilege and, besides, unnecessary), only of making him incapable of functioning as pope. Imprisoned for a couple of months, Leo had escaped last August and fled to Paderborn in Germany to get help from Charlemagne, To help his memory continually, Leo now has one blind eye and a half-controlled tongue that jumbles his words. The bell of St. Peter's starts to toll: the king is near.

To give Leo his due, once the agony and imprisonment were over, his personal fear gave way to a bigger fear. Returning under Frankish armed escort here to Rome on November 29, he was a changed man. Charlemagne himself arrived two days ago, held a trial in which Leo's enemiee were convicted and banished, and decided to stay for Christmas. Now Leo sees his own brush with death and his rescue by Charlemagne as a mirror-image of what threatens the church, the See of Peter, and the only world Leo has ever known. And he remembers the peculiar effect of Charlemagne in Paderborn—the same effect that a brilliant flash of lightning has over a dark and dangerous landscape: All became suddenly, unmistakably clear in Charlemagne's presence. Leo did not know why. But he sensed the message.

The world of Leo and Charlemagne, their Europe, from Britain to the Danube, from the Baltic to the Mediterranean, is being battered to pieces like a worn piece of metal held in a pincers. One northern claw of that pincers is the Norseman threat. The southern claw is the long Arab empire stretching from Gibraltar to the Indus. Held inescapably down on the anvil of a defenseless Europe, this world is being beaten, flattened, and shredded by a rain of hammer blows—disease, wars, disunity, treachery, hunger, burnings, enslavements, massacres, lawlessness, corruption, assassinations. "These," said Alcuin, chief counselor of Charlemagne, "these are the loveless days of the world's last age."

Charlenagne enters the basilica bareheaded, carrying his helmet in the crook of ore arm. "A Frank is born for the forest," Alcuin had said. Charlemagne stalks deer in his native forests with the same watchful ease. He is a seven-foot, bull-necked, pot-bellied figure with the girth of a Japanese sumo wrestler, seven-foot, bull-necked, pot-bellied figure with the girth of a Japanese sumo wrestler, a long straight nose, thin lips, narrow black mustache, full beard. Now forty-eight years old, Charleagne was king at twenty-six. He eats eight platters of meat a day, downs six bowls of wine, sleeps briefly; and when he laughs, he roars while his big ears work back and forth and the rafters shake.

Bowing to Leo, Charlemagne goes straight to the door of the crypt and kneels to pray. No one is deceived by the white tunic, purple cloak, and light slippers Charlemagne is wearing today (Leo had urgently asked him to wear the dress of a Roman patrician). He, Charlemagne, complied, but insisted on carrying his battle helmet. And under this aristocratic clothing is the chain-mail undervest that Charlemagne never removes.

Even kneeling, with bowed head and clasped hands, Charlemagne is still formidable. No one forgets what he is, what he promises, what he has done. He exudes the power of a man who has never lost a battle during sixty campaigns waged west to Spain, south to Sicily, north to the Baltic, east past Poland and Hungary, deporting ten thousand here, massacring forty-five hundred there, baptizing whole populations into Christianity with the sword or with water—it was one or the other—governing 1,615 states all over Europe, not fearing anyone on the face of the earth. Men have never known a power like his. They say: When the earth shakes, when the sky darkens, when the air is filled with the thunder of hooves, with clashing shields, with shouts of warriors, when forests ard cities fall, when all animals run for cover, then you know the great shield of Charlemagne's armor is near you.

Charlemagne's purpose here today: to be crowned emperor by the pope. All last night, he has discussed this with his counselors, Theodolf, Arno, Angilbert. Their opinion is the same as Alcuin's: your Europe is Christian Europe. Accept. "But I have all power now," he kept retorting to them. And they: "Yes. But as emperor you will unite all Europe and give them hope." The prayer of all is for hope. We all need hope. Give us all hope, Golden Charles!

Leo has a double purpose in crowning Charlemagne. One: to assert publicly that all political power, all power on earth, comes from God—and is only given to individuals and governments through God's representative, the bishop of Rome, the successor of St. Peter; today, through him, Leo, Peter's ninety-seventh successor. The other: to make possible the dream that all things human should be renewed, and that Jesus will come again. Charlemagne by the power of the pope will be emperor of the West, of Rome, of Britain, of Constantinople, of the Holy Lands, of Africa, of Asia, of Europe, of the whole world.

What neither of these two powerful men knows or intends is that they are building into the soul of the Roman Church and the civilization of Western Europe a principle of organization and a way of thinking that one thousand years later will lead both church and civilization to cannibalize themselves. They will end up, not assailed from the outside, but devouring the good in themselves, the very substance of themselves.

In spite of their best intentions, both Leo and Charlemagne have been pushed into "hard-line" positions by the logic of a history they did not initiate and would not have time to contol, much less finish. Events set in motion by the long-dead Constantine were now out of control.

First as to empire. The emperor of Constantinople, since Constantine's time, had always been called the Roman emperor, the Holy Roman emperor. Defense and propagation of the political welfare of the world was his duty and privilege. And, true, the Byzantine emperors had fulfilled their duty in the past. But by Christmas 800, no longer. The onslaught of Norsemen from the north, Slavs and Asiatic barbarians from the east, Islam from the south, all this had reduced the once Holy Roman Empire to a shrunken territory. The Mediterranean was an Islamic lake, at least from Italy eastward to Palestine. North Africa was Muslim. Spain, Egypt, Palestine, Syria, Persia, Arabia, were all under Islam.

Constantinople ruled over only one third of Greece, one third of Italy, Sicily, Cyprus, Corsica, Sardinia, and most of Turkey. Constantinople was barely holding on. It could defend no one.

Only one man could take Constantinople's place: Charlemagne. Who else could guarantee Leo's exalted position as patriarch of the West and supreme political authority? Leo III also resented the fact that the emperor of Constantinople had confiscated Leo's revenues from Sicily and Calabria. The emperor needed the money. But so did Leo.

Then as to spirit. Monarchic Rome and collegial Constantinople were worlds apart. The two sides did not even speak the same language. "Latin," said Emperor Michael III of Constantinople, "is a barbarian and Scythian language." (Scythian for Michael was roughly equivalent to our saying "piggish oinking.") Charlemagne, who could not read any language and did not write a word, said Greek was like "the hissing of vipers." And in the renaissance of arts and letters that he started at his court—the Carolingian renaissance—Charlemagne instilled a very deep anti-Greek prejudice. For many reasons. Jealousy of Byzantine splendor. Fear of Byzantine arrogance. Greed for Byzantine wealth. Dislike of Byzantine beliefs. Conviction that Byzantines were heretics, almost idolatrous.

For over one hundred years the Byzantine Greeks had been fighting among themselves about their painted pictures of Christ, the Virgin, the saints, the angels—their ikons, as they called them. One faction (the iconoclasts, the "ikon-breakers") said that use of ikons in worship was tantamount to idolatry. Eventually, by 840, the Byzantines decided in favor of their ikons and against the iconoclasts. From what we know of Charlemagne, he had strong opinions in theology; he was, for instance, against ikons. He even repudiated the decrees of the seventh ecumenical council of Constantinople which championed ikons, probably because his main enemies were idol-worshiping nations north and east of his empire. He had another theological bone to pick with the Byzantines: the famous (or notorious) *filioque* clause regarding the status of the Holy Spirit. Charlemagne insisted on the use of it rather than the Greek version, *dia tou uiou*.

Once Charlemagne made up his mind that the Byzantine Greeks were

95

the enemy, anything was permissible to beat them with. Even accusations of heresy and an alliance with a beleaguered pope in Rome. Charlemagne assembled his Latin bishops in council at Frankfurt in 794. Under his determined prodding, they turned around and did the unspeakable— what no Roman authority had ever done: they condemned the Greeks for using their phrase (*dia tou uiou,* literally "through the Son," which is how they conceived the origination of the Holy Spirit) and asserted that only their own Latin clause, *filioque* ("and from the Son") was acceptable for Christians, east or west. Then Charlemagne and his bishops petitioned Pope Adrian I to take their side. Adrian wrote back that there was nothing wrong with either formula, provided you understood them correctly.

The farce could have stopped right there, if it weren't for other allies of Charlemagne and the chauvinism of Byzantine clerics. French monks, who always chanted the *filioque* clause at Mass, settled in Jerusalem where the Byzantine Greek clerics had been for centuries. The Greeks heard those Latins chanting their *filioque,* and screamed heresy. The French monks screamed heresy right back. And the fight was on again.

The pope by now was Leo III. Like Adrian, he told the monks to stop screaming; that the Greeks were all right in their way; yet to keep on chanting their *filioque* in Latin ceremonies. Leo, in fact, inscribed the Nicene Creed on silver plaques and hung them in St. Peter's Basilica in Rome. He omitted the *filioque!* But by now the Greeks were calling all the Romans heretics.

Besides these differences (and those others concerning fasting, married clergy, unleavened bread, the proper way to make the sign of the cross, and so on), the chasm between Greek and Roman had been hugely enlarged because they had developed for centuries in isolation, one from the other. Romans treated religion juridically; Greeks treated it liturgically. Rome stressed the unity of the Godhead; Greeks, the Trinity. Romans spoke of redemption in Christ; Greeks of deification in Christ. Romans put a crucified figure on their crosses, and stressed Christ's function as victim for men's sins; Greeks had no crucified figure, and emphasized Christ's victory by enduring the crucifixion.

At Christmas 800, what it came down to was this. The most powerful Western military and political potentate, Charlemagne, found his only real obstacle on the path of empire to be Byzantium. The most powerful religious potentate, Leo III, found his only real obstacle on the path of absolute authority to be Byzantium. In addition, Charlemagne and Leo thought and believed in an identical way. Their alliance was inevitable. But it was one more fateful step downhill for the Roman popes. They were now ready to abandon one half of Christianity (and the more ancient, the more flourishing part) for the sake of wordly ambition.

Leo reaches over to a cushion placed near his throne and picks up a thin gold crown glistening with tiny jewels. Pope Adrian had told him, following the notions of Gregory the Great: "We must reign alone without kings." Gregory himself had written: "Peter's successor is ruler of all." Gregory was right. And wrong. Leo's other predecessors—Victor, Celestine, Gelasius—none of them had ever thought of doing what he now is doing. Never had a pope accepted a king or emperor as co-ruler. Yet only this will give hope. Yes. It is again hope that the whole world needs. It is always hope.

Charlemagne is on his feet, making the sign of the cross. Leo stands up, goes over quietly to his side, and wordlessly places the crown on his head. On signal, the bystanders break into a shout: "Long life and victory to Charles, Augustus, crowned by God, great and peace-giving emperor of the Romans!" Once more they repeat that shout. Charlemagne has not budged. Leo and his attendants place a purple cloak around his shoulders. Then, looking Charlemagne straight in the eyes, Leo kneels down and bows before him. Everyone in the basilica does likewise. There are a few moments of utter silence. The emperor must now act, signify his mind. Charlemagne has yet to say or do anything. He stands stockstill.

The enormity of the step being taken this Christmas Day by Leo the pope and Charlemagne the king is only more emphasized by the utter dissimilarity between the two men. Leo, Roman son of the elegant Roman Azuppius, Roman in his bones, from a three-hundred-year-old Roman family. Charlemagne, German son of the fierce bullet-headed Pepin, an Arnulfing Frank, descendant of Clovis, of Dagobert, of Charles the Hammer, and remotely of the eagle-god of northern forests and of Me-

97

roveus, son of the sea. Leo, perfumed with the onyx powder and musk water of Sicily, smelling of candles, of incense, of planned activity. Charlemagne, scented with horse-sweat, with Burgundy wine, with the rough lye soap he washed in, smelling of the forest, of straw beds, and of unplanned success.

Leo, a cleric from the age of eight and reared in the library, the church, the papal court; a cardinal at the age of thrity with an unblemished reputation for celibacy, elected pope unanimously at the age of forty-eight. Charlemagne riding bareback at eight years to hunt in the German forests, fighting in battle at thirteen, commanding troops at eighteen, at twenty-six king of the Franks, married four times, divorced twice, and now a widower with a mistress. Leo speaks pure Latin and Byzantine Greek in a resonant basso. Charlemagne speaks only Frankish fluently, has learned an execrable Latin dialect from ploughmen and foot-soldiers, and is famous for the thin, high-pitched, squeaky voice with a snarl in it that comes out of his ponderous frame. Leo, only mindful of Rome, of Peter, of his ninety-six predecessors on the throne of Peter, of Jesus' promise and of the *Romana Comunitas,* of the *populus dei,* "the Roman commonwealth of the people of God." Charlemagne, unable to forget the nations in his care, Frisians, Saxons, Franks, Visigoths, Lombards, Slavs, Celts, Angles, Jutes, Burgundians, Gascons, Greeks, Avars, Basques, Catalonians, Vandals, monks, farmers, weavers—"The whole Christian folk" was his own expression for them (he disliked the terms "empire" and "emperor").

Yes, despite these enormous differences, a common day and a common danger and a common faith has now brought Charles the Warrior and Leo the Fisherman together. The invisible guests at this ceremony are three:

The Muslim perched in Spain and Africa, harassing the sea lanes, rending the southern shores all around the Mediterranean, waiting for an opening.

Irene, queen in Constantinople, she-devil, magically beautiful; Irene who has put out her own son's eyes, thrown him in prison, surrounded herself with devoted eunuchs castrated by her orders, seduced the patriarch, and three months ago has written to Charlemagne: ". . . if the king should wish to marry, of course . . ." (The king did not, and that finally dashed any hope of a reconciliation between Rome and Byzantium.)

And the Norsemen. Charlemagne has seen their long boats with the grinning dragon prows nosing up the Meuse and the Seine. Leo in Rome receives every month the monks and nuns and priests who have fled their monasteries before the merciless Norsemen.

Both men understand, each in his way. Charlemagne quotes and adopts one of the few phrases from St. Paul's letter he has learned by heart: "I, Charles, apostle of Jesus Christ, by the will of God." He accepts.

The High Mass starts. At its end, the emperor bows to Leo. Charlemagne had always called the previous pope "my sweet co-father." This pope, Leo, is "my brother." Then, to the shouts of the people, Charlemagne strides out of St. Peter's. In his lodgings, he removes the crown, the purple cloak, the white tunic, the light slippers, never to wear them again. He remains in Italy until Easter, then rides west to the Adriatic with his troops, up the coast to Spoleto, Ravenna, Pavia, and on to the plain of Lombardy. As they approach the Alps, his daughters start singing the old Valkyrie songs of the Franks. After the Alps, he is in his homeland.

He will never return to Rome, never again pray in St. Peter's. He does not accept finally the Roman ideal. He retains his own: "The whole Christian folk of Europe." And he will give it tangible shape in his new internationalism: a common coinage; an international communication medium—the round, tidy Carolingian script—which will become uniformly used throughout Europe; his creation of agrarian communities; his price-fixing; his development of a merchant class of Jewish middlemen; his legal code; his irrigations, road-building, fortresses, monasteries, schools, libraries, churches, artists' workshops, homes for the destitute. And, above all, his huge protective shield. There shall be hope—until he dies. And even after he goes, the reviving rhythms of life will keep on until that shield explodes, galvanizing the twelfth and thirteenth centuries. So much hope, that it will afford Europeans the luxury no other continent has ever produced: the goal of chivalry, the nobility of gentleness, the tranquil dream of human love expressed in the love poem, the haunting beauty and mortal sadness of death with honor. Neither the Niebelungenlied of the Germans, the Ossian poems of the Celts, the poets of ancient Greece and Rome, nor the prolific writers of India, China, and Japan will ever produce the equivalent of Charlemagne's ideal of the citizen, which will animate the Italian "borghese," the Edwardian gentleman, and the big-hearted American of the twentieth century.

Leo will travel to France in 804 in order to get more protection from Charlemagne. This pope will survive two rebellions by the serfs on his estates and yet another assassination plot against his own life by Roman nobles in 815, suppressing the conspirators with the ferocity of a Byzantine master-torturer. And he will watch his Frankish "brother" from afar. "Have a Frank as a friend," it used to be said, "but not as a neighbor." Leo will die in great distress of body and soul on June 11, 816, and be buried a few paces from where Peter, Linus, Clement, Gregory, and all the others lie. Later his ashes will be mingled with those of Popes Leo I, Leo II, and Leo IV in a common tomb. He will be called St. Leo and have a little-celebrated feast day each year on June 12. Only ten of his letters are extant and they speak only of his troubles. His only real claim to remembrance will be that crowning of the Frankish king.

Charlemagne will lose his two sons in death, Pepin in 810, Charles in 811. After forty-six years of uninterrupted reign, and none too sorry to die himself, Charlemagne succumbs to pleurisy at the age of seventy-two in January 814. He will be buried sitting bolt upright, fully armored, sword in hand, the cross of Jesus on his chest. But his is one name that belongs to all Europeans. The meaning of his power and the immense stature of his idea of "all the Christian folk of Europe" will exert an almost mystical magnetism for a little over eleven hundred years. Constantine had conceived the idea of the temporal power spreading and legitimizing a spiritual vision. Gregory had created an empire of the spirit. It was Charlemagne who planted the idea of a dual control in the sociopolitical life of European men and women: the king and the priest, the temporal and the spiritual.

Charlemagne will be canonized as saint by the Germans, pictured in the stained glass of Chartres Cathedral, and claimed as ideal, as patron, as godfather, by the Holy Roman emperors (Frederick II exhumed the huge body and wrapped it in a new imperial cloak), by Napoleon in the nineteenth century ("our predecessor, Charlemagne"), by Hitler with his *Festung* Europa in the 1940s, by Pope Pius XII in his vain hope for the "New Order of Europe being founded by Herr Hitler and Signor Mussolini," by Jean Monnet and the post-World War II "Europeans," and by Pope Paul VI in his initial zest for a "reborn Christian Europe of all Christian peoples." Leo was quite right in the year 800: the great Frank, "Golden Charles," by his very presence, did throw a sudden flash of light over the darkened face of his Europe. He showed Europeans the ideal and the hope of being one.

Each of the succeeding popes from Leo III to Boniface VI (896) were elected in a tortuous fashion. The Roman factions battled among themselves and with the ordinary people. A candidate emerged from these always rough, frequently bloody, often fatal encounters between the various contending parties who used money as well as arms and sexual subversion to enforce their wishes. This candidate was then confirmed and ratified by Charlemagne's successors. Before he was crowned, the candidate swore loyalty to the Frankish ruler. At times, that ruler imposed his own pope-candidate on all the factions.

Pope Nicholas I endeavored to rectify the one-sidedness by excommunicating anyone who even disputed the right of the clergy and Roman nobles to participate in the election of a pope. The decree was aimed both at Frankish rulers, and at the Roman people.

In his *Constitution* of A.D. 827, Pope Valentine, who was pope only for six weeks, allowed Roman nobles to take part in the papal elections, making no distinction between clergy and laity in his decree. And he conceded to the emperor what no pope had ever dared concede: partial control over the validity of the papal election. Hitherto, any emperor could propose his own favorite candidate, or he could reject or approve the candidate of the Roman assembly. He could not, however, make a pope himself. Valentine also decreed exile (and, in certain cases, death) for any non-Roman who interfered with the election or tried to participate in it without special permission.

When Charlemagne's empire had been divided and his royal line had died out, the power of local politicians and nobles came to the fore. Lambert, the Lombard duke of Spoleto, first, and then his wife, Agiltruda, imposed six popes: Stephen VII (896–897), Romanus (897), Theodore II (898), John IX (898–900), Benedict IV (900–903), and Leo V (903). Then the local House of Theophylact seized control. Theophylact's wife, Theodora, imposed five popes from Sergius I (904–911) to Leo VI (929). Then her daughter, Marozia, with one of her sons, Alberic, influenced the next six, ending with John XII in 963, who was her grandson.

Despite the wholesale corruption involved in the selection of popes, the range of possible candidates had by this time been greatly enlarged. It was everybody's wish. Pope John IX had decreed in 898 that the papal electors should include, of course, primarily the Roman cardinal-bishops and clergy but also bishops from dioceses near Rome. The dukes of Spoleto and the counts of Tusculum wanted their own local clergy, their appointees, to be in the running for pope. The electors, John decreed, should consult the good wishes of the Roman Senate and people (who usually desired to have a pure-bred Roman as pope), but they could also elect a non-Roman.

It may be puzzling for our twentieth-century minds to think that the men and women of those far-off days clung to the papacy and that, despite what seems to us to be wholesale corruption and unworthy morals in the representatives of religion, the Christians of those days continued to hold the papacy and the Church of Rome in total veneration. This was only possible because Christians had succeeded in creating a heartland of their own, infused with a new anthropology replacing all that Greece and Rome had anciently supplied. Rome and its pope formed the centerpiece of that heartland. As long as that heartland held strong, the power of Rome in the social and political sectors of human life was paramount.

The Christian
Heartland

By accepting the gift of Constantine in the fourth century, and by dint of unswerving efforts to capitalize on that gift, Christians automatically made a fatal adaption, so far, the only basic adaptation of the original "good news," the Gospel of Jesus: they locked their message of salvation into a highly specific socioeconomic and political system. Within four centuries they produced a new Christian anthropology, a blend of Bible teaching and the revelation made by Jesus; and this and this alone made possible the rough, brash ebullience of medieval Europe, the pride of the Renaissance, and the culture and civilization of the West in modern times.

Now the linchpin of that lock on human affairs was the city of Rome, the city *par excellence*, and all that Rome stood for. Already, Rome was the place where the acknowledged chief representative of Jesus had lived, Peter, the rock on which Jesus said he would build his church. Peter and his successors now represented the channel of the new hope, the physical point of contact with the invisible and all-saving Jesus. So, the Rome of the Roman bishops became central, and everything connected with it. Rome's people became the *sanctus populus*, the holy people; Rome itself became the *sancta civitas*, the holy city. The bishop's domain was Jesus' domain, his government and authority now became civil, legal, military, economic, and diplomatic. But it remained Jesus' authority. The very language of Rome, Latin, became the language of Jesus. The assembled will of Roman citizens through which each new successor of Peter was chosen became the voice of God; and there arose the quasitheological principle, *vox populi, vox dei*: the voice of the people is the voice of God, on which all subsequent ideas of democracy in Europe and America were originally founded.

What the church and its leader the pope actually did take over from old Rome was the imperial idea, the idea of a landed political empire.

We do not know of any people prior to the Romans who possessed the idea of a political imperium. The word in their mouths meant "power" rather than "empire". For their minds it was a system of political control and administration which took in all local traits of tribe, language, color, religion, nationality, culture, military arms, and aimed at uniting all under one central and centralizing *political* government, by safeguarding local interests and conceding the benefits of universal Roman law and Roman citizenship. At the back of our quite modern idea of the "state" lies this primary Roman idea of political *imperium*.

At one stage of their history, Jews believed in and aspired to a moral *imperium* throughout the world. The great Hebrew prophets made this the object of their most impassioned pleas and exalted pronouncements. The Greeks were the first to discover the universal empire of the human spirit. Many ancient empires—Pharaonic, Assyrian, Persian, Babylonian—attempted to set up an economic-military *imperium*. None, but the Romans, evolved a political formula for a universal *imperium*.

Until Constantine, Christians viewed this Roman order as the physical arm of the devil himself. Besides, to the eyes of Christians the Roman world was falling to pieces. In Constantine's time, Romans guarded 10,000 miles of frontier against the barbarians, and maintained a regular army of over 500,000 men. But when the German crossed the Rhine one night in the winter of 406, it was all over.

Yet under Constantine's protection, the Christians had a new vision. The promise by Jesus of final victory was now rooted in a very earthly context: the old centralized political system of classical Rome was to become the earthly framework of Christ's universal rule. All the attributes of classical Rome were now seen as attributes of Roman Christianity. And within a hundred years the Roman Church was the only source

104

of authority, culture, and military help left in the old empire. By 440, when the old Roman title Pontifex Maximus (Supreme Pontiff) was assumed by Leo I, the pope was the effective ruler, not only of Rome but of numerous territories.

Within three centuries, the Roman Church had transformed the administrative organization of the Roman Empire into an ecclesiastical system of bishoprics, dioceses, monasteries, colonies, garrisons, schools, libraries, administrative centers, envoys, representatives, courts of justice, and a criminal system of intricate laws all under the direct control of the pope. His Roman palace, the Lateran, became the new Senate. The new senators were the cardinals. The bishops who lived in Rome and the priests and deacons helped the pope administer this new *imperium*. This bureaucracy elected the head of the *imperium*, and they carried on the tradition from pope to pope.

Roman pride of place went very, very far. When Pope Gregory III bought back the town of Gallesa (near Viterbo) from the Lombard duke of Spoleto for a huge sum of money, the Roman chronicle states solemnly: "Gallesa has now returned once more into the corporate structure of the Holy Roman Republic [Rome] and into the visible body of the beloved Christ [the Roman army]." Rome would be sacked at least seven times (by Alaric the Hun in 410; Genseric the Vandal in 455; the Ostrogoths in 546; the Saracens in 847; Barbarossa of Prussia in 1107; the Spanish-led German army in 1526; Napoleon in 1799). It would be deserted by popes for nearly two hundred years. But, in the end, the popes came back to settle there, in the holy city of the people of God.

This constantly recurring phrase, the holy Roman people, with its emphasis upon the "people," expresses the change which Christians introduced into the old Roman imperial idea. For the Romans, the source and the repository of all power was the Roman people and its Senate. For the Christians, the Roman Christian people and their clerical leaders were a channel of power from God. The Christian community, beginning forty days after the departure of Jesus when they elected a new apostle to replace the traitor Judas, and then later in Rome, had been accustomed from their earliest times to voting in assembly on all important matters and especially on the identity of every new Roman bishop who was to

105

govern them and, they were convinced, to govern all churches. Primarily, the Roman elective assembly chose a bishop from among themselves. Automatically, their choice was accepted as God's choice, and the candidate so chosen became pope of the universal church. Power to rule came to him through the people from God, so they believed.

Whether they chose the new bishop by direct individual voting in assembly, or whether they merely confirmed or respected the nominee of a previous pope or that of a powerful prince, the new bishop had authority only if the Roman community accepted him. And so the special dignity and power attached to the oft-repeated phrase: "All the Senate and the entire membership of the citizens of this Roman city which God preserves" rang down the ages with awesome authority from the fourth to the eighteenth century.

Calvin in his theology of the church, the Pilgrim fathers of Plymouth Rock in 1620, the American revolutionaries of 1776, the French revolutionaries of 1789, all took this idea of power coming *through* the people and converted it into a "democratic" model. But gradually a subtle change was made: the people in their outlook became the source and the executive, not a mere *channel*, of all power.

In the church from the fifth century onward, the new *imperium* of Jesus was housed within a very tangible and concrete form: vast real estate holdings in Rome and outside the city, together with an extensive grip over the loyalty of other temporal rulers in Italy, France, and Spain. By the end of the sixth century, the holdings of pope and church had become vast around Rome, in Naples, Calabria, and in Sicily. The revenues from Calabria and Sicily amounted to 35,000 gold florins per year. By A.D. 704, Pope Paul I was speaking of *pars nostra Romanorum*, "our ecclesiastical Roman state"; and the pope's title was *dux plebis*, "leader of the people."

Every pope called the Roman state the "patrimony of Peter," and the "Holy Roman Empire." Before the end of the 700s, the Roman ecclesiastical state was considerable: cities and towns conceded by emperors to the pope; church estates and colonies annexed or bought by popes; other portions of territories and cities donated by local princes to the pope. Faithfully, all these were said to be added to what was called the "Roman army," or the "Holy Roman republic." Around the pope in Rome there

106

grew an entire bureaucracy of clerics, bishops, priests, deacons, laymen, to administer papal farms, papal towns, papal armies, papal fleets, papal treasuries, papal caravans, papal tax collectors, papal justices of the peace, papal police, papal envoys and missions, applying papal laws— civil and ecclesiastical.

By the end of the century, the pope was the most powerful temporal ruler in his part of the world. By 726, he felt strong enough to deal harshly with an emperor: "We can only address you in rough and uneducated style," wrote Gregory III to Emperor Leo, "because you yourself are rough and uneducated." By 754, Pope Stephen made a peace agreement with Pepin of the Franks on behalf of the Roman people and thereby acquired extensive territories from Pepin. What remained of Byzantine possessions in Italy became the popes': a huge central swathe of the Italian peninsula bordered on the east coast by the land from Venice to Ancona with its hinterland, diagonally across central Italy to the west coast from around Livorno in the north down past Naples in the south, including the "toe" of Italy and Calabria. It covered 16,000 square miles and in its better days held a population of about three million.

The popes also received large territories lying in what is now Yugoslavia. Pepin had the keys to all the cities and towns in these territories taken and placed on the high alter of St. Peter's in Rome. The Roman Christian heartland was now in existence. And every Roman senator and noble had to swear to defend with his life the Basilica of St. Peter, the Castle of Sant' Angelo, the Pantheon (now called Santa Maria Rotondo), the Trastevere district of Rome, and the Leonine City (roughly the present Vatican city).

By the end of the eighth century the pope was, in fact and practice, a temporal ruler of gigantic proportions. The papal states had been established. As time went on, in addition to the papal states which were ruled directly by the popes as their own possessions, the Roman pope gained feudal power over other states: they were obligated to pay yearly tribute and to contribute to the defensive and offensive policies of the popes. The Roman pontiffs also acquired political control in still other lands: the rulers were appointed with papal approval, and they were bound by offensive-defensive alliances with the papacy.

By 1216, Pope Innocent III could define three categories of papal claims on the heartland quite clearly for the German emperor: five papal states in Italy (essentially that huge central swathe of Italian territory, all governed centrally from Rome by the pope); papal fiefs—most of Portugal, the Navarre and Aragon provinces of Spain, England and Ireland (England alone paid 1,000 marks sterling as its annual feudal tribute), Bulgaria, Corsica, and Sardinia, and the Kingdom of Sicily, which took in the southern half of Italy as well as Sicily; and, thirdly, countries bound politically to the pope—Armenia, Hungary, and Poland.

On November 18, 1302, Boniface VIII could issue a famous statement of papal claims which stands as the ultimate expression of the Christian heartland and profound Roman claims on it. "The Church," declared Boniface, "has one body and one head, Christ and Christ's Vicar, Peter and Peter's successor . . . In his power there are two swords, a spiritual and a temporal sword . . . Both kinds of power are in the hands of the Roman Pontiff . . . And furthermore we declare and define it to be believed as a necessary condition for salvation that everything created in the human universe is subject to the Roman Pontiff."

The popes made impressive displays of this power. Alexander III gave Portugal exclusive rights for trading and colonization on the west coast of Africa between Cape Bohadan and Guinea, in 1479. In 1493 Alexander VI laid his index finger on a globe of the earth with all countries and oceans marked on it. He traced a boundary line from north to south, 100 Spanish leagues west of the most westerly island of the Azores. All east of that line would belong to Portugal, he decreed; all west of it would belong to Spain. The line was pushed 270 leagues further west by the Treaty of Tordesillas on June 7, 1494—a change supervised and sanctioned by the pope.

Hand in hand with this elaboration of political geography, an entirely new geography of the spirit was elaborated. Heaven with God and his angels and saints was placed high above the skies, dislodging the ancient gods from Olympus along the way. Beneath the earth lay the domain of Satan, of evil. In the middle was the Roman world, Roman in the new, Christian sense, bounded by dangerous seas and by shadowy lands, Africa, India, China, where strange semihuman and nonhuman beings lived and to which missionaries would be sent as to the outer darkness where

Satan ruled. All had been created by God and mysteriously renewed by Jesus on his cross.

Time spent on the new earth was sanctified. Time, which had been a tyrant, was now the period of personal salvation. Space was now filled with the presence of God. Death, still the final pain of the living, was no longer a mystery. Afterlife happiness was no longer the privileged purlieu of a handful of gods, goddesses, and heroes.

In the meanwhile, a new psychology evolved, based on that new anthropology. Each human being was composed of body and soul. The soul had spirituality, liberty of choice, and immortality. The body had senses, passions. In his soul, man was like God. In his body, he resembled animals. To help the soul grow in love of God and to govern the rebellious passions and wayward senses, there were, Christians believed, seven rites called sacraments: baptism to make him a Christian, confirmation to strengthen him in faith, penance to wash him clean of sins, the Eucharist to unite him with Jesus, marriage to sanctify his union with another being, holy orders to create priests who could forgive sins in the name of Jesus and offer the sacrifice of the Mass, and extreme unction to prepare him to die in such a way that he reached the paradise of God and his chosen ones. The outward world of man was to be sanctified by things called sacramentals—holy water, statues, relics of the saints, medals, pictures of the saints, and special blessings for all the objects a person used in life.

Within the heartland of Christendom, all became sanctified: water, earth, trees, rivers, cities, houses, clothes. Within Christendom, one could be on familiar footing with God, with Jesus, with the Virgin Mother of Jesus, with Angels, with saints, with the all-holy. "Tell us, Mary," runs the medieval Easter hymn with astounding directness, "What did you see on the way?" And they heard Mary answering: "I saw the tomb of the now living Christ, I saw the glory of Christ, now risen."

The most delicate of man's arts, music, was translated into a special form, church music, which became common and international language of divine worship. As music, and as a religious expression, the form devised by Pope Gregory the Great, and called Gregorian chant, has never been surpassed. The soul of the chant was precisely the new union of Heaven and earth through the great hero, Jesus. And Gregorian music conveyed the message of Jacob's Ladder, on which the angels ascended and descended and ascended continually from man to God to man and back to God.

The music appears at first to be the voice and utterance of this world as if all the elements on land, on sea, and in the skies had blended their different tones into a rising and falling cadence of adoration recalling the undulating perpetuity of ocean waves, the high-soaring flights of cloud and sky, the triumph of winds blowing across the earth—all as a unique voice of creation, with human beings included, chanting before their God with the joy God's creatures must have known before—it was their conviction—sin and darkness and death entered the universe through man's sin and the Devil's evil. For it was with all this sentiment that Gregorian chant filled Christians everywhere.

The physical relics of their dead holy people became important to Christians. Shrines were built to house them—the bones of the Magi in Cologne Cathedral, the head of John the Baptist, and the head of St. Balduino, the hand of St. Gregory, the robe of Jesus, the Virgin's cloak, Mary Magdalene's foot, even the foreskin of Jesus (the only relic of him, preserved in a ruby and emerald-studded casket supported by two silver-gilt angels—still visible today in Calcata, north of Rome). That they were essentially all phony is not the issue. The point is that people believed in them.

When Pope Boniface IV consecrated the old Roman Pantheon as Sancta Maria Rotondo in 610, he had thirty-two wagon loads of martyrs' bones brought from the catacombs and placed in the various shrines within the newly consecrated church. And, according to popular song, in the pommel of Roland's trusty sword, Durendal, there was a tooth of St. Peter, a drop of St. Basil's blood, a hair of St. Denis, and a thread from the Virgin's cloak, so that Roland could rely on the intercession of those saints as he smote the infidel "in the name of God and of Sweet France and for the Golden Emperor Charles."

A new militarism was born: this Christian heartland, Christendom, must be defended by Christian arms. Wars could be holy, would have to be waged, would be a holy duty. Cruelty to enemies of Jesus within and without the heartland could be God's vengeance. "Neither sex nor age nor rank have we spared," was the statement of the general who conducted the war against medieval heretics called Albigenses. "We have put all alike to the sword."

The new cry was on the lips of Roland, the perfect Christian and the model knight, as he fought at Roncevaux against the hated Moors: *"Paien unt tort e Chrestiens unt droit!* (Pagans are wrong. Christians are right!)" And when the first crusaders came over a hill in Palestine and caught sight of the walls of Jerusalem, they dismounted from their horses, tore off their boots, and fell to the ground groaning and crying tears of joy in a delirium of desire, thanking God for allowing them to live long enough to reach the Holy City where Jesus lived, was crucified, and rose again from the dead. Then they put on their shoes, besieged the city, and took it by storm, convinced that the angels of the Lord were fighting by their side. They put to death by sword over 17,000 Muslims on the site of Solomon's Temple and burned all Jews inside their synagogues.

Between the years of Leo I (440—461) and the end of the eighth century, there developed a whole body of thinkers, preachers, writers, philosophers, theologians—the Fathers of the Church, as they are called. They codified the new anthropology, explaining, elaborating, defining, giving expression to all the aspects of the New hope: the life of the soul, the value of the mind, the meaning of the body, the idea of human personality, the fundamental concepts of guilt and innocence, the function of the universe, the idea of love, the significance of all human history. Men and women and nations were nourished for over a thousand years with the thoughts, the conclusions, and the precepts of Gregory of Nyssa, Augustine of Hippo, John of Damascus, Hilary of Poitiers, Ambrose of Milan, Chrysostom of Constantinople, Basil of Caesarea, and Cyril of Alexandria.

True to the recommendations of Basil of Caesarea ("You must chirp all day and evening like the cicada"), the "Fathers" of Christian thought poured out a new stream of literature. They were media men. No matter that to us their language seems abstruse, their thinking convoluted, their tomes inaccessible to all but a few. They worked in a society of severely restricted literacy. But it was a society of the spoken word and oral tra-

111

dition, of vast leisure for all. The ruminations and disputes of scholars were actually the subject matter of talk and discussion and partisanship in the marketplace, the wine shop, the public baths, the inter-city convoys. What the new anthropologists taught filtered down through preacher, teacher, itinerant monk, cathedral school, parish prayers, guild functions, extended family activities, folk songs, theater, agricultural methods, church music, university, seminary, down into the daily lives of peasant and king and warrior and artisan. Men and women had no other way of thinking about themselves except in terms of this Christian message.

True, the new anthropology produced such far-out calculations as the number of angels in the whole universe. There were, in all, 399,920,004, of whom exactly one third—133,306,668—had sided with Satan against God and therefore now worked against Jesus, his church, and all Christians. The same anthropology enabled Pope Alexander III to use for his own advantage the visible destruction of a giant meteorite against the upper horn of the crescent moon on June 18, 1178, in order to frighten the German Emperor Frederick who was supporting Alexander's enemies. And Christians were puerilely wrong, because woefully misinformed, in their calculations concerning such things as the age of the world. The Jews of their day dated the world from October 7, 3761 B.C. Eastern Orthodox Christians latched on to September 1, 5509 B.C. Western Christians quoted the year 5000 B.C. as the starting date for everything. And as late as the seventeenth century, Protestant Bishop Ussher determined that it all began at 6 P.M. local time on October 22, 4004 B.C.

In all this, Christians were not overly interested in analytic problems. And what elaborations they produced were "medievalisms' were mere aberrations. The central achievement of the new order was incredibly vast and solid. When, unknown to most of its inhabitants, this ancient world arrived at its sunset in the late 1500s, a living European commonality, a veritable commonwealth in spirit, had been created which flourished and predominated from the Arctic Circle down to North Africa, and from Galway in Ireland over to Vladivostok in the Far East and eastern Turkey in the Near East, with extensions in Spanish and Portuguese America. We find it intact today in the remnants of its popular art, in frescoes, paintings, triptychs, enamels, etchings, stained glass windows, sculptures in wood, stone, marble: King Dagobert's tomb at Saint-Denis (France), the Rymätilä paintings of Finland, the Tiele paintings of Sweden, the Celtic crosses of Ireland, the ikons of Kiev, the triptychs of Flanders and Italy, the wood-carvings of Paraguay, the Chinese biographies of Jesus, the medallions of the eastern Russian steppes, and the embroidered Madonnas and saints of Tierra del Fuego.

Throughout, we find the same personages—Jesus, the Virgin, God the Father, the Holy Spirit, the pope, the angels and saints, Judas, the apostles, Satan, the church—and the same themes of sin, virtue, Hell, Heaven, Purgatory, death, marriage, baptism, loyalty, love, grace, hope, illustrating the same events of Jesus' life. What is singularly impressive is that these personages and events and themes are depicted in identically the same way in places as diverse as Scandinavia and Sicily, Colmar in France and Edinburgh in Scotland, Salonike in Greece and Guadaloupe in Mexico. The themes and events have the same details.

And we know the reason why. Even as early as 787, the Second Council of Nicaea laid down rules for depiction in art. Artists and craftsmen led nomadic lives wandering through cities, towns, villages, and hamlets, where they exhibited their notebooks, their "catalogues," showing what they could do for the parish church, the village square, the town cathedral, the castle chapel, the convent cloister, the wayside shrine. Bishop and prince and priest and lord and monks enforced the rules laid by successive church councils and popes; these had listed the specific canons of taste, of detail, of proportion, which were to be universally accepted, and which ensured that the beliefs of Christianity were accurately and adequately mirrored in the media of the time.

Without benefit of electronic media or mechanical transport, a monolithic and unitary mind was created, accepted, elaborated, perpetuated. This formed a womb of demographic settlement, economic power, political aspiration, cultural optimism, and aggressive thinking from which sprang the direct forebears of all we moderns have become: the early experimental scientists in Cambridge and Paris during the eleventh to fourteenth centuries, the explorers of the thirteenth to sixteenth centuries, the Renaissance men, the empire builders and the first nationalist leaders, the scientists of the Enlightenment, and the champions of democracy

113

in Europe and the Americas in the eighteenth and nineteenth centuries. They were all nourished by the new anthropology within the Christian heartland.

This new familiarity and intimacy with Heaven on earth drew its inspiration and encouragement from Rome and from the vicar of Jesus, the pope, who lived there. Rome and its bishop became the focal point of this vast intricate translation of the message of Christian hope. Its central shrine, St. Peter's, built over the tomb of the apostle, was the first church of Christendom.

From the Palace of the Popes, the Lateran, issued all legitimacy in civil government and political succession, validity of marriage, inspiration for learning and exploration and experimentation. As the real estate possessions and dominions of the popes grew (the state of the church, or the papal states, as they came to be called), the idea of Christendom, of the Christian heartland, emerged. It was co-extensive with papal authority— either in the direct governmental authority of popes or the feudal dependence on popes under which most of Europe lay at the opening of the thirteenth century.

When the pope appeared in public procession, he wore the diadem of Jesus' power, symbolizing power over man's spirit and power over man's temporal condition. Before him was carried the sacred host of the Eucharist, the body and blood of the Savior. All of Christendom knew of Rome and of the man who lived there bearing the words and the authority of salvation won by Jesus. Pilgrimage there was the most noble act anyone could perform. The very walls of Rome were venerated. The pilgrims came to catch sight of the pope, to get his blessing, and then to visit the churches and the catacombs, to worship at the tomb of St. Peter, to venerate the relics which only Rome possessed, or claimed to possess— the steps up which Jesus had to labor in order to be condemned by Pilate, the handkerchief of Veronica with which she had wiped his face during his Via Dolorosa to Calvary, the chains that had bound St. Peter, the head of St. Paul, the arm of St. Luke, the robe of St. John Evangelist.

At the first Jubilee in 1300, 30,000 pilgrims entered and left the city daily, while at any given moment there were 200,000 pilgrims staying within city boundaries. By contributing to the saying of Masses, the lighting of votive lamps over the tombs of saints, the pilgrims could get assurance of forgiveness for their sins. It did not bother them that night and day during the pilgrimage two smiling priests stood at the alter of St. Paul's, for instance, shoveling in the gold and silver offerings like hay.

For at the center of all this there sat the pope, Jesus' vicar on Earth, occupying the highest throne of the West, the most extensive real estate owner, the most universal lord of all vassals and feudal serfs, the rector of all princes, the sole legitimizer of all governments and dynasties, holding the keys of the Kingdom of Heaven, and ever mindful of the words Jesus spoke to Peter: "Thou art Peter . . . to thee I will give the keys of the Kingdom of Heaven. . . . "

In short, a giant step had been taken in a relatively short time. Peter the Apostle, writing from Rome about A.D. 66, refers to Rome as "Babylon" (a term loaded, for Christians, with connotations of corruption and deviltry); and, with obvious contempt and disgust, tells his Christians, "The end of all things is close at hand. . . . Wait eagerly for the heavens to shrivel up in fire and earth to melt in its heat. . . . We have a new heavens and a new earth, and look forward to the dwelling-place of holiness. . . . "

The forty-fifth successor of Peter on the throne of Rome, Leo I, wrote just four hundred years later: "God's providence previously brought the Roman Empire into existence so that many kingdoms should thus be confederated in a single empire and the evangelization of mankind should be able to make unimpeded and rapid progress among people held together in one political system. . . . " And, far from decrying Rome as the unspeakably corrupt "Babylon" which Peter loathed, Leo apostrophized the city: "Rome! You holy family! You chosen people! You priestly and royal city! You have become the capital of the world by being Peter's See. . . . You have extended your rule far and wide over land and sea. . . . Your empire of peace is greater than the old Roman military empire. . . . "

But this Christian heartland contained the seeds of its own disintegration. The pairing of religion and politics, of the sword and the spirit, never produced peace on earth—nor even deeper religion or more inspiring leadership from Roman popes.

In 963, a brand new force with a vested interest in papal elections

115

entered the arena of international politics: the German emperor, Otto I. Uncontested overlord in Italy and central Europe for the moment, Otto assembled all the Romans, nobles, clergy, people, in the ancient Forum on November 12, 963. His soldiers ringed the city and held every gate, every strong fort, every entrance to the Vatican treasury. He made them swear "never to choose a pope without his [Otto's] or his successor's approval." Over the following 280 years—up to the election of Celestine IV in 1241—the election and confirmation of forty-eight popes was usually in the hands of German emperors. In that whole period, the most astounding episode in the election of popes concerns a woman named Marozia.

RIPENESS
AND
DECAY

The Nymph Who Made Popes

The marriage undertaken in the year 800 by Leo III and Charlemagne, linking the temporal power of the emperor to the spiritual power of the pope, did promote the well-being of "the Christian folk of Europe," but did little to enhance the spiritual growth of the papacy. To say the least!

Consider a woman called Marozia and her involvement with the papacy of the tenth century. The high point in Marozia's career came at the end of her very long life when she was visited in her Roman prison by an emperor who had just seized possession of the city—Otto III, a successor of Charlemagne. He had only one reason for visiting Marozia—to lay his eyes on the woman who was the mother of one pope, whom she conceived by another pope, and who was the aunt of a third pope, the grandmother of a fourth pope, and with the help of her own mother, the creator of nine popes in eight years, of whom two had been strangled, one suffocated with a cushion, and four deposed and disposed of in circumstances that have never come to public light. Otto, who himself was to make and unmake popes, just had to see this woman before she died. Of course, he was going to see to it that she died, make no mistake about that.

It is the last evening of May, a Thursday, in the year 986 in Rome. On May 3, Otto saw his own choice, his first cousin Bruno, aged twenty-three, consecrated as Pope Gregory V. On May 25, Pope Gregory dutifully reciprocated and crowned his cousin, this same Otto, aged fifteen—

yes, fifteen—as emperor. The legacy of Leo III is still with Rome. Church and state are bound together.

On May 25, Gregory V and Otto held a synod of cardinals, bishops, lower clergy, and councilors in St. Peter's. Among other things, it was decided to send a bishop to the prison where the old woman, Marozia, had been locked up for fifty-four years. She should be granted the benefits of confessing her sins and receiving the last rites before her execution. Otto can do nothing else to help her. She is the pope's prisoner. And Gregory is not willing to do more. This night, after Otto's visit with the bishop in her cell, another and irresistible visitor is coming to her cell: death. A cushion will be held firmly over her nose and mouth, until she stops breathing, "for the well-being of Holy Mother Church and the peace of the Roman people." So they decide.

Marozia's cell is at the end of a corridor in the lowest basement of the tallest and strongest building in Rome, the mausoleum of Emperor Hadrian. The bulky red-brick building created by that ancient pagan ruler as his grave is now the fortress-palace of the popes. It has six towers and 164 battlements, and is popularly called the Castel of Sant' Angelo, for on the summit stands a bronze statue of St. Michael Archangel, sword in hand, guarding Rome from all her enemies.

The iron door of the cell swings open and the biship, a young man in his twenties, enters first; he is followed by the jailer and a representative of the pope—both carrying candles. Otto then enters preceded by two personal bodyguads. The young bishop could not be blaed if he is nervous, he has to read the document of accusation and pardon to the woman, elicit her repentance, perform an exorcism over her, declare her excommunication lifted, and give her absolution fo all her sins. Thus she will be ready to die.

"*Marozia! Daughter of Theophylact!*" the bishop begins, addressing the huddled mass of rags lying on the straw in one corner. "*Marozia, are you among the living? I, Bishop John Crescentius of Portus, comand you in the name of Holy Mother Church. Speak to us! . . .*" His voice trails off. All six men peer into the corner. The old woman is lying on her side, facing the wall.

Without stirring, she whispers: "Living, my Lord Bishop, living."

Then after a pause: "For all my sins, forgiveness . . . forgiveness." The young bishop plunges into the reading of the document: "*Inasmuch as you, Marozia, did from the beginning and at the age of fifteen conspire against the rights of the See of Peter in the reign of Holy Father, Pope Sergius. . .*"

Nonsense! Marozia's career had begun when she was six years old! The big eye-opener for her had been in March 897. Agiltruda, the queen mother of Spoleto, took her by the hand to the Lateran Palace. They stood outside in the bright sunshine with a crowd of Romans. Inside, the reigning pope, Stephen VI (nicknamed "the Trembler" by his contemporaries because of his nervous disease), surrounded by his cardinals and bishops, conducted a trial. Agiltruda, a Lombard, with her luxuriant blond hair, blue eyes, impressive stature, and imperious voice, wanted everyone, including the child Marozia, to witness the degradation of her most foul enemy, a dead pope, a Corsican, Formosus by name. Pope Formosus had deprived Agiltruda's son of his due honor by crowning instead a hated German, Arnulf, as Holy Roman emperor in February of 896.

Agiltruda had led an army, seized Rome, and installed herself in Hadrian's Mausoleum. But Emperor Arnulf had sent her packing home to Spoleto, breathing vengeance and hate. Pope Formosus had then set out at the head of his own army to capture Agiltruda's beloved Spoleto. But he died of a stroke (or perhaps Agiltruda's poison) on April 4, 896, and was buried in Rome as befitted a pope. The next pope, Boniface VI, was put on the throne by armed Roman citizens. Within fifteen days Agiltruda made sure Boniface was stone dead (after all, before becoming pope, he had been twice defrocked for unseemly behavior). She then put her own creature on the throne as Pope Stephen VII. Everyone, including Agiltruda, knew that Stephen was insane and subject to violent paroxysms of black rage. He was therefore perfect for Agiltruda's scheme.

The venom and malice of that scheme were monumental. Formosus had been dead and buried for over eleven months. On Agiltruda's suggestion, Pope Stephen had the rotting corpse dug up, brought to the Lateran Palace, clothed in pontifical vestments, placed sitting on a papal throne, and then tried for capital crimes by Stephen and his cardinals and bish-

121

ops. This was the famous Corpse Synod. Agiltruda had looked forward to it for a long time. This was why she came to the Lateran Palace with Marozia. This was why she was smiling and gay.

Inside the synod, all went according to plan. Pope Stephen himself and a papal accuser cross-questioned the rotting corpse (a trembling eighteen-year-old deacon stood beside the corpse and answered for the voiceless Formosus). The conviction came when Pope Stephen, livid with fury, shouted: "Why did you usurp this See of the Apostle?" And the young deacon answered for the dead Formosus: "Because I was evil." At that crucial confession, Cardinals Sergius, Benedict, Paschalis, Leo, John, and the others rushed on the corpse, ripped the pontifical vestments from it, tore off the first three fingers of the right hand (Formosus, like every pope, gave the papal blessing with those three fingers), and then dragged the corpse from the hall.

Marozia was there as the cardinals and clergy dragged the corpse out of the palace and along the streets. The shouts of the crowd, the smell of the putrefying flesh, the stones and the mud she and the others threw at the corpse did not let up at all. And then there was the dull splash as they threw the remains of Formosus into the River Tiber. Pope Stephen then sent the three torn fingers to Agiltruda, by the hand of Cardinal Sergius. This was Agiltruda's request. As the cardinal gave her these grisly trophies, he noticed the child by her side. Their eyes met. It was the first known meeting between the two, but far from the last. She was then six, he thirty-six. Then Pope Stephen and his retinue emerged from the palace. At that precise moment—first to the astonishment, then to the great fear of the gathering—the Basilica of St. John adjoining the palace in the vast Lateran complex literally collapsed in ruins with a tremendous roar of falling masonry. It had been abandoned as dangerously unstable years before, but still the timing was exquisite, and certainly suggestive. Sergius, always in control, just grunted in disquiet. Agiltruda turned white with fear, although only momentarily.

In Marozia's early years, the fortunes of Rome were in the hands of such rich families as hers. Agiltruda had lasted a few years more, seized the city of Rome once more in 897, put Pope Romanus on the throne after Pope Stephen VII has been imprisoned and strangled, then did away

122

with Pope Romanus after four months and installed Pope Theodore II. But in the same year, Lambert, Agiltruda's son and only heir, her pride and joy, fell off his horse at Marengo, broke his hip, and died of gangrene. Pope Theodore turned against Agiltruda: so he lasted only twenty days— . Agiltruda still had power. But she was a broken woman. Besides, the German emperor imposed a Roman-born German cardinal as Pope John IX. He lasted two years and, to everybody's surprise, died in his bed. Meanwhile, Agiltruda's House of Spoleto had lost out, and it was now the turn of Marozia's family, the House of Theophylact.

At the papal court and in the Vatican during this time, the most important and weighty official of the pope was called the *Vestarius* or (in vulgar Latin) *Vestararius*. In actual fact, the incumbent of this office combined the duties of treasurer, chancelor, secretary of state, general chief of staff, governor of Rome, and chief senator. On January 25, 904, when Pope Sergius III was consecrated, Theophylact was *Vestararius* and *Senator*. His wife, Theodora, was *Vestararissa* and *Senatrix*. They had two daughters, Theodora and Marozia, the latter now this old woman lying in the cell listening to her sentence. Frankish in origin, the powerful House of Theophylact controlled the Church of Rome for nearly sixty years.

Marozia, having learned valuable lessons from Agiltruda, was taken over by her own mother, Theodora, now powerful enough to become pope-maker. She put the mild and priestly Benedict IV on the throne, but he lived only three years and two months, dying in the summer of 903. Theodora's next two popes were tragic: Leo V was pope only for July of 903, and then was imprisoned by Cardinal Christopher, who took his place. Then Christopher was imprisoned by Cardinal Sergius, who assassinated both Leo and Christopher in prison, together with all the other cardinals who opposed him. He had his enemies at the papal court strangled and himself declared Pope Sergius III. In engineering all this, Theophylact and Theodora had one aim: their daughter Marozia should be empress-queen of all the Romans.

In 906, when Sergius had been pope for two years, Marozia, aged fifteen, became his mistress. They had only one child, John (subsequently Pope John XI).

123

This was the "defilement" of the papacy of which she is now accused, ". . . *following the example of her Satanic mother. Theodora*", according to the document Bishop John is reading over her. By the time of which he speaks, Theodora was the mistress of an earlier Bishop John, Bishop John of Ravenna. (Theodora was aways thinking of the next pope.) Sergius III had seven years as pope. He behaved in a spiteful, brutal, merciless way all his life, yet he rebuilt ruined churches in Rome, restored the Lateran Basilica (it had lain in ruins since the Corpse Synod), condemned Pope Formosus in yet another full synod, endowed the Convent of Corsarum with several estates so that Abbess Euphemia and her nuns could sing one hundred *Kyrie Eleisons* for his soul every day, and died peacefully in May 911.

Marozia's mother made the next two popes, Anastasius III (who reigned for two years) and Lando (a bare six months). Their modes of dying were chosen by Theodora. Then, on March 8, 914 Theodora by force of arms put her lover, Bishop John of Ravenna, on the throne as Pope John X. Marozia was then just twenty-two, at the height of her beauty and charm.

In those far-off days, her life was spent either in the Lateran Palace of the popes, in her favorite retreat on the Isola Tiberina (an island in the middle of the River Tiber), or in her family mansion. Her companions were young nobles and prelates—bishops, most of them, who said Mass with their spurs on, their hunting daggers in their belts, their horses saddled and ready outside the church. When Mass was finished, they rode off immediately to fly their falcons and hunt boar with bow and arrow. They lived sumptuously in houses filled with celebration, dueling, dice-playing, lechery, their walls draped in purple and velvet; dining from gold vessels, entertained by dancing girls and musicians, sleeping on silken pillows in beds inlaid with gold and mementos of their loves, traveling in luxurious carriages surrounded by a mob of parasites, and perpetually served by vassals, serfs, and retainers. Marozia had been through it all. It had all been *so* exciting! And good training, too.

Then an unknown Lombard prince, Alberic, suddenly appeared unchallengeable in Rome. He frightened Pope John X so much that he and Theodora delegated Marozia to take care of him. Marozia therefore married Alberic and a few months later they had a son (also called Alberic). The elder Alberic tried to capture Rome itself by arms, but failed. Marozia was forced by Pope John and his Roman militia to look on her husband's mutilated body.

Theodora, her mother, died shortly afterward, and Marozia then married a certain Guido. She joined with Pope John's enemies, and they threw John into prison where they had him suffocated. They named a man of their own as pope, Leo VI, in May of 929. How Marozia disposed of him is not known, but in December 929 she replaced Leo with Pope Stephen VIII. He similarly disappeared in March 931. For now, Marozia's own son by Pope Sergius III was old enough—barely, at sixteen—to be pope. She had him consecrated in March 931 as John XI. As the accusation reads, *"She and her son by the upstart Alberic now plotted to take over the whole world . . ."* The whole world—yes, that was their dream. *"She dared, like Jezebel of old, yet again to take a third husband."*

When Guido, her second husband, died, Marozia married King Hugo of Tuscany, had her son Pope John XI marry them with pomp and ceremony in Rome, and then settled in to connive for an imperial coronation. Her dream: she as queen-empress, Hugo as emperor of all the Romans, and her son, Alberic, as the emperor to succeed Hugo.

But all her plans evaporated when her son Alberic revolted with the Romans in 932 and became ruler of the city. Poor little Hugo, her third husband, fled over the walls of the city hidden in a basket and wearing only his nightshirt, and hurried back north to his native Lobardy. Her son, Pope John XI, was put under house arrest in the Lateran Palace by his half-brother Alberic, where he died five years later. And she, Marozia, was thrown into this prison cell by that same son, Alberic! She was never to emerge again except in death. All that had happened fifty-four years ago in 932, when Marozia was forty.

Alberic ruled Rome for twenty-two years (932-954), appointing five popes of his own choosing, and calling himself "Alberic by the Grace of God, humble Prince and Senator of all the Romans."

Sensing his own approaching death in 954, Alberic had a meeting called in St. Peter's of all the Roman nobles and clergy together with the reigning pope. Agapitus II, whom Alberic had appointed. Alberic had all of them swear a solemn oath on the head of St. Peter the Apostle that, when Agapitus died, they would unanimously elect Alberic's young son and Marozia's grandson, Octavian, then aged fifteen, as next pope. Alberic wished to make the papacy a hereditary dynasty. All present in St. Peter's that day swore the oath, which the church later condemned as a double sacrilege, double because it destroyed a free vote of Romans, and it meant appointing a new pope while his predecessor lived, both fatal violations of church law. Pope Agapitus II died one year later in the autumn of 955, and a month later, on December 16, the youthful Octavian was consecrated pope and took the name of John XII.

Octavian as Pope John XII was the absolute nadir. Becoming pope, he did not change his way of life. Surrounded by boys and girls of his own age and rank, he spent his days and nights eating sumptuously, playing at the tables, hunting, and in love affairs. The pope's palace was frequented by courtesans and prostitutes. And, even though John XII ordered the monks at Subiaco Monastery to chant every day one hundred *Kyrie Eleisons* and one hundred *Criste Eleisons* for his soul, the story in Rome said that the monks prayed that many times for his speedy death.

For Marozia, the reading of Pope John XII's sins must have provided a paroxysm of personal suffering. Every word is accurate: ". . . *your grandson, Pope John XII, perjured himself, breaking his oath to the Great Emperor . . . he stole the Treasury of the Popes and fled to Rome's enemies . . . was deposed by a Holy Synod and replaced by Pope Leo VIII . . . then the apostate returned to Rome, evicted Pope Leo VIII, cut off the nose and tongue and two fingers of the Cardinal-Deacon, flayed the skin off Bishop Otger, cut off the hands of Notary Azzo, and beheaded sixty-three of Rome's clergy and nobility. . . . During the night of May 14, 964, while having illicit and filthy relations with a Roman matron, he was surprised in the act of sin by the matron's angry husband who, in just wrath, smashed his skull with a hammer and thus liberated his evil soul into the grasp of Satan. . . .*"

The bishop finishes his charge and quickly gives Marozia absolution. Then he and Emperor Otto III go out into the fresh warm air of the courtyard.

Later, two men, cowled like monks, will enter the prison. One will carry the telltale red-velvet cushion.

There will be little sound when they come for her. Just the click of the key turning in the lock and the creak of the door. And it will all be over in a very short time. The only thing, Marozia would know, would be not to panic, not to struggle, let it happen.

High up in his palace, Pope Gregory doubtless consoles himself with the thought that now the young German emperor will be a new Charlemagne for the church and will protect him, Peter's successor. But Gregory will be poisoned two years from now, at the age of twenty-six. Otto himself will be dead in six years' time, before he is twenty-two. And the leadership of the church will pass into the hands of other popes who will continue on in the persuasion that the salvation of Jesus must be protected by warriors' spears and cozened in wealth and magnificence.

While the corruption of absolute power was feeding on the greed and sensuality of the men who succeeded Peter the Apostle as popes in Rome, it also fed on the ambition and jealousy and exclusiveness that form the heart and soul of the tendency in absolute power to corrupt absolutely.

No happening illustrates more clearly that dreadful tendency than the break between Rome and Constantinople. At the bar of history, the two great nations of Christianity, Roman and Eastern Orthodox, are convicted of murderous—fratricidal—intentions.

The Mark of Cain

By the opening of the 1000s, the stage was set for the final break between Rome and Constantinople. From then on, every Roman pope and every partriarch of Constantinople "would forever carry the mark of Cain, the primitive murderer, on their foreheads," one Roman commentator later observed.

In the two centuries separating the 1000s from Leo III and Charlemagne, the breach between pope and patriarch had continued to widen. While Rome flourished militarily and economically, Byzantium shrank territorially, barely survived militarily, and staggered economically. When Constantinople fell in 1453 to the Islamic Turks, it was a moment long overdue.

Particular incidents poisoned the relations between pope and patriarch. The Photian incident, for example. At the time he was elected patriarch of Constantinople in 861, Photius taught that, in the Christian Trinity, the Son had nothing to do with the origin of the Holy Spirit. In this, Photius was heretical in the eyes of his own church as well as Rome's. But in the heat of mutual enmity, his unconventional teaching passed unnoticed for a while. When Photius informed Pope Nicholas I of his appointment, Nicholas rejected it and nominated a rival, Ignatius, infuriating the Greeks. "The Pope has authority over all the earth, that is over every church," Nicholas told them. The Greeks replied by excom-

129

municating Nicholas for violating an agreement dating back to Constantine's time, forbidding one patriarch to interfere with another.

But in 869 the ax fell on Photius. A council of his own bishops deposed him for his teaching on the Holy Spirit, which they condemned as heretical, as Nicholas had said. And they replaced Photius with Ignatius, as Nicholas had wanted. But during all this adjustment, there was no thaw in relations with Rome. In time, Photius was reconciled with his church, however, and when Ignatius died, Photius was again made patriarch.

The religious dispute between Rome and Constantinople was real enough, but its effective props were territorial and economic. Both churches were sending out waves of missionaries. By the end of the ninth century, Constantinople had converted the majority of Bulgars, Serbs, Moravians (inhabitants of modern Czechoslovakia), Albanians, many Poles and Romanians to Eastern Orthodoxy. Within another hundred years, there was a national Orthodox Church in these places tied politically and culturally and religiously to Constantinople. And, by then, too, Vladimir of Russia had converted and Greek missionaries started on the conversion of Russia's Slavs. The "New Rome," "the Second Rome," was expanding to the north and west even as it withered in its original heartland.

Roman popes as well as their German emperors saw clearly where all this was leading. The initiative leading directly to the ultimate break was started with Pope Sergius IV in 1009. Sergius, on his election, flauntingly sent "statutes of faith"—a declaration of Christian tenets as he saw them—to the patriarch of Constantinople for acceptance. The "statutes" included the contentious *filioque* clause abhorred by the Greeks. It was a direct provocation. Not only did the patriarch refuse to answer Sergius directly, he refused to inscribe Sergius's name in the official Diptychs, or list of patriarchs. In the complicated protocol of the time, this was tantamount to declaring Sergius an imposter.

When Pope Benedict VIII crowned the German Henry II as emperor in Rome in 1014, he used the *filioque* clause in the ceremonies. The Greek envoys rose and left. Venice and Genoa, by now starting their careers as powerful maritime city-states with fleets of men-of-war and commercial transports, began at this time to encroach on what little remained of Greek territory in the Mediterranean. Successive popes and their families had considerable sums invested in the Venetian and Genoan enterprises. The Normans, with papal connivance, started to overrun Greek colonies in southern Italy and in Sicily, and the popes' representatives forced Latin rites on the Greeks captured there. In retaliation, Patriarch Michael Cerularius of Constantinople forced Greek rites on the Latins living in Constantinople. The fighting and bickering and plotting went on without cease.

The Greeks, no innocents, in addition found Roman morality too pungent for their nostrils. We still have documents of Byzantine ambassadors reporting on the four questions ritually put to every priest about to be consecrated as a bishop of the Roman Church: "Have you sodomized a boy? Have you fornicated with a nun? Have you sodomized any fourlegged animal? Have you committed adultery?" These questions accurately reflected the standard required of would-be bishops. St. Peter Damian wrote a famous book, the *Liber Gomorrhianus (Book of Gomorrha)*, graphically describing the venality, lechery, bestiality, and homicidal fecklessness of his fellow Roman clerics.

And the ordinary events the Greeks saw in Rome nourished their contempt for all papal claims. They saw Pope Silvester II murdered on May 17, 1003. Pope John XVII, who succeeded him, died by poisoning seven months later. Again, in 1009, Gregory of the Crescentii family was made pope by the force of his family's arms. But Theophylact of Tusculum attacked Rome, defeated the Crescentii and Gregory, expelled Gregory, and put himself on the papal throne, calling himself Benedict VIII.

When Benedict VIII died, his brother Romanus seized the papal throne. He had himself ordained priest, consecrated bishop, and crowned as pope, all in the space of one day, June 24-25, 1024, calling himself Pope John XIX. Nothing about John XIX is interesting except for one moment in his life as pope when Patriarch Eusthathios of Contantinople made very sincere peace overtures, offering to submit to Roman claims of overlordship. For a moment, apparently, John was tempted to do the right thing. But his closest advisors were Cluniac monks. With the interests of Cluny in mind, they quickly dispelled any of John's ideas of reconciliation.

131

Cluny was a monastery founded by a very religious man, Duke William of Aquitaine. From being a simple monastery in east-central France, the Cluniac order spread to over one thousand other monasteries all over Europe. Cluny became a quasifeudal family centralized under the rigid control of its powerful abbot, who commanded great wealth, vast territories, and held a close alliance with the German Holy Roman emperors. The Jesuits of their times, Cluniac monks were advisors to popes, became popes themselves, and wielded great influence in the church throughout medieval times.

When John XIX died under suspicious circumstances in 1033, a relative of John's took his own twelve-year-old son, also called Theophylact, had papal clothes made to fit him, lifted him bodily onto the papal throne, and had him consecrated pope as Benedict IX. The spectacle of this twelve-year-old issuing excommunications, giving his papal blessing, formulating decrees, consecrating bishops, deciding theological matters, was ludicrous enough, but it took more than that to shake the impassive Greeks.

Benedict shook them, though. First, the child was bisexual, sodomized animals, and ordered murders. He also dabbled in witchcraft and Satanism. Within less than a year, there was a plot to strangle him. He escaped, and his big brother, Gregory, put him back on the papal throne. The Roman citizenry revolted against him and elected John of Sabina as Pope Silvester III. But Benedict's family again put him back on the throne, and Silvester III had to flee.

In May of 1033, Benedict found a buyer for the papacy—John Gratian, a rich archpriest. Benedict and John Gratian signed a formal document according to which Benedict, when he resigned the papacy in John's favor, would receive for the rest of his life the entire tribute of the English church—it was called Peter's Pence. John Gratian became Pope Gregory VI. Benedict IX became Theophylact once again, but continued to live in the Lateran Palace, which he converted into the best brothel in Rome. At the same time, living in Rome were Silvester III in St. Mary Major's, and Gregory VI in St. Peter's.

Yes, that shook even the Greeks.

In September 1046, Holy Roman emperor Henry III came to Rome, expelled the two popes and the ex-pope and appointed one of his own German bishops, Suidger of Bamberg, as Pope Clement II, whom the Byzantines took to be a stooge of their mortal enemy, Henry.

Clement didn't last long, however. Theophylact (our former Benedict IX) had Clement II poisoned on October 9, 1047, and once more he climbed back onto the papal throne as Benedict IX. He lasted exactly eight months and nine days—until the Emperor Henry returned to Rome. Benedict took to his heels and Henry put another of his German bishops on the throne, Poppo of Brixin, as Pope Damasus II, on July 17, 1048. But Theophylact's poison acted again, and Damasus II died twenty-three days after his elevation.

Fortunately, Henry had a goodly supply of bishops. He put still another, Bruno of Toul, a member of the powerful Egisheim family, on the throne as Pope Leo IX. Besides receiving King Macbeth of Shakespearean fame in the year 1050, Leo inadvertently slammed the door on Constantinople. Partiarch Michael Cerularius, noted for learning, arrogance, and plotting, wrote to Leo proposing peace and offering to write the pope's name in the official Diptychs. Fine, Leo replied. Just begin using the *filioque* clause, too, and we can all be friends. In his ignorance, Leo even demanded that the Greeks restore the *filioque* to the Nicene Creed when it had never been there in the first place. So that was the end of that. But it wasn't the end.

The end was that Leo sent a delegation of three cardinals to Constantinople, led by the fierce, uncompromising, Greek-hating Cardinal Humbert, bishop of Silva Candida. They landed one afternoon and marched straight to the Basilica of Hagia Sofia, where the patriarch was presiding over a Mass. Without nod or say-so to anyone, all three, booted and robed, marched into the basilica, tramped up solemnly to the central altar and, to the utter consternation of the clerics present, laid a document of excommunication on the altar. Then without a word or look at anyone, the three turned around and tramped out. Outside, Humbert pronounced his only recorded words on this occasion: "Let God look and judge!"

By this time, the patriarch had scanned the document and realized its import. He sent a deacon running after the three cardinals, who caught up with them in the street, stopped them, thrust the document at Humbert, and implored him to take it back. Humbert shook his head and kept on, and the document fell to the ground.

It was over. By this quick and lethal act, Rome declared the patriarch, the emperor of the East, all Eastern bishops, priests, nuns, monks, and layfolk to be excommunicated and damned to hell-fire unless they repented and submitted to Rome. What the patriarch had done to Pope Sergius IV and his church in 1014, Pope Leo IX now had reciprocated. The mutual fratricide would stay in force for more than a thousand years.

The Crusades started in 1098 and continued for two centuries. Antioch and Jerusalem, both under the jurisdiction of the Greek patriarch but held by Muslims, fell into crusader hands. The popes insisted that all Greek churchmen be replaced by Latins with Latin rites. The Greeks in Constantinople retaliated by massacring every Latin they could find within the city limits.

In 1204, the Fourth Crusade was diverted and directed against Constantinople. These crusaders, each with a red cross of Christ painted over his shoulder armor and on his shield, stormed the city, took it, went through the streets and houses and churches and palaces methodically raping, massacring, robbing, and burning. They installed a famous French prostitute on the high altar of Hagia Sofia, where she sang ribald songs. In Rome, Pope Innocent III crossed himself in pious fear, and spoke of God's vengeance on recalcitrant heretics who refused to obey God's vicar. One Byzantine historian, Nicetas Choniates, wrote: "Even the Saracens [the Muslims] are merciful and kind compared to these men who bear the cross of Christ on their shoulders." Constantinople was made a Latin kingdom with a Latin patriarch subject to the pope. Kingdom and patriarchate lasted until 1261, when the Byzantines retook Constantinople.

After this, all efforts at reunion of Rome and Constantinople were futile. Rome made two more efforts, one in 1274 and another in 1438, to force a union on its own terms. But it was all useless. "I would rather see the Muslim turban in the middle of this city than the Latin miter," said the Grand Duke Lucas Notaras of Constantinople in 1452. One year later, he did. Sultan Mehmet II stormed and took Constantinople on

May 29, 1453. Byzantium as empire ceased. The "New" or "Second" Rome was finished. The Eastern Church became a *millet*, or division, of the Ottoman Empire, the patriarch becoming what the Ottomans called the *millet-bashi*, or commander, of the Christian *millet*. The Eastern Church was protected by sultan after sultan, and it continued on with its undying hatred and distrust of Rome and its church and its empire.

The consequences of this Roman imperialism ran further than the end of Byzantium. Within seventy years of the fall of Constantinople, the "Third Rome" arose under the rule of the grand dukes of Muscovy. "Our ruler, Czar Basil III, is on earth the sole Emperor of the Christians, the leader of the Apostolic Church which stands no longer in Rome or in Constantinople but in the blessed city of Moscow. . . . Two Romes have fallen, but the Third stands. A fourth there will not be." These words of the monk Philotheus of Pskov, written in 1510, stand as a stark reproach to the mercilessness of Roman imperialism and the fecklessness of Byzantine ambition. By their fratricidal behavior, Rome and Byzantium made possible the rise of yet another contending leader for Christians in the world. After the break, the Roman popes went on blithely occupying themselves with their Renaissance of arts and letters and their temporal power. For none of them ever forgot that, for two glorious centuries, the hated Byzantines had created in Constantinople the artistically richest and theologically most evolved religious society the world had ever seen. Rome wished to do better. It never did. Even today, no Roman pope will accept the blame for the split with Byzantium.

In their greed and jealousy, the Roman popes asserted an absolutist primacy that Eastern Christians will never accept. The damage went even further. Once Rome was willing to sacrifice the oldest and most substantial part of Christianity to its own concept of power, it is small wonder that they couldn't be bothered by an obscure but loudmouthed Augustinian monk called Martin Luther who was as full of hatred for Rome as the Greeks were. The popes, blindly and without thinking, cast off half of Europe and made straight the way of the Protestant reformation. What stuck in the throat of Luther and his followers was the same indigestible lump on which Constantinople had gagged: Roman imperialism.

The curse of Constantine has reached down to our day. A historian coolly surveying the development of Europe down to 1960, will trace the clear beginning of the rift between Western Europe and Eastern Europe in that trench that Rome and Byzantium dug between themselves in the name of religion. That deep division made the fall of Constantinople inevitable and confirmed the rise of Russia as the "Third Rome." The line that separated East from West then is virtually congruent with the line that separates the West of the 1980s from the Soviet Union and its Eastern European satellites.

The historian would also point out that the ideograph that Western Europeans and Americans have of the Eastern European—mystical, suspicious, threatening, plotting, unreliable, shifty, backward—corresponds again almost exactly to the way the Romans thought about Byzantium.

The sins of the fathers!

With the realization that the Eastern Church was now cut off definitively from the Church of Rome, it was inevitable that a pope should arise who would claim absolute power over all things temporal and spiritual. This was Pope Gregory VII.

Lord of the World

High upon the knobby Appennine spine of Italy is the isolated spur named Monte Cenis. Its flat top is almost 2,000 feet above sea level and sits at the halfway mark on an imaginary line drawn between the proud cities of Parma and Modena. Roman emperors built a fortress here. Hannibal surveyed Italy from here.

The Lombards, a conquering German tribe, built a stronghold here. Centuries later, the counts of Tuscany, Lombards too, enlarged the stronghold, heightening and tripling its walls, crowning it with defense towers and turrets, narrowing the windows of the lower stories, fitting it with ditch, moat, drawbridge, and portcullis. This castle of Canossa, as they called it (from a Lombard word meaning "lair"), became impregnable until gunpowder came into use. High winds always howled around Canossa. In winter, it was hidden in the clouds, and approaches to it were iced over. In summer, it could be seen for scores of miles around. On January 25 through January 28, 1077, Canossa witnessed a sight the like of which the world never before saw and will probably never see again:

Canossa's triple walls bristle with armed men. Knights in full armor. Crossbow archers. Spearmen. Macemen. Cauldrons of boiling oil smoke on the topmost battlements. Piles of rocks and stones, and pitch firebrands ready to be torched, lie at hand in piles. The weather is seasonal: cold, blustering, merciless winds; occasional sweeping sheets of hail and rain;

137

dark, glowering skies on all sides. Nothing can be seen of the world in the plains beneath Monte Cenis. Canossa is above the clouds and mist.

The windows of Canossa's upper stories are filled with staring faces. Gentlemen in court attire and battle gear. Ladies in full dress regalia, be jewelled, bewigged. All are staring and chattering in the Tuscan dialect, a mixture of coarse Latin, Lombard German, and a Greek that Demosthenes would not understand. All eyes and all fingers are pointing at the figure of a man outside the portcullis.

He is young, about five foot five in height. He wears the armor of a knight covered with a rough brown sackcloth robe. By his side on the ground, helmet, sword, and shield. His face and hands are blue with cold. His head is bare except for a thin gold band that only kings wear. For this is the twenty-one-year old Holy Roman emperor, Henry IV of the German Salian family. He is the most powerful single ruler in Europe between Ireland and Constantinople, between Norway and North Africa. Continually, he lifts his arms. He keeps talking and shouting by turns, and he is weeping copiously. Real tears. Every fifth word on his lips is either "pardon" or "sorry" or "repentant" or "penance" or "mercy" or the like. He arrived here on the morning of the 25th, and has been kneeling most of the time, standing occasionally to relieve himself, all the while his eyes fixed on one window high up in Canossa's walls.

There is always a cluster of people at that particular window. But two people in particular keep coming and going. One is a slim thirty-one-year-old lady, handsome rather than beautiful, wearing the clothes and insignia of nobility. She is Mathilda, countess of Tuscany, a Lombard by birth, exclusive owner and ruler of a huge central swathe of Italian territory running from the Adriatic in the east to the Mediterranean in the west. Her husband, Godfrey the Hunchback, who had lived for some years in perpetual exile with her enemies in Germany, was murdered one year ago. Now Mathilda, childless, rules here absolutely. Beside her at the window there is an imposingly tall, narrow-shouldered, ascetic-faced man. Around his shoulders an ermine-trimmed scarlet cloak. On the index finger of his right hand, a ring bearing a cross—the Fisherman's Ring. On his head, a conical hat—the tiara of popes. For this is Pope Gregory VII. It is his eyes that contemporaries remember: black, blazing, perpetually taking in all details around him, perpetually examining your face, perpetually running you through.

Gregory was born fifty-two years before this date, the son of an unknown Lombard carpenter called Bonipert (Gregory and Napoleon had the same family name, country, and ethnic origin). Named Hildebrand (or Yldebrand or Ildebrand—Gregory spelled it at least three different ways), as a boy he became a monk of Cluny, where he learned all about discipline, celibacy, order, organization, and centralized authority. He emerged from there, fanatic, unforgiving, devoted to religion, to serve as a minister for five popes and as legate for four of them. Most of them were monsters in his eyes—and would have been in the eyes of any civil person.

Pope Alexander II died on April 10, 1073, the last of a half dozen popes who had tried to reform their church but had failed. That same day, while Alexander's unburied body lay in the Lateran Basilica, without waiting for the approval of the German Holy Roman emperor (Henry IV), the cardinals had picked this fiery stark-minded Hildebrand as Pope Gregory VII, to the acclaim of the Romans. People said later he and his friends had bought the election with gold.

It did not matter. He was now pope and had exactly 12 years, 1 month, and 26 days to live. In that time he would fill Europe with a war that created more dead bodies and ruined more cities than the Thirty Years' War. It lasted fifty years and filled his church with strife, but Gregory dazzled all with his ruthless, single-minded strategy. He endured the vilest humiliations and died a failure in his great enterprise. But he overturned that medieval world he had inherited, and changed the fundamental thinking of all his contemporaries. In fact, he led them to think in terms that have made possible our modern concepts of "state" and "nation." He was an original.

None of all this, of course, was Gregory's intention. He had a grand enterprise; and when we now look back on it, we see he had to fail. He tried to do in a few years something that would have taken centuries—or a miracle—to accomplish.

But certain odds were in his favor. Disgust at the corruption in Rome over the span of six popes had produced a powerful reform party of cardinals, bishops, priests, noble families. Gregory's chief ally was Mathilda, the single most powerful noble person in Italy of the time. Never before and never since in the history of the papcy did a pope and an energetic, young, and powerful woman stand side by side in a world-shaking alliance. (Not even Gregory's enemies, by the way, tried to make Mathilda anything more than a devoted ally and supporter of Gregory.) It was the times and the spirit of the times that made success for Gregory possible. Men could not think of life without Rome, without the pope, without religion. Church, pope, religion represented at the time the highest ideals for men and women.

The world of Gregory was dominated by the church and the German Holy Roman emperors. Church and state. The spiritual and the temporal. Pope as monarch of the spiritual, emperor as monarch of the temporal. The relationship between the two passed through many variations, pope or emperor trying to encroach here or there on each other; but essentially the two remained equals, sharing the world of mankind. Gregory's grand enterprise: to bring the temporal, *all* temporal power, under his own spiritual control. It was as simple a proposition and as impossible a venture as that. We still have today the twenty-seven prirciples of Gregory. Some of them are harrowing:

> The Pope alone has the right to make use of imperial insignia.
> The Pope alone offers his foot to be kissed by princes.
> The Pope alone has the right to depose emperors and kings.
> The Pope can be judged by no one.
> The Pope can release subjects from allegiance to unjust rulers.
> His name, Pope, is unique in all the world.

Before persuading the emperor to the righteousness of this view, Gregory had to overcome three preliminary obstacles. By Gregory's time, the pope's hold over his traditional lands and rulers and bishops had been weakened by an ingenious system called "investiture." Kings, princes, noblemen, strongman rulers (and in certain places strongwoman rulers) had acquired over the centuries a so-called right to appoint bishops, abbots, and priests to benefices, or landed estates. Western Europe was dotted with such ecclesiastical real estate holdings that had fallen under the control of local rulers. The cleric or layperson who was given the living, as the English called a benefice, naturally became the creature of the ruler in matters spiritual as well as temporal. Gregory was determined to break this custom of lay investiture, and restore Roman authority.

The next two obstacles sprang from investiture. Local rulers could be bought even more easily than popes. Every man had his price. Bishops and abbots and priests regularly bought their abbey or bishopric. We know of over forty popes who bought their way into the papacy. Because the first man who tried to buy spiritual power with money was named Simon Magus, this practice of buying ecclesiastical appointments was called simony. Gregory was determined to abolish simony.

Allied to simony was the question of clerical celibacy. Throughout Western Europe, the majority of priests were married. Simony was closely tied to clerical marriage, because a man with a wife or mistress and children (and perhaps grandchildren) needed a living and had in his family a very compelling reason to seek it by simony if necessary. A married bishop or priest who had bought his living naturally felt a stronger obligation to his benefactor than to the pope.

Once Gregory was pope, therefore, he set out immediately to abolish lay investiture, simony, and clerical marriage. He called a first council of bishops in Rome in 1074. With Countess Mathilda sitting by his side, he mercilessly deposed all the married and simonist clergymen he could ferret out.

Rome presented him with a particular problem. Sixty married laymen called *mansionarii* guarded St. Peter's Basilica. Every day they put on cardinal's vestments and pretended to say Mass for the pilgrims who came to worship, collected the rich offerings of money and valuables, and lived off them sumptuously—and sometimes riotously. They held sexual orgies on the steps of the basilica, joined by their wives, children, mistresses, and the local streetwalkers. Gregory summarily dismissed them,

141

but the now dispossessed *mansionarii,* their numerous families, dependants, friends, and associates, joined the already vast throng of Gregory's enemies at home and abroad. For his initial decrees about simony and celibacy had produced a wave of horror throughout Europe. The clamor against Gregory arose across the continent like the "howling of wolves," one contemporary wrote.

His enemies tried kidnapping and assassination. On Christmas Eve, 1075, Gregory was saying Mass in the Basilica of St. Mary Major's in the middle of his cardinals and clerics and in the presence of a full congregation. As he started reading the Gospel, the doors were flung open by the governor of Rome, Cencius, accompanied by his fellow conspirators, all in armor and with drawn swords. Cencius rushed up to the altar, seized Gregory by the hair, slashed at his legs, and dragged the pope down the main aisle by the hair, vestments and all, down the steps, threw the cleric over his horse, mounted, and rode off at a gallop to his family house in southwestern Rome. All that night, Cencius with his sisters and friends mocked and tortured Gregory. In the morning, the Roman citizens attacked and liberated Gregory. The pope returned to St. Mary Major's, took up the Gospel where he had left off, and finished the Mass. Cencius he spared for a later death.

Nothing daunted, one year later, Gregory called a second council at which he forbade under the direst penalties all and every and any investiture of any cleric (bishop, priest, abbot, deacon, subdeacon) by any lay ruler from the Holy Roman emperor down to the most impotent village squire in Haddam-Haddam, England. Now, to forbid the sale of abbeys and bishoprics was one thing. To enforce a law of celibacy was still one thing. But to forbid every and any ruler in Europe from investing the local clerics as his feudal serfs and servants was to strike at the feudal system itself—the only system Europe of that time knew. It was also to free the enormous real estate holdings of the church from control and possession by kings and princes. Revolt against Gregory boiled over everywehre.

In between these two councils, Gregory had been hard at work whipping up support for his new system of international government. Gregory saw the world as passing and unimportant in its politics but eternal and divine as the outer clothing of Christ's church. Even from our much enlarged and so-called "internationalist" mentality of today, we still find Gregory's proposal breathtaking in scope and daring—almost fantastic. Given the religious faith of the day, he might have succeeded if he really had proposed his plan selflessly. But Gregory was a man of the world, and was looking out for himself. "Cursed be the man," Gregory declared, "who holds back his sword from shedding blood." In Gregory's cause, of course.

Gregory did not, therefore, propose the shortest and surest way to his noble goals, namely that the church and its clerics give up their worldly acquisitions and address themselves to spiritual matters as Jesus had done. As Peter had done. As Pontian had done. No. Gregory said that *all* wordly things must belong to the church and its pope. Small wond/.r that Europe seethed with revolt.

In his letters (we have hundreds of them) Gregory made it clear to all and sundry that every country and very nation in Western Europe was to be his vassal. Gregory did not want merely the shreds of the former ecclesiastical estates returned to the church. Bohemia was the pope's, he wrote. So was Russia. And Hungary, as well as Spain, Corsica, Sardinia, Dalmatia and Croatia (Yugoslavia), Poland, Scandinavia, Germany, England, Ireland, France, Italy. All!

Further, Gregory proposed, he would assemble a gigantic European army, attack and expel the Normans, Greeks, and Muslims, push east beyond Constantinople, finally destroy the Muslim Caliphate, invade Palestine, and retake Jerusalem and North Africa. He himself would command the army. Even though he assembled fifty thousand Italian and trans-Alpine troops south of Rome, the project came to nothing. For by now, 1075, he and Emperor Henry IV were in dire collision. And actually Gregory had maneuvered Henry onto that collision course.

Henry, despite Gregory's prohibition, kept on investing clerics with lands and properties. Gregory addressed an imperious letter to Henry demanding an acknowledgment from the emperor that he was a grave sinner. Further, Gregory demanded, Henry would have to put his repentance, confession, and sorrow in writing and have it notarized by a bishop of Gregory's choosing. Gregory's trap is clear to us: he was tempting

143

Henry to resist a purely spiritual weapon. Henry had only armies and gold as weapons. And he fell into the trap. He summoned a council of his own pandering bishops at Worms, deposing Gregory. "Henry, King by God's will," was the way he wrote to Gregory, "says to Hildebrand who is not Pope but just a treacherous lying monk! Get down off the Throne of Peter! Get down! Get down!" Gregory did nothing. He waited.

In his youthful brashness (Henry was barely twenty), the German emperor sent a priest called Roland to confront Gregory—in Rome of all places! "My Lord Bishops," the hapless Roland began speaking to the bishops sitting around Gregory in the Lateran Basilica, "this man is not a pope. He is a ravening wolf! Come all of you to Germany with me. There our gracious emperor will give you your pope!" It was the culmination of Henry's mistake. History has drawn a veil over what they did to Roland.

Gregory excommunicated all and everyone associated with Henry. Henry himself he put under a special ban: no one henceforward owed the emperor any allegiance in anything. In those rough days when life was cheap, this was one way of putting what we moderns would call a "contract" on Henry. Just as any baron in Henry's empire, when he acquired a new sword, was allowed to try it out on the back or neck of the first serf he met, so anyone who could do so was entitled to seize Henry's property and kill Henry.

The effect of putting the emperor under such a ban is difficult for us to appreciate. It might be comparable, say, to all sources of civil authority in the U.S.A. suddenly being struck powerless. The whole world of Henry, wrote one chronicler, shook and trembled.

Trouble from down south was one thing. But Henry was taken from behind his back. His rambunctious nobles and tribes started to revolt. His bishops began to feel the pinch. In dribs and drabs, they started to desert him and slink back to ask Gregory's forgiveness. "Unless the Emperor," declared a gathering of German bishops, "is released from the Pope's ban and excommunication before February 2, 1077, then the Emperor stands condemned, deposed, and exiled by his own subjects."

Worse news came. "We are coming to Germany in person," Gregory sedately announced, "to set the Church in order." Henry understood. He flew to his horse and made his way south. By the time he crossed the Alps and descended into the plains of Lombardy, Gregory had already reached Mantua. Fearing Henry would attack and kill him, he took refuge in Mathilda's triple-walled castle of Canossa. But Henry climbed up in the depths of winter, left his troops at a respectful distance, and on January 25, 1077, started his three-day, three-night vigil in the bitter cold. His pleas and weeping were interrupted only by the arrival of more and more bishops from Germany and France and Italy, all seeking forgiveness from that man whose face glared down from the topmost story of Canossa.

When on January 28 Gregory finally admitted the frozen Henry to the castle and forgave him, he carried the scene to the utmost point of theatricality. Henry would obey him in everything, he stipulated. At Mass, with Henry standing miserably by his side, Gregory took the consecrated bread (then, in the eyes of believers, the body of Christ), broke it in two portions, held out one to the emperor and the other portion to his own lips. "We declare, my Lord Emperor, that we are innocent of all wrongdoing. If we lie with these words, may this sacred bread choke us to death here and now." Gregory swallowed his portion amid the cries and huzzahs of the congregation. Only then did poor Henry realize that the spiritual weapons Gregory wielded far outdid all his armies and imperial power.

But Gregory's victory was hollow and short-lived. Henry, once back in Germany, disposed of the more ungovernable of his subjects, gathered his forces, and invaded Italy. He besieged Rome four times. Gregory ended up as a refugee with a few followers sitting in the gloomy vaults of that old forbidding mausoleum of Hadrian, the Castel Sant' Angelo. The world outside, all its rulers and people, had seen finally where Gregory wanted to go and what he intended to achieve. Gregory might have broken forever the old feudal system of thought and government. But he could not impose his own spiritual monarchy. Instead, he freed the minds of his contemporaries, who started to think of other and new formats for government, for religion, for civic life. On Gregory they piled abuse and calumny. "Ally of Satan!" . . . "Defecator-in-chief!" . . . "Enemy of the Church!" . . . "False Pope!"

145

Eventually, Gregory was rescued and liberated by his Norman allies (who in the process sacked, burned, looted, and desecrated all of Gregory's Rome), and conveyed into exile to Salerno where he died on May 25, 1085. "I have loved righteousness and hated iniquity," Gregory's last words were from the Bible, "therefore, I die in exile." The ending was his own addition.

But although Gregory failed personally, he changed his world forever. He buried the notion of a "Christian republic" under the concept of the Privilege of caste. From that came the dogmatism and the clerical domineering that necessarily implied the Reformation and the breakup of Christianity. There is not one monument of Gregory's or to Gregory's memory in Rome. Yet, the emergence of "states" and "nations," the formation of the papal chancellery that has outlived all other chancelleries—those are Gregory's monuments. Only one fifteen-word inscription in Rome mentions Gregory's name in passing. But he set up the circumstances that led to the millions of words poured out by the sixteenth-century reformers. Without Gregory, Martin Luther would have remained an obscure, whining monk of doubtful morals, twisted psychology, and bizarre theology. For Gregory's attempts to universalize Romanism evoked the local spirit everywhere. It would take four centuries to arise in force. But once born, it would blow away forever the hierarchy of Rome.

Gregory also set the papacy on another path. Within a hundred years of his death, his clerical imperialism had sharply and forever separated the clergy from the laity. By the time Pope Innocent III died in 1216, the papacy was organized as a monarchy, served by a fully-fledged chancellery, a "Curia" complete with a foreign office, a domestic office, a financial department, a school for diplomats, a school for Roman law, a regular and organized control exercised by Rome over bishops, abbots, cathedrals, seminaries, monasteries, and parishes, and finally the definitive emergence of the Roman cardinals as a 'college" of powerful counselors who decided on all important matters, exclusively elected each new pope, and ensured continuity in papal policy from pontificate to pontificate. Gregory's idea of a papal monarchy limited to the hierarchical organization was completely implemented. The papal states in Italy—a substantial territory in the center of the country—were now firmly in the hands of the popes. It was within this new Roman Curia that the papal mechanism of conclave was born.

Within a hundred years, German political and military power waned, and that of France, England, Sicily, Spain, and of various northern Italian states grew stronger. Papal elections started to be a matter of dispute between the various clerical factions which represented the interests of these emerging new national powers and city-states of Europe.

While these forces played on the election of popes, papal legislation about the election process was still being refined. In 1059, Nicholas II decreed that only cardinal-bishops could be papal electors; the lower clergy and the people merely acclaimed the candidate chosen. He also ruled that, if the condition of morality in Rome was bad to intolerable, the election could be held outside the city in any suitable convent, monastery, church, or meeting-hall.

Nicholas also fulminated against the great vice of his day: simony, the buying and selling of the papacy and other ecclesiastical offices with money or for money. "If anybody attempts to obtain his own election by money, by human patronage, or by force of arms, without the peaceful and canonical election and blessing of the Cardinal-bishops . . . let him be anathema."

Even the Roman municipal authorities (consuls, Senate, and people) got into the act, decreeing in 1145 that no one, even if elected, had to accept the office of pope. And, in 1159, at the Lateran Synod, Alexander III gave legal form to some further details: only cardinals (bishops, priests, deacons) could be papal electors; to be elected, a candidate had to receive two-thirds of the entire College of Cardinals' votes; the candidate elected need not belong to the diocese of Rome, need not be a Roman citizen, need not even be a cardinal.

In the beginning, the cardinalitial title had been simply *Dominus Cardinalis* (Lord Cardinal). The title *Reverendissimus* (Most Reverend) was added later. Pope Innocent IV (1243–1254) instituted the Red Hat as symbolic of the cardinal's office and duty. Red was chosen as the cardinalitial color, because, as leaders of the church, cardinals were to be ready

147

to shed their blood for the faith. Pope Urban VIII decided in 1623 that all cardinals should be addressed as *Eminentia* (Eminence) or *Emminentissimus* (Most Eminent).

The number of cardinals increased enormously after the twelfth century. Between the years 1200 and 1491, thirty-six popes created 540 cardinals in all. Between the years 1431 and 1794, forty-five popes created 1,275 cardinals. Some popes (Celestine IV, Clement IV, Innocent V, Alexander V, Leo XI) created no cardinals. Others, like Honorius IV (A.D. 1285) created one. Pope Adrian VI, a Dutchman, was so disgusted with Rome and all foreigners, that he made only his close friend, Enkevoirt, a cardinal. But most popes made cardinals several times during their pontificates. Prior to the twentieth century, the highest numbers were created by Urban VIII (74 cardinals between 1623 and 1643), Pius VI (73 between 1775 and 1794), and Clement XI (70 between 1703 and 1720). But until February 1965, the number of cardinals at any given moment was always in or around seventy. This particular number was chosen in order to commemorate the seventy ancient scholars of Alexandria who were traditionally thought to be the translators of the Hebrew Bible into Greek. In 1965, Pope Paul VI raised the number to 101; and by 1976, in spite of the cardinals who died in the intervening time, Paul had raised the number of cardinals to 136.

In the hands of the cardinals, the Roman papal court and administration became a vast bureaucracy which at certain times became as oppressive as any bureaucracy could be—with the added spite and malice that clerical castes seem to develop. A thirteenth-century poem bemoans the fact that the truth and love of Christ are no longer to be found in the "Roman Curia with its fulminating condemnations . . . its thundering judges, its oppressive sentences, its gold, its luxury. . . ."

Cardinals were holy, profane, learned, ignorant, worldly, meek, arrogant, politicking, pious. Speaking of the College of Cardinals in the early 1500s, a chronicler named Antonio Baudino notes that "you are taken to be a boor, unless you express some false or heretical beliefs about church doctrine." Cardinals' characters ran the gamut of human achievement and human error, from excellence of all kinds to evil of a deep kind. Cardinal Robert of Geneva was expert in the tactical use of Breton pikemen, wielded no mean pike himself, marched at the head of a contingent of these butchers over the Alps, and massacred every man, woman, and child he could find in the town of Cesena, Italy—all in all, about 6,000 people. The statesman most responsible for the rise of Protestant England, Protestant Germany, and Protestant Sweden was Cardinal Richelieu, who was not at all bothered by the cannibalism and terrorism of the Thirty Years' War which he fomented, and who died as he crawled about on all fours, neighing and persuaded that he was a horse.

Down through the centuries there were a series of cardinals who were scholars of the highest repute or holy men who worked in obscurity and whose names are never mentioned. More often than not, it is one like Cesare Borgia, brother of Lucrezia, and son of Alexander VI, who is remembered. Cesare was a huge bull of a man who always wore a mask to hide the deformity of his face (due, some said, to the ravages of venereal disease). He could behead a bull with one stroke of his broadsword. He employed his own personal assassin, Don Michelotto. Cesare was definitely bisexual. He assassinated his own brother (Alexander VI's other son), and stabbed Alexander's favorite boy mercilessly to death as the favorite cowered under Alexander's papal cloak and Alexander tearfully pleaded with Cesare to spare the boy. He was made a cardinal by Alexander, but then was given a special dispensation so that he could make a good marriage with Charlotte d'Albert, daughter of the king of Navarre. When he deserted this wife, he took various mistresses, and ended his days in the dungeon of a Spanish prison. Cesare Borgia is the only man known to us in history to whom a book on syphilis (*Tractatus contra Pudendarga*) was gratefully dedicated by the author, a Spanish doctor, with Cesare's permission. Cesare had allowed the doctor to try out some new cures for the disease on himself; and the doctor gracefully noted in the dedication of the book that "in Your Person, you have afforded mankind the chance to find a cure for this illness."

The nationality of cardinals remained for a long time restricted to southern Europeans, and to Italians in particular. Except for the eighty years that the popes spent in Avignon, France (when most cardinals were Frenchmen), Italians were the preponderant bloc in the College of Cardinals down to the twentieth century. Side by side with the huge Italian

149

preponderance, there were since the fifteenth century a steady number of French, German, Spanish, Portuguese, and Austrian cardinals; and then at a certain point there was included a limited number of Dutchmen, Hungarians, English, rarely a Greek, an Oriental, an African, or a Middle Easterner. Only in the twentieth century did the College of Cardinals become truly international.

By the twelfth century, the technique of papal election had also developed to a more refined form. Once the election became an issue between a limited number of electors, and not a matter of popular assembly, it fell into two main phases. The *tractatio* (general presentation) was a period of time during which the various candidates were named and their qualifications were described. This was followed by the *deliberatio* (debate) in which the various factions argued their case. The election was ended by the voting. With few electors, each one signified his vote *ore et manu*, by voice and hand-signal. There were only seven electors present in 1059 when Nicholas II was chosen.

By contrast, in 1136, there were fifty present to elect Innccert II. With an increased number of electors, it was found necessary to use written ballots and to institute the "scrutiny": a careful examination of the ballots by representatives of each faction to discourage cheating.

The widening of the scope of papal elections in the choice of candidate, and the new two-thirds requirement, only increased the difficulty of arriving at the election of one man. More and more, papal elections became a microcosm in which European princes battled with each other through the cardinal-electors in their pocket in order to get their own candidate elected. And another major factor had emerged by the opening of the 1200s: the most important landowner in Europe was the pope; the most important parts of Europe were fiefs of the pope. He commanded their military support, their political loyalty, determined who their rulers were to be, and could call on their financial contributions. Most importantly, the men and women of the age knew no other means of discerning legitimate government except by the approval of that one resident bishop of Rome who claimed ceaselessly to be the successor of St. Peter and the Vicar of Jesus. On his will depended, therefore, their civil order and the legitimacy of their laws.

Besides, the pope possessed spiritual weapons he could use against his enemies. He could excommunicate individuals and whole communities. As a consequence, nobody could be forgiven their sins or receive the sacraments. He could place the whole city, the whole country, if necessary, under interdict: all other Christians were forbidden to have any intercourse with them, even in cases of necessity. All trading was illegal. All business deals were invalid in law. It was the churchly version of the old classical Roman punishment meted out to fugitives, traitors, and criminals, the refusal of "fire, water, bread, and roof." And no one could long survive under an effective interdict. Every ruler wished to have some control or call on the man who sat on the throne of Peter in Rome, and whose cardinals were princes in their own right. These very circumstances—the powerful temporal dominion of the pope, his spiritual overlordship, and the irreconcilable clash between these two claims—inevitably produced a new way of choosing a pope: the conclave. Nothing illustrates more graphically than the lives of certain popes why and how the conclave method arose.

How They Invented Conclave

The most telling facts about the conclave system of electing popes are the least obvious to the modern mind. Layfolk, not clerics, were the inventors of conclave, and their reasons for doing so were not religious or spiritual, but political and economic. In fact, reluctant and recalcitrant clerics were literally dragged, howling and kicking, into the first conclaves. But once the efficacy of the system was demonstrated, it was a pope who made it the official mode of electing popes.

One inescapable fact of the thirteenth century led to the invention of conclave: Europe was dominated by the papacy. The legitimacy of all rulers in that Europe depended on their relationship with the Roman pope. The political life and therefore the economic well-being of all European peoples revolved around that single bishop of Rome, his policies, his preferences, his family interests, and the dynasties he personally supported. And whenever for one reason or another the chair of St. Peter stood vacant—sometimes months, even years, intervened between the death of a pope and the choice of a successor—political relations, international trade, and civil order were threatened. There had to be a validly elected pope for day-to-day life in Europe to go on.

By the end of the twelfth and the opening of the thirteenth century, the political conditions of Europe were so acute and the personal loyalties of the cardinals were so divided, that they could not agree among themselves; and, by now, only they were empowered to elect a pope. At this juncture, they dithered too long over political stakes that were too high,

153

too explosive. The tides of civil tension, economic stagnation, political stress, territorial disputes, and military duress were running too high. So the ordinary laity took the law into their own hands. They literally locked up the cardinals in one large room ("conclave" means "with key"), progressively harassing and starving them until, in desperation, the cardinals elected a pope. Conclave had been born.

It was not a new idea. The Lombards, who invaded Italy in the sixth and seventh centuries, locked up their chief men until they agreed among themselves to pick one supreme commander. At least once in the early history of Venice, the Doge was elected in this fashion. And, in 644, the Muslims kept six of their officials impprisoned until they elected a successor to the Caliph Omar.

The first, impromptu papal conclave came about after July 16, 1216, the day on which Pope Innocent III died of malaria in the Italian city of Perugia. During his reign of eighteen years, Innocent brought the papacy to a great peak of power. He reestablished Roman authority over the Eastern Orthodox churches. He had issued feudal patents of nobility and power to an enormous and exhaustive list of kings, princes, counts, bishops, cities, lords, and nobles throughout Europe. As Innocent himself wrote coyly but accurately to King John of England: "As the rod lay beside the table of the Law in the Ark of the Lord, so lies the terrible power of destruction and the gentleness of mercy in the breast of the Pope."

The pope's words were more than mere metaphors. The facts were brutally obvious to his contemporaries. At Innocent's death, the throne of Peter in Rome was not merely the only dogmatic and canonical authority of the peoples of Europe. It was their only and supreme political tribunal. There was no inhabitant, high or low, in that now far distant Europe who did not recognize that the pope and his church contained the center of gravity for all political and moral order in their lives. Without a pope, Europe was impossible. It would have fallen apart.

Within a few days of Innocent's burial, therefore, the cardinals gathered in Perugia to elect his successor. When it became clear that the reverend prelates were dawdling and feuding, the Perugian civil authorities and the citizenry locked the doors of the house where the cardinals were meeting. In sheer fright, the electors quickly chose an aged cardinal,

154

a citizen of Rome named Cencius Savelli, as Pope Honorius III. It was not a formal conclave but the seed had been planted.

When Honorius III died in 1227, the electors quickly elected his successor, Gregory IX; and nobody even thought of locking them up. But Gregory's feckless career brought the church and therefore Europe to a supreme crisis that conclave emerged to solve.

By a series of hotheaded and ill-conceived political and military moves, Gregory soon lost the autocratic hold that Innocent III had forged. Gregory made a mortal enemy of the ambitious German emperor, Frederick II, who invaded Italy with his armies, occupied most of the important cities, and laid siege to the city of Rome. Gregory also mismanaged his relations with France, Spain, and England. And at home, in his own papal states of Italy, he alienated many powerful noble families and the ordinary people in some of the biggest city-states. Innocent III's empire was in a shambles of divisive factions, and Gregory lacked the power to control them. In the hindsight of history we can now see that these troubles were inevitable. The pie of papal power was big and appetizing. Kings and princes and nobles found that their lands, their palaces, their wealth, and their power depended on who was pope.

Inevitably, too, the divisiveness affected the cardinal-electors and their supporters. Some backed Gregory. Others saw their interests in the French, German, or Spanish claims. Still others ambitioned the papacy for themselves. When Gregory died on August 21, 1241, at the age of 100, he left a legacy of enmity and bitterness to the church, to his twelve cardinals, and to European rulers. The German emperor, Frederick, had invaded Italy, captured and imprisoned two of the cardinals in the northern city of Capua, and encamped with his armies at Tivoli some miles from Rome.

Rome itself was a divided city. Besides the individual cardinals themselves and their vast households, armed retainers, and followers, the noble families and the Roman populace were divided into as many opposing camps as the ten cardinals. The streets and squares of the city became extremely dangerous in the daytime and very lethal after dark. Popular markets, business transactions, sanitation, civil jurisdiction, religious worship, all began to flag and fail. Reports of a similar chaos throughout the papal states filtered into the city.

155

Surveying this wreckage was the powerful and now dismayed governor of Rome, Senator Matteo Rosso Orsini, the most powerful layman in the papal organization. His power and prestige were at stake. Matteo was determined that a pope would be elected as soon as possible. He knew the alternative included his own death, the impoverishment of his family, as well as foreign—probably German—rule over Rome and Italy. He set about taming the fractious cardinals.

First, he had the cardinals brutalized by his own men. Each cardinal was tied hand and foot, flung to the ground in the presence of eyewitnesses (to instill a sense of shame), struck and beaten as if he was a thief and a felon, stomped on by the soldiery, and abused with foul language: *"Sacco di mierda! Reverendissimo Cardinale!"* was the expression each cardinal heard as a military boot ground his face into the mud.

Untied, the cardinals were then thrown bodily into the main hall of the Septizodium, a huge, three-tiered, columnar structure built at the end of the Via Appia one thousand years before by the ancient Roman emperor, Septimius Severus. Matteo ordered the doors of this one big room locked, its windows blocked up. No one was allowed to enter or to leave. Armed guards were posted all around the outer walls and on the roof. The senator gave public orders to kill on sight anyone who tried to get in or out. He then commanded the ten cardinals to get on with it and pick a new pope. The first genuine conclave had begun.

The living conditions were abominable. There were a few chairs and benches, some broken-down cots, insufficient bedclothes. No exceptions were made for the sick or the ailing or the very old cardinals. They lay around the floor among the healthy. No doctors were allowed in. No special food was permitted. Primitive latrines were provided inside the hall, but they were not to be emptied until a pope was chosen. A modicum of cold water was allowed for drinking purposes, but no hot water, no change of personal clothing or of bed sheets. The summer heat was still at its height, and the air inside the room was humid and fetid with odors.

When one cardinal started to die, he was hastily stuffed into a long box while still breathing, and he listened while the other cardinals sung over him the Latin hymns which were normally chanted at the funeral services after death. Upstairs on the roof, the armed watchmen who were forbidden by the senator to leave their posts, used the gutters as garbage dumps and as latrines. When sudden summer squalls during the frequent Roman thunderstorms, or *temporales*, poured gallons of rainwater onto the roof in a short space of time, the inevitable happened. The clogged gutters poured food detritus, feces, urine, and rainwater down on top of the cardinals and their sleeping-places.

In spite of all this, it was only in the last days of September that the cardinals made any real effort to elect a pope. They were divided into two factions: one trying to elect the favored candidate of Frederick, the other intent on choosing as pope a man who would give his blessing to the French, the Spanish, and the Sicilians who intended to make war with Frederick. After all the bickering, both factions compromised and chose a candidate, Cardinal Humberto Romano, who had bound himself by oath not to offend either faction and to abdicate the moment they were freed from their prison. Then the senator was summoned. Told the news by the cardinal-dean, he saw the ruse immediately and went white with rage. Humberto would do nothing to relieve the church of its miseries, and the cardinals knew as much, the senator shouted. Did they think he did not know their clever little game? Once freed, they would scatter to the four winds: the peace party to the safety of Frederick's camp, the war party to their allies in France, Italy, and Sicily. "No," the senator swore at the cardinals in Latin. "By the Sacrament, I swear it! No. Here is what your Eminences are going to do right now: Pick another candidate!"

If not, he went on, he would dig up the recently buried pope and put the cadaver in the middle of their hall. They could live, sleep, eat, talk, while they looked on and smelled the cadaver in its decay. If they still persisted in evading their responsibilities, he concluded, he would kill them all. Cardinals Sinibald and Richard of Sant'Angelo were already critically ill, he noted. "They will be ill unto death, if we haven't a new pope soon," the senator said, as he left the hall.

Even so, it took the cardinals over three weeks more (until October 25) to pick the gentle Milanese, Godfrey, bishop of Santa Sabina. Matteo concurred, and the first conclave was over. The cardinals had spent over fifty-five days within that single room.

Some days later, Godfrey, who chose to be called Celestine IV, fell ill. Two weeks later, on November 10, he died—a pope-elect who had never actually been consecrated. In the meantime, the cardinals fled for refuge,

157

some to Anagni a couple of miles from Rome, some to their own fortresses and palaces. From there, they communicated by messengers with each other about the identity of the next pope. Occasionally, they met together. But it was all to no purpose. Time passed. By February 1242, they had not reached an agreement on the next pope. Apparently, they had not yet learned their lesson.

By now, it was Emperor Frederick of Germany who was intent on having a new pope. From his armed camp at Tivoli, he sent a message to the cardinals at Anagni: "We are sending you the two cardinals we imprisoned at Capua (Oddo Colonna, Jacopo of Praeneste), and the other cardinals who are in their palaces and fortresses. Get together! The church needs a pope."

Another year passed, and in April of 1243 the emperor decided on violent measures. His armies laid waste to all the properties belonging to the cardinals. And he sent one army corps to besiege Rome. The majority of the cardinals fled for safety to Naples. By the beginning of June, the want and starvation was enormous, and all revenues were drying up. In desperation, the leading cardinals held private discussions with Frederick, with the result that on June 25, 1243, at Anagni, the eleven cardinal-electors chose Sinibald Fieschi as Pope Innocent IV. Frederick's sword had served instead of the conclave key. And a secure decade passed.

Innocent IV died in Naples, in the house of a certain Peter di Vinea, on December 7, 1254. According to the ancient rule, the cardinal-electors should have remained in the city and elected the next pope in the place where the previous pope had died. But, fearing for their safety, they planned to leave Naples in secrecy. The governor of the city, Bartolomeo Tavernano, got wind of their plans. He, together with a German knight, Berthold von Vohburg-Hohenburg, closed and locked the gates of Naples, and on December 10, the two noblemen locked the cardinals into Peter di Vinea's house (the dead pope's body had been removed), and announced that the cardinals would emerge only when they had a new pope. Thus began the second conclave.

By now there were thirteen cardinals: seven Italians, two Frenchmen, one each from England, Spain, Burgundy, and Hungary. Only eleven of the thirteen were present in this second conclave.

The eleven cardinals had no intention of exposing themselves to such rigors as their predecessors had endured in the Septizodium. Within a couple of days, therefore, they elected Bishop Rainald of Ostia as Alexander IV, on Saturday, December 12. When Alexander IV died at Viterbo seven years later, on May 25, the eight cardinal-electors almost immediately elected Patriarch Jacques Pantaleon, a Frenchman, as Urban IV. There was no time—and no need—to lock them up in conclave.

But when Urban IV died at Perugia on October 2, 1264, the twenty-one cardinals present could not agree for six months on a successor. Urban had made fourteen of them (seven Italians, six French, and one Burgudian). But the question of Sicily's political future divided them. Some favored the German emperor's claim to Sicily, some favored the French or Spanish or Italian point of view. Six months passed before the German emperor rattled his sword and whispered the dread word "conclave!" Immediately the main two warring factions (pro-French and pro-German) agreed to appoint official compromisers—three cardinals from each faction who would then pick one candidate each. The cardinals would then choose one of these two.

This compromise resulted in the election of Guido the Fat of Fulcodi, cardinal of Santa Sabina, as Clement IV, on February 5, 1265. It was bad news for the emperor. Guido had one consuming interest: his hatred of, and desire to kill or see killed, every member of the emperor's family, the Hohenstaufens, who threatened to take away the material possessions of the papacy. The "patrimony of St. Peter" was in danger, Guido said. And, in his three and a half year reign, he wreaked much of this hatred on the Hohenstaufens.

When he died at Viterbo in the early hours of November 29, 1268, the cardinals met in the Archbishop's Palace in Viterbo where he had died. They were eighteen in number. Eleven in the Italian party were supported by the German emperor and wanted a restoration of papal lands. Seven in the French party wanted a French pope and were supported by King Charles of Sicily and King Philip III of France. Reunion of the Roman Catholic and Greek Orthodox churches was also an issue.

There was no way that these eighteen cardinals could have agreed. Among them were the toughest prelates in the whole history of the church—John of Toledo, Allobuoni, Oddo of Tusculum, Gaetano Orsini, Hugo of Santa Sabina, Richard of Sant' Angelo, Stephen of Palatine.

159

They and the others had all lived successful if quite dangerous lives. They were enormously rich and pleasure-loving and power-struck. They were princes in their own right who owed obligations of one kind or another to princely families and royal houses around Europe. They lived by their wits, wielded power of life and death over their own vassals and servants, were unrelenting in enmity, stubborn in their views, completely persuaded of their own righteousness. The issues splitting them into two factions concerned the power-centers of their entire world: Who would rule Sicily? Who would be emperor of Germany? Which of them could satisfy his jealousies or further his ambitions? Which of them would be supreme pontiff? And complicating all this were the innumerable family ties that linked each cardinal with powerful families besides his own and with other economic and financial interests throughout Italy, France, Spain, Germany, and England.

Almost three years passed, and by January 1271, it was clear to the three major parties (Charles of Sicily, the emperor of Germany, Philip of France) that the cardinals were not going to agree. True, in December 1270, they did agree on the one holy man known to them all: Philippo Beniti, a non-cardinal and head of the religious Order of Servites. But Philippo was told that he would not survive his election very long. Wisely or unwisely, but certainly prudently, he refused to accept the honor of being elected pope of the universal church. And, to emphasize his refusal, he took off by night for the solitude and anonymity of the nearby mountains.

At this point, the kings and princes started to gather. Charles, who had been in Rome in late February, proceeded to Viterbo, arriving there early in March of 1271 accompanied by Prince Henry, son of King Richard of Cornwall. Soon, King Philip of France together with his viceroy of Tuscany, Guido of Montfort, arrived from Tunis bearing the dead body of King Louis IX who had died in Tunis while on crusade. Guido, a tall, hulking, hot-tempered man with a taste for blood, had a personal vendetta against Prince Henry. Guido's father, Simon of Leicester and Montfort, had been slain by Henry's family and his corspe had been mutilated and disfigured.

Charles and Philip and the others first tried persuasion on the cardinals. But it did not work. They and the townspeople of Viterbo grew sullen. All municipal activity came to a standstill. The city was invested by two armies, and the countryside around was more dangerous than "walking among the Muslims of Africa," as the saying went. The roof of the Archbishop's Palace where the cardinals were meeting, was occupied by the Viterbo magistrates and their guards. Every morning, a litter of bloodied and mutilated bodies around the streets underlined the frailty of life and did nothing to dispel the cardinals' fear of reprisals—no matter what they did or whom they chose.

To intimidate the cardinals all the more, they were given an object-lesson on how to die bloodily in public with no hope of being helped. On March 13, in the Cathedral of Viterbo, Charles and Philip with their retinues and servants attended High Mass in the presence of all the cardinals and clerics of the city together with the magistrates and nobles and their ladies. The bull-like Guido found himself behind Henry of Cornwall who was just about to go up to the sanctuary near the altar in order to receive the Eucharist. It was too much for Guido. He jumped up, pulled a dagger from his belt, leaped on top of Henry, and stabbed him eleven times drawing great gobs of black-red blood all over his clothes, the floor, and the nearby spectators, all the while shouting "with the voice of a female wolf defending her cubs," says the chronicle. It was all over in seconds: Guido dragged the dying man by the hair of the head down the central aisle between the worshipers, kicked open the main door, and threw the dying Henry headlong out the main portico down the steps to roll in the dust and the bright sunlight and his own blood. The cardinals and kings and their retinues had only time to stare dumbstruck and help-lessly at it all.

Although King Charles removed Guido from his post as viceroy of Tuscany, twelve years later Pope Martin IV made Guido ("our most beloved son") commander-in-chief of all papal armies. The future Martin IV was one of the cardinals who gazed on the assassination of Henry that March 13. At least Guido was decisive and efficient, Martin doubt-lessly reasoned. Rulers needed decisive and efficient soldiers and com-manders.

But the incident did not help spur the election of a pope. The cardinals became even more bitter and divided and fearful. No matter what they decided, somebody powerful was bound to be offended. Now, the Viterbo townspeople intervened. The governor of Viterbo, Albert de Monte-buono, together with the magistrates and the Savelli family and Ramiro Galli, captain of the Viterban militia, locked all the cardinals with their servants into one room of the Archbishop's Palace. Thus began Conclave 3. They ran rough beams from wall to wall. From these they hung sheets of canvas, thereby creating cubicles for the cardinals. The holes hacked in the walls for that purpose can still be seen today in the building at Viterbo. The Viterban authorities refused to send in any food to the cardinals except bread and wine. When this did not induce the cardinals to elect a pope, the Viterbans sent in only water, and they removed the roof of the building so that the cardinals were exposed to the heat of the day and the cold of the night, and the occasional heavy rainfalls. John of Toledo cracked a grim joke about their incarceration: "Sure! They had to take off the roof. How else could the Holy Spirit enter among us?"

Nobody laughed. Instead, the cardinals retaliated as best they could. They threatened to excommunicate their jailers, and to punish Viterbo by forbidding all religious ceremonies—baptism, Mass, marriage, confession, blessings, and forbidding the outside world to have any communication with Viterbo and the Viterbans. The roof had to go back on the palace, the cardinals insisted. The locks had to be opened. Food had to be supplied.

But matters had gone too far by now. The members of the Savelli family announced themselves as "Custodians of the Conclave" and vowed to cut down anyone who dared put back the roof or open the locks or supply food to the cardinals. And the Savelli, together with Governor Albert, the magistrates, and the townspeople, told the cardinals: "We may live excommunicated and without religious worship. But your Eminences will surely die of hunger, disease, and hardship. Choose a pope!" It speaks a lot for the cardinals' stubbornness that by September of the same year they still had not elected a new pope. Many of them, of course, had high hopes that one of their kingly supporters would come and break the conclave.

It took a sermon preached at them on September 1, 1271, by a certain Father Bonaventure (later canonized as St. Bonaventure by the church), to galvanize the cardinals. Bonaventure had been the first to insist with the civil authorities that the cardinals be locked up. He now told the

162

cardinals that the needs of the church were great. He also outlined in vivid medieval terms the penalties in store for those who betrayed Christ's trust. Did they all want to burn in hell-fire when they died—and die they surely would within this very palace, if they did not choose a pope. Directly after Bonaventure's fiery sermon, the cardinals appointed six compromisers. And by the late evening, the compromisers had chosen a non-cardinal, the sixty-one-year old archpriest, Toebaldo Visconti, a northern Italian with a great reputation for holiness and reportedly in extremely bad health (a distinct advantage in the electors' eyes). The third conclave was over.

There had been no pope for exactly 2 years, 9 months, and 2 days. When the convlave ended, the pope-elect, Teobaldo, officially archdeacon of Liege in Belgium, was on crusade in Palestine with King Edward I of England. Messengers reached Teobaldo in November, and on March 13 of the following year he entered Rome and was consecrated as Pope Gregory X on March 27.

Gregory's main achievement was to call a general council of the church at Lyons in France. He wished to introduce reforms into the church. At the end of the council, he laid down the conditions under which popes should be elected in future. It was the first detailed ceremonial for papal elections. Conclave (Gregory was the first pope to use the term), the weapon of desperate laymen and irate princes, was now consecrated as the official church method for electing the successor of St. Peter.

Wherever a pope died, Gregory ordered, there all the cardinals were to gather under the direction of the cardinal chamberlian who presided over the church until a new pope was elected. The cardinals already there were to bury the dead pope with due ceremony, waiting ten days for their brother cardinals to arrive. Then all were to enter one papal palace together. Each cardinal could have one personal servant to wait on him and, if a cardinal was ill or very old and feeble, an additional attendant. The cardinals were to be "conclaved": the doors were to be locked, all windows were to be barred, and there was to be no communication by word or by writing or by signals with the outside world.

Gregory gave the Savelli family a pepetual right to be custodians of every conclave. That right passed to the Chigi family in 1712 when the last Savelli died, and it remains with the Chigi to this day. The custodian

163

was to watch outside the conclave. The papal chamberlain was to guard the interior. Both were to hinder all infraction of conclave secrecy. For as long as there was no pope, all papal revenues were confiscated; no cardinal could receive any money; papal affairs, courts, tribunals, missions, envoys, banking arrangements, dispensations, state councils, all was to cease.

Gregory was unremitting in his detailed rigor. The cardinals and their servants were to live, eat, wash, discharge their personal functions, discuss candidates, and elect a new pope in one large room. No one was to have a separate room or "cell" or "cubicle" or even a special corner of his own. Food was to be passed in daily to the conclave through a heavily guarded window, and all food was to be examined thoroughly before being allowed into the hands of the cardinals. Gregory wanted to avoid what he had often seen—messages hidden in bread, weapons like poison in fruit or stilettos in steaks, and written communications between the cardinals and temporal rulers.

No cardinal was to touch the plate or the food or another cardinal. Each one ate alone and by himself. For the first three days, the food was to be plentiful and as the cardinals needed, demanded, and paid for. If no valid election had taken place after three days, then for the next five days the cardinals were to be given only one meal per day. (Gregory did not specify how many courses in that one meal, however, so that in later conclaves when this rule was applied, the cardinals observed this rule by ordering one meal consisting of nine courses!) If the five-day period was fruitless, then the cardinals were to be given only bread, water and wine. At the extreme, when a deadlock continued, the roof of the palace was to be removed and the cardinals exposed to the vagaries of the weather day and night.

Gregory also established a minute code of voting and scrutiny of votes. To be elected, a candidate had to win two-thirds of the total vote. There were to be two main voting sessions, one in the morning and one in the evening. On each occasion, the cardinals could take a second vote, if the majority so decided. Three cardinals, elected each time, were to read the votes, and three others (also elected each time) were to watch the first three. If a cardinal received two-thirds of the total election vote, the presiding cardinals must make sure the pope-elect had not voted for himself.

If so, the vote was invalid. And voting would have to start all over again.

Gregory laid the responsibility for the observance of all these rules on the magistrates of the town where the conclave took place under the custodianship of the Savellis.

He did not specify that the election should take place in Rome, as later became the rule. He followed the long established custom that it take place where the previous pope died. Theologians had taught that elections should only take place in Rome. "Nowhere else in the world," wrote Peter Damien in 1057, "but within Roman walls shall the Pope be elected." But for six centuries (from the ninth to the fifteenth) the location varied around Italy and France. Only from 1431 onward did the election again take place regularly in Rome.

The severity of Gregory's rules, of course, was in perfect keeping with that pope's whole character. An incident at the close of his life demonstrates even better than his conclave rulings the unyielding harshness of Gregory's outlook. Returning from the Council at Lyons in 1275, he arrived outside Florence in December. The weather had been extremely severe for weeks. The River Po, which stood between him and the south of Italy was flooding over its banks and impassible. He could pass southward only by going through the city of Florence. Because of a bitter dispute between him and the Florentines about civil government and tribute-payments, he had excommunicated the whole city and forbidden anyone to enter it. To enter the city, he would have to lift his own ban. He had no alternative, and so he did. He was then able to enter the city.

On January 1, he left Florence by the main gate on the southern bank of the Po. Immediately, he turned around on his horse, lifted his hand, and again threw the city and all its inhabitants back into excommunication. There is no more telling portrait of the medieval popes than that of the fiery Gregory on horseback, with flashing eyes and hand upraised, turning his head for a brief instant, glancing at the walls of Florence under the murky skies, and casting the whole city back into outer darkness, before he passed on southward. Arriving at Arezzo on the 10th of January, Gregory suddenly took ill and died. Conclave was his monument.

165

To an outside observer it would seem that the conclave system as a mechanism of papal election should eliminate all but the rarest of dangers that could possibly arise from the interplay of human ambitions and the prize of earthly power that the papacy represented. Yet, as history unraveled, this was not the case. Conclave, after all, was devised as a very human way of bringing men (the electors) to a vivid sense of their responsibilities. And they, presumably, being ordained and consecrated chruchmen, would retain a sense of their mission and their churchly duty. This must have been the mind of the fierce Gregory X who canonized conclave as the official method of electing popes.

Yet, as history shows, this was not the result. Conclave merely focused the power struggle within a narrower arena. As long as earthly power was involved in the office of pope, conclave elections became living examples of what men will do in order to gain power. Two popes—how they came to be elected in conclave, and what they did with the power they acquired—illustrate the corroding influence of that earthly power conferred by the papacy. In a very true sense, conclave became the sport of princes—the princes of the church, the cardinals.

Pope Celestine V could not assume his responsibilities; he deserted the papacy. Pope John XXIII of the fifteenth century was willing to assume the responsibilities of the earthly power; but, in the judgment of the whole church in his day, was incapable of assuming its spiritual duties, and he was deposed. Small wonder that in the twentieth century another pope would reassume the name, John XXIII, in order to re-sanctify that papal name.

In between Celestine and John, conclave elections became such a power arena that the popes left Rome and lived in France under the very French protection of the French kings.

166

The Pope Who Wouldn't Trust

In the year 1294, a pope who had been validly elected, chose to resign, was imprisoned, and awaited execution. His name was Peter Murrone.

Once he had been elected as Pope Celestine V, Murrone found that he simply could not live with the worldliness of the papacy. He would not exercise its political power, use its wealth, wield its influence. Neither was he strong-minded enough to even attempt to cleanse the church of its ugly encrustations, and he was one of the bare handful of popes in all history who could have reversed the fateful trend begun by Silvester that transformed the church into a temporal power.

And Celestine *could* have made that effort, and *would* have had a good chance of success, because he was a candidate of desperation and could have named his own price for acceptance. But he rejected the chance, and he rejected it for a reason that infuriates: as the first widely recognized charismatic in the church's history, he lived in his own ideal world, occupied with imagining where the Holy Spirit might appear to create a new Pentecost—and, Peter expected the Holy Spirit to do all the hard work entailed. In this, Peter was quite comparable to twentieth-century charismatics. He believed in the promise of Jesus to Peter, but he did not trust in it; and because he had no trust, it was more than a century after his death before there was another chance of true reform.

The youngest of eleven children, Peter was born and reared in the

167

valleys of the Abruzzi. He was a Benedictine monk at thirteen, founder of his own order of monks—the Celestines—at twenty-two on the limestone mountain of Murrone (hence his name). Mystic, devoted to the Holy Spirit, given to fearful asceticism in fasting, prayer, bodily lacerations, and solitude, Peter left Murrone only once in sixty-three years—to obtain approval of his Celestines from Pope Gregory X, at Lyons in France. Peter always regarded himself and his monks as the first "spiritual men" of the new age, a special age when the last phase of salvation would be achieved. He believed in the prophecies of one, Joachim de Flore, and practiced the fearful asceticisms recommended by Joachim. Peter awaited the fulfillment of Joachim's prediction of a new pope of holiness, and of an end to the world. Peter and his monks spent their days and nights waiting for the call and for the advent of paradise on earth in the prophetic age.

One fine day in the year 1294, Peter had some visitors. Climbing laboriously up his mountain came three bishops, a Roman senator, a cardinal with his retinue, a group of noblemen and knights, and several thousand people. They suddenly invaded the mountainside clamoring for his approval, begging him in the name of Jesus to utter the magic words: "I accept the grade of Pope." The only reason Peter did what they asked was his reasoning: nobody but the Holy Spirit could have made three power-hungry bishops, one arrogant Roman senator, and one stiff-backed cardinal climb that hard-faced mountain on foot in search of him. What Peter did not know was the crisis preventing the choice and election of a new pope. Even so, he could have named his price for accepting the papacy, but he did not.

Pope Nicholas IV had died in Rome on April 4, 1292. The conclave to elect the new pope got together in late May. From the very beginning, this conclave was a shambles. First of all, the factions. There were thirteen cardinals in conclave: eleven Italians and two Frenchmen. The Italians were split into three diametrically opposed factions. The Colonna cardinals (Jacopo, Peter, John Boccamazi), who wanted Roman independence from outside political interference, opposed the Orsini cardinals (Latino, Matteo Rubeus, Napoleon). In disagreement with both were the remaining four Italians (Benedict Gaetani, Gerard Bianchi, Matteo d'Acquasparta, Peter Peregrossi), who were in the pay of the king of Naples. The two Frenchmen (Hugo of Sabina, John Chalet) wanted, each one, to be pope and opposed all others.

Secondly, there was the weather. It was unbearably humid. Rome was full of flies and mosquitoes. Cardinal Latino, dean of the cardinals, moved them around from St. Mary Major's to the Aventine Palace to Santa Maria Sopra Minerva in a desperate attempt to pacify them. In vain. Five of the six cardinals from Rome fled to Rieti for cooler air. The other Roman, Cardinal Gaetani, went to Anagni. People feared Gaetani. He had a reputation for cruelty and unpredictable moods. His very appearance frightened, with those little glaring points of light in the center of his eyes. In September, all returned to Rome and started the conclave again. But the fierce wrangling continued. For one year. In Rome. In Anagni. In Perugia. For a second year. In Rome. In Perugia. The summer always brought a disbanding of the conclave. Besides, the cardinals had to attend to political and family matters.

Finally, during one of their tumultuous meetings at the beginning of July 1294, Cardinal Latino Orsini threatened his fellow cardinals: "The holy hermit of Mount Murrone has had a vision, Messires! Severe punishments await us all, if we do not give the church a new pope!" And then Cardinal Peter Peregrossi remarked: "No offense, my brothers, but Peter is the only man whom the ordinary Christian regards as holy. We're all tarred with the brush of corruption." Cardinal Napoleon Orsini saw an end to his miseries of being cooped up with the others. He screamed: "I propose Peter for Pope!" Napoleon Orsini never spoke. He always screamed. These wordly-wise clerics in their high boots and silken vests and unbreakable pride paused.

Every one of them knew of Peter. The whole world knew of Peter. But the electors had other suspicions. Did Napoleon Orsini actually know Peter personally? Had he made a deal with Peter? Peter's reputation was assured all over Europe since his interview with Pope Gregory at Lyons in 1294. Eyewitnesses swore that Peter had removed his monk's cowl and hung it on a sunbeam before the pope's eyes. The miracle had won Gregory's approval of the Celestines. In the conclave, it only took these cardinals one day more to realize that Peter was the way out of their difficulty. On July 5, all votes were unanimous: Peter was to be pope. The document of election was signed, Cardinal Latino Orsini and three hardy young bishops were dispatched to find Peter and tell him the good news. It was not all that easy. First, the site of Peter's monastery was not known. Then, to get to it involved climbing on foot up gulleys, through thickets, over streams. As the news spread, the crowds accompanying the clerics grew greater and greater. Eventually they all arrived.

Peter must often have recalled that first moment. A young monk rushed in whispering that the "Saracens were invading the monastery." Up the mountainside outside Peter's tiny hut about 7,000 people were led by mounted knights, the three bishops, and the cardinal, all at the end of their tether, each one intent on being the first to reach the pope-elect. Peter's hut was obvious to them. The oldest of the bishops advanced, peered in through the little opening and found himself looking at the haggard face and timid gaze of a very old man. "Peter, our beloved brother, it has seemed good to us and to the Holy Spirit to choose your Excellency as successor of Peter the Apostle, Rector of the Universal Church, and Father of all mankind. Do you accept?" A shout went up from the 7,000: "Long live Pope Peter, our Father. Long live the Bishop of Rome! Long live Peter!"

It took Peter only a few minutes. His monks, now free of their initial fright, ran from their hiding places, shouting: "The Call! The Call! The Prophetic Kingdom is here! The Call! The Call!"

The waiting cardinal and bishops saw Peter's eyes gazing meditatively on the crowds, then up over their heads to the surrounding mountains and the skies. Certainly there was peace in his hermitage, the face of the sweet-smelling earth and shining skies, the nights alone with the stars and the whispering winds, his colloquies with streams and flowers. Could it be that the Lord wanted him to leave? The cardinal and bishops who were nearly beside themselves with worry that he would not talk, much less leave his hut, finally heard the long-desired words: "I accept the grade of Pope."

Everything was suddenly transformed. The cardinal and clerics ran in through the little door, fell on their knees, and kissed Peter's filthy rags—"*Chiffonibus vilosis,*" wrote Jacopo Stefaneschi, the senator's son, in the Latin verse he started to compose then and there.

The monks all ran about in a veritable ecstasy, chanting: *"Paradiso! Paradiso!* Come all ye Turks and Jews! Believe in Jesus Christ. Rise, Christian soldiers! Kill all infidels!"

The crowds knelt down, extending their hands and shouting: "Blessing! Blessing! Holy Father! Blessing!"

At length, Peter appeared around the corner of his hut. He raised his hand and blessed them in an immense silence.

Then they placed him on a donkey and the procession set out. By the time they reached the town of Aquila, Peter's donkey was led by two kings. He was surrounded by barons, princes, knights-at-arms, dukes, bishops, clergy of all sorts, choirs of monks and children singing hymns, and a flood of ordinary people quite beside themselves.

Peter, still in his old leather tunic and shoeless, was lost in meditation. Jacopo Stefaneschi, continuing with his poem, craned forward to catch every prayer the new pope said.

At Aquila, old Cardinal Latino Orsini died. The other cardinals invited Peter to come and be consecrated at Perugia, where they were comfortable. He would not budge. They came to Aquila in dribs and drabs; Cardinal Gaetani was the last. Finally, they all gazed with horror on this taciturn, pleasant-faced, timid man who now, thanks to them, was the most powerful man in their world. These polished and learned gentlemen paid homage to the pope-elect, backed out of the room, and went into a huddle. What on earth have we done? What's going to happen to the church? they ask each other.

Gaetani stayed apart. He had his own counsel. While he watched it all grimly, he made his own assessment: this farce must end, bloodily or unbloodily. But how? How best for everyone concerned? Whatever happens, Peter must never see Rome, much less reign there.

King Charles of Naples arrived and took possession of Peter. Charles decided who would and who would not see Peter. Gaetani thought a long time about Charles, who was his paymaster.

On August 24, they clothed Peter in vestments, placed him on a white mule, and led him through the town in procession as far as a small chapel where they consecrated him as Pope Celestine, his own choice. Was he not the pope at the beginning of the celestial period? *"Paradiso! Paradiso!"* his followers kept chanting.

171

Immediately he created new cardinals—the old ones supplied him with suitable names. He revived the conclave rules of Gregory X. He signed every document the wily papal chamberlains put in front of him. Then, after some weeks' rest, King Charles led Peter on a triumphal tour: Salerno by October 6, Isernia by October 14, San Germano by October 18, Capua by October 27, and finally Naples by November 8 where Charles installed the pope in his own castle in a special papal hermit's cell constructed high up in the tower. For Peter this was a special time of the year: Advent, the time of waiting for the birth of the Lord and of the new age. At Cardinal Gaetani's suggestion, Peter entrusted all affairs of state to three trusty cardinals.

But there was no peace for Peter. They extracted him from his cell periodically, set him on a throne, surrounded him with clerics, quick-witted, wily, smiling, obsequious, whispering, always whispering. The people who came to see him never got to him. The clerics were always talking monies or politics or plots. Between him and the people there was woven a labyrinthine web—a wall—of intrigue, of lies, of servitude, of deceit. And always Gaetani in the background. Gaetani whispering, eyeing him sideways, never smiling, bowing his head at everything Peter said.

By mid-November of 1294, Peter knew Gaetani was in cahoots with King Charles to replace him. He also had decided that there was no way to restrain the greed and plotting of the clerics, no way to reform the papacy as he found it. "Paradise" or "the new prophetic age" would not come about by his being pope. Peter's prayers then changed radically. He now saw himself trapped. All he could achieve would be silent heroism of a particular kind: to be plotted against, to be laughed at, to be held a fool, to be deceived, to be treated like an idiot by the great and the mighty. Even to be done to death. Could *that* be what Jesus wanted?

Late one night in that November of 1294 when he was still pope, Peter was wakened by a sepulchral voice talking in the darkness of his papal hermit's cell. "Peter! Peter! My servant! Peter!"

Automatically, Peter said: "Yes, my Lord." Then he began to realize the pit of insane foolishness into which they intended to shove him. "Peter!" the voice went on, "this is the Lord himself!"

The undertones of that voice began to strike an eerie note of familiarity in Peter's consciousness. "Arise, Peter! Abandon this position! Retire to Murrone! Pray! Peter! Pray! Pray! Pray!"

There was much more of the same. Peter could not mistake those accents after a few moments. Gaetani had never been able to pronounce the "t;" it always came out sounding like a "d." He even called himself "Gaedani."

Peter was not fooled, but Gaetani's trick worked to the extent that by the following morning, Peter had made up his mind. He would abdicate.

Told about the decision, Gaetani's haughty face never changed a muscle. His eyes rested unblinkingly on Peter's like a hawk's on a cornered rabbit's.

It was all concluded very rapidly on December 13. All the cardinals assembled. Gaetani shoved a long Latin document into Peter's hands. He was resigning, the document said, for important reasons of soul. Then, Peter as Celestine V stood up, left the hall in his papal robes, and a few moments later returned as Peter Murrone, barefoot and clad only in his original tunic.

But when he attempted to leave, two pikemen took him by the arms, ever so gently, and placed him back in his papal hermit's cell. Peter was in "protective custody."

To William d'Estendard (William the Constable), chief military officer of King Charles, who visited him in his cell, Peter merely said of Gaetani: "He will enter like a wolf, reign like a lion, and die like a dog."

Outside the palace in Naples that day, a crowd of about 15,000 chanted: "Papa Celestine, Papa Celestine! Do not leave us to their mercy! Papa Celestine! Papa Celestine!" But it was all over. Charles sent his pikemen to disperse the crowds and arrest the leaders.

Alas, Peter was more correct in his prophecy about Gaetani than Joachim de Flore had been in his prediction of a new pope of holiness. Old Gaetani had himself elected pope four days after Peter abdicated. King Charles of Naples made sure that the weak cardinals were too frightened to resist and that the strong ones were too well bribed to object. Gaetani

173

had entered the papacy like a wolf. Then Gaetani decided to set out for Rome, taking Peter with him and planning to be consecrated pope in Rome on January 23.

William the Constable sent two henchmen on the night of January 6 and freed Celestine—he had known of Gaetani's plan to take Peter to Rome; and he knew that if Peter ever reached Rome in Gaetani's custody, he would die shortly afterward. Gaetani set out anyway, entered Rome in a triumphal procession, threw a sumptuous banquet for all the cardinals and courtiers, was consecrated Pope Boniface VIII, and then set about eradicating all opposition to his reign. Charles sent an armed posse to catch Peter. Alive or dead. It did not matter now.

For five months Peter ran like an animal seeking cover in the woods and thickets of Apulia, then back to Murrone, then to the Adriatic where he caught a boat, intending to take refuge in Dalmatia (in modern Yugoslavia). But the sea threw him back on the shores of Italy. And at Vieste, the crowds kissed his hands and screamed at him, "Declare yourself lawful pope, Holiness!" William (yes, the same William who had let him escape; one has to live, after all) caught up with him, brought him back in chains to the papal states. On May 16, Boniface sent the patriarch of Jerusalem and a knight to convey Peter to the penitentiary of Fumone. "For the good of the church, you must be put in prison." Pope and king could not have a live pope wandering around free—not this pope anyway. All of Europe knew about him. The majority of his contemporaries revered him as pope still, as saint. But the others, the powerful ones, feared him. They brought him to Fumone in order that he die without any fuss.

Fortress Fumone, the state penitentiary of the Vatican, stood on a steep hill. From his cell window in the northeast tower, Peter could look down each day over the roofs of Alatri and out across the plain eastward where Rome lay under the rule of Boniface VIII, southward toward Naples where Charles reigned, northward toward Aquila where he himself had been consecrated pope and further on, in the same direction, toward the country of his beloved Mount Murrone where his own community of monks, the Celestines, lived in the monastery he had built with his own two hands. Within that triangle of territory, and in a mere matter of two years, Peter's life and fate had been played out.

The day they executed Peter was May 19, 1296. On May 16, three days before that, Peter is visited in Fumone by William the Constable. Peter is now eighty-six years old, scrawny, big-boned, wide-foreheaded, bearded, with unkempt hair and weather-beaten face lit up by big luminous brown eyes. He wears no shoes. His one-piece belted leather tunic hangs from shoulders to knees. Except for two months of his life, he has worn such a tunic continuously since his early twenties. He will die in it. They will bury him in it. "This is my Calvary," he tells William. "God bless you and forgive you your sins." Three days later, they come for him, and find him kneeling by his cot. There is no struggle at all as they hold the cushion over his face and stop his breathing within a minute.

Now Boniface is free to reign like a lion. Apart from individual killings and torturings, he will wipe out one whole town. In October 1298, he will have every man, woman, child, and animal killed, and every building—except the cathedral—flattened in the town of Palestrina. "We ploughed the earth of Palestrina with salt," Boniface will write in his papal bull of June 12, 1299, "so that nothing, neither man nor beast, be called by that name, Palestrina." Boniface will shower the world with excommunications and anathemas and interdicts, will torture and massacre, will breed hate and jealousy. He will glory in his honors, be unsparing in his ferocity, and immovable in his sense of dignity.

It will take Pope Boniface VIII another nine years before he dies like a dog, a mad dog. In between he will be captured, maltreated, tortured, imprisoned, accused of "heresy, tyranny, unchastity, intercourse with the Devil" (they said he wore a ring on his left index finger in which an evil spirit lived and talked with him and came out at night to sleep with him), and finally he will be locked up in the Vatican for thirty-five days where on the last morning they will find him dead on the floor, his skull smashed open, his brains on his shoulders and all over the floor. Did Boniface bash out his own brains in a frenzy of despair and furious anger? Or was this done for him by the usual pair of mercenary executioners employed by one's rivals in those days?

In true Roman fashion, Boniface VIII was buried in the Vatican which he disgraced. Peter's remains were hidden in Aquila where he had been consecrated pope-for-a-time. The poet Dante, who had spoken with Boniface in 1300 to plead for his native Florence, placed Boniface in his

175

Inferno. Of Celestine (who, the poet thought, had let them all down and whom he also placed in his *Inferno*), Dante spoke bitterly as the one "who out of vileness of soul made the enormous mistake of refusing to be pope." Dante spoke for the ordinary people who depended on the pope to save them from the oppression of their rulers and to keep the clergy—and Christendom itself—in order.

And this was the tragedy of Pope Celestine V, as it continued to be the tragedy of the Roman Church until the Reformation of Luther and, then, the Treaty of Westphalia, when the tragedy turned into gross failure. At Westphalia, in 1648, the European nations decided to go their way religiously, each according to its own desire. The old unity of Europe was gone forever. For until that date, the peoples of Europe depended on the Roman bishop for definition; definition of their civil order, of their political authority, of their economic well-being, of their humanist development, of their religious security—in a few words, definition of the meaning of their very existence. Men had sensed about Celestine V that he, possibly, could have heightened that meaning, revivified its spirit, and reversed the slow downard slide toward fragmentation and disunity. Hence Dante's bitterness—a reflection of his contemporaries' mind. And what brought Celestine V to reject his responsibilities was precisely the worldly stance that the papacy and its Vatican had assumed since the time of Silvester.

Popes in Babylon

Pope Boniface VIII, as Gaetani chose to be called, died in Rome on October 11, 1303. Conclave 13 met there in St. Peter's on October 18. Factions were divided among the families of Orsini and Colonna, supporters of Charles of Naples, and the agents of King Ferdinand of Sicily. On October 22, a pro-French Italian, an attorney's son, Nicholas Boccasini, emerged as Benedict XI. He wasted no time in leaving Rome where his life was in danger, stayed for a while in Italy at Montefiascone and Orvieto, then settled in Perugia where, in the following July, at the age of fifty-six, he was assassinated with a plate of poisoned figs.

Conclave 14 opened in the Archbishop's Palace at Perugia. It lasted almost a year. Outside pressures were intolerable. Civil war raged among the Gaetani, Orsini, and Colonna families. Inside, Colonna and Orsini fought among themselves and with the pro-French and pro-Italians. King Philippe of France put pressure on every cardinal. The Italians proposed three of Boniface VIII's cardinals. The French cardinals, now more powerful than the Italians, promised King Philippe they could get the archbishop of Bordeaux, Bertrand de Got, elected as a compromise candidate. Philippe made his own arrangements with de Got, who was elected in June 1305 as Clement V and was crowned in Lyons, France. In genuine fear of his life, he never went to Rome. Instead, for three years he wandered among the French cities of Lyons, Cluny, Bordeaux, Toulouse, and Nîmes, finally settling in Avignon. The papacy owned two vast estates

177

there (both make up the *department* of Vauduse today). At Avignon, a preponderance of French cardinals was created, and seven popes in succession were French. We know very little about the Avignon conclaves except that, for sure, every pope who emerged from them was the choice of the French king, and this fact proved disastrous.

Rome was Peter the Apostle's diocese, and the popes were supposed to be Peter's successors. Why were they in Avignon? people wondered. Further, the developing nation-states of Europe began to deprecate the papacy—correctly—as just another instrument of French national policy rather than as a shared international institution. In a purely secular way, it made the popes absentee landlords of the vast papal states in Italy. In sum, the sojourn of the papacy in Avignon was a terrible wound to the Christian heartland.

Avignon is a region of snow-peaked hills dominating dry plains and green valleys full of vineyards and orchards. It was locally known as Paradise Corner; and the night air was perfumed with lavender, jasmine, rose, thyme, rosemary, basil, and a thousand natural wildflowers. The city of Avignon, at the confluence of the rivers Rhone and Durance, was renowned for its architecture and crafts. It was pleasant and peaceful compared with the violence and hate and rabid rivalries of Rome. It is easy to see why the popes were tempted to go—and to stay.

But in doing so they let the focal point of Christendom collapse. No longer the center of politics and trade and finance, Rome was left to the mercy of thieves, smugglers, kidnappers, and killers. Grass and weeds grew in the streets, and water ducts clogged. The marble, carved wood, and stone of derelict churches were stolen to be sold. In the late 1300s, the only marble remaining in any church was to be found in the steps leading up to the church of St. Maria Ara Coeli. "Whenever I entered a church in Rome at that time," wrote one visitor, "I found tax-brokers and the clergy." The shame of Rome was the scandal of Europe. In the jubilee year of 1350, fifty thousand pilgrims a day arrived to pray at the tomb of St. Peter only to find cows pasturing on the grass in the main apse, dog-droppings in the crypt, and all over Rome the filth and detritus of an anarchic population.

178

Clement V, who founded Christian bishoprics in India, Nubia, Abyssinia, Barbary, Morocco, Basra, and China while Rome began to slide into decline, died in 1314, and was succeeded by John XXII, who moved from Avignon to Chateauneuf-du-Pape. This pope has left 80,000 documents that testify to his worldwide interests. But he also gallicized the College of Cardinals, creating twenty-three French cardinals between 1317 and 1332, and only five non-French cardinals in the same period. For this, the poet Dante consigned John to the pit in his *Divine Comedy.*

Clement VI, who succeeded John after the reign of Benedict XII, bought the town of Avignon for 80,000 gold florins, and built the mammoth three and a half acre Palace of the Popes, which still stands on a solid rock foundation called Notre-Dame des Doms. He built it as a fortress with five-yard-thick walls and machicolated battlements, towers, and gateways, and surrounded it with further battlements flanked by eight towers. He filled it with chapels, halls, salons, dining rooms (the banquet hall is 156 feet long), private apartments, business offices, storage space, military barracks, and servants quarters. One can still admire today the fresco depicting nymphs and hunters at pastoral play that Clement commissioned for the papal bedchamber.

Over a period of seventy-two years (1305-1377), however, pastoral play at Avignon corroded the very core of the papacy. The popes decorated and enriched this palace with paintings and other art treasures. They and their cardinals amassed great wealth and spent huge sums, acquired by heavy taxes on church estates ii France and Italy. When Cardinal Hugo Ranieri died at Avignon in 1364, his personal coffers yielded twenty-two purses each containing 500 gold florins and several others with thousands of gold and silver coins from Italy, France, England, and Spain. At Pope Urban V's death, 200,000 gold florins lay in his personal treasury.

"You have neglected," Dante wrote in a letter to Clement V, "to guide the Chariot of the Bride of the Crucified along the path so clearly marked for Her." Dante called the papal court at Avignon the *gasconum opprobrium,* or the Gascon shame, a reference to Clement's nationality. Petrarch described Avignon as "the fortress of anguish, the dwelling-place

179

of wrath, the sink of vice, the sewer of this world, the school of error, the temple of heresy, once Rome, now the false and guilt-ridden Babylon, the forge of lies, the horrible prison, the hall of dung." Clement's city and court of Avignon was "home to wine, women, song, and priests who cavorted," Petrarch said, "as if all their glory consisted not in Christ but in feasting and unchastity." "Wolves," screamed poet Alvaro Pelago, "have become the masters of the Church." And St. Catherine of Sienna stated: "At the Papal Court which ought to have been a paradise of virtue, my nostrils were assailed by the odors of Hell." Petrarch's characterization later became a label conveniently affixed to the papal years at Avignon—"The Babylonian Captivity of the Papacy."

Finally in 1367, the pressure from all over Europe became too much. Urban V decided in the spring to return to Viterbo, Italy. By October he was in Rome. He remained there for three miserable years. Then he and his cardinals, homesick for France and the lush lowlands of Avignon with its palaces and culture, left for Avignon on September 24, 1370. Ten years later, with great difficulty, Gregory XI returned definitively to Rome on January 17, 1377. The Romans lit up old St. Peter's in its decrepitude with 18,000 lamps of joy and welcome. "Twenty more years," said Cardinal Albornoz, "and the [Italian] States of the Church would have perished entirely."

In late March of 1378, Gregory's time to die had come. We have rather detailed accounts of the events in those fateful months of March–April 1378. Even now, they make a stirring diary.

March 18:   Pope Gregory XI, forty-eight years old, the last French pope, is dying. His servants say he looks like a man of ninety-five. Yesterday, his doctors bled him with leeches; but the pain in his lower abdomen and the hemorrhaging continue. Rumor has it he wants to return to France to die either in his family castle (he is the son of Count William of Beauport) or in the Palace of the Popes at Avignon, built by his uncle, Clement VI. But Gregory is too weak for travel. Even so, the rumor is that Gregory is writing a papal bull about the next election of a pope.

March 19: The bull is published. In it, Gregory commands: When I die, the candidate elected by the majority is to be accepted by everyone. There are sixteen cardinals in Rome, six at Avignon, one at Sarzana attending a congress. Of the sixteen in Rome, eleven are French, one is Spanish, four are Italian. Gregory is afraid the small Italian minority will impose an Italian candidate.

March 20: All cardinals in Rome assure Gregory they will abide by his rulings.

March 21: Gregory is confined to bed. The Roman people are making ugly demonstrations, crying: "We want a Roman! We want an Italian!" The eleven French cardinals and the one Spanish cardinal bring all their valuables to the fortress of Sant' Angelo (it is under a French commander).

March 25: Confrontation today between the cardinals, on the one hand, and the senator of Rome, his magistrates, the army captains, many clergy, and respected citizens. They march in a body to the Palace of the Holy Spirit, and tell the cardinals they must have a Roman pope. Or at least an Italian. Nobody else must be elected as pope now.

March 27: Gregory dies in great pain during the afternoon. Made cardinal at the age of seventeen, Gregory's life has been nothing but suffering. His body is taken to St. Peter's.

March 28: Gregory's remains are taken to his own church of St. Maria in the Forum. Obsequies follow. They bury him there. It will be two hundred years before they erect a monument over his grave. After the ceremonies, the cardinals barely succeed in getting back safely to their palaces. The Roman mob is quite ugly. Protocol and ceremonial require that during the next nine days they go each day to the St. Maria Church for the obsequies and mourning rites for Gregory. They do it always under armed escort.

181

March 29:   The majority of the cardinals made secret plans to leave the city at night and get to France for safety. The plan is leaked.

March 30:   The cardinal of Eustachio and the archbishop of Arles fill Sant' Angelo fortress with Breton pikemen. The Roman city authorities call in their own troops (about 6,000 foot-soldiers) from Tivoli and Velletini outside Rome. All bridges and gates are blocked so that the cardinals cannot escape. There is nothing for it now but to hold a conclave in the Vatican.

March 31:   Just to be sure, the cardinals empty the treasure room in the Vatican and send its contents to Sant'Angelo.

April 4:   Today, the cardinals have a headman's ax and block erected outside the Vatican doors. A clear warning to all: any violators of their rights will pay with his life. The Vatican is surrounded on all sides with militia.

April 5:   In the hall of the Vatican set aside for conclave, cubicles were created today by means of curtains.

April 6:   The hall and the partitions and furniture were damaged today when lightning struck the hall. Workmen set it all up again. Bad omen, say the Romans.

April 7:   In the evening, sixteen cardinals enter conclave: four Italians, one Spaniard, eleven Frenchmen. The crowd outside keep shouting, "A Roman or an Italian!" There are two front-runners: the infamous Cardinal Robert of Geneva, and Bartolomeo Prignano, archbishop of Bari.

April 8:   Robert of Geneva wants to be pope. The French do not want an Italian or a Roman. The Italians do not want a French pope. The demonstrations outside continue: "A Roman or an Italian!" There are endless fights among the cardinals. The French, led by Robert of Geneva, do not want an Avignon cardinal; nor will they accept a Roman: Tibaldeschi is too old, Orsini too young. Nor anyone else—Simone Borsano was a Milanese, Peter Corsini was a Florentine. At one point, the captains of the Roman militia enter the conclave and state firmly: "We demand an Italian."

Some of the people break into the hall beneath the conclave hall and shove lances through the floor as a threat. Others pile up combustible materials in the room beneath the conclave hall and are ready to set it on fire. "Burn the traitors!" is the cry. All the cardinals get up early this morning. The bells of all Rome's churches are tolling. The cardinals agree that they must elect someone quickly. By midmorning, 20,000 people are milling around the Vatican. All the cardinals except Orsini elect Bartolomeo Prignano as pope. At about eleven o'clock, they decide not to announce the election quite yet. They sit down to eat breakfast. The crowd outside are tipped off that a pope has been chosen. They break down the main door and mill into the Vatican. "Tell them that Cardinal Tibaldeschi [a Roman] has been elected," shouts Cardinal Robert, as all the cardinals run for sanctuary to a nearby chapel. "That will buy some time." But by noontime, the crowd is yelling: "Show us our pope. Show us our pope!" Robert and the others hurriedly dress the aged Tibaldeschi in papal clothes—miter and cloak—seat him on the papal chair, and shove him out at the crowd. Everyone begins to kiss his hand and feet. It is all too much for Tibaldeschi who breaks down and tells the people about the hoax. But by then, the cardinals have escaped: six run to Sant'Angelo fortress; four of them leave the city, six lock themselves in their strong palaces at home. "We have no Roman!" shouts the crowd. "Death to the traitors!"

April 9:   Calm returns to the city during the night when extensive conversations take place between the civil authorities and

183

the remaining cardinals. The authorities accept the election of Prignano as valid, and they tell the people this. Nine days later, Prignano is consecrated as Pope Urban VI. He will make twenty new cardinals. When he dies in St. Peter's on October 15, 1389, he will be described as "the worst of men, cruel, most scandalous."

Immediately on his consecration as pope, dizzying divisions set in, which will only be resolved years later by the General Council of Constance, whose findings are used here to characterize popes as real or as anti-popes. Sixteen cardinals leave Rome and hold their own conclave at a nearby place called Fundi, where they elect Robert of Geneva as (the General Council of Constance will later decide) anti-Pope Clement VII. Clement returns to Avignon. On Urban's death in 1389, fourteen cardinals hold Conclave 22 in Rome and elect the thirty-year old cardinal of Anastasia as Pope Boniface IX. Meanwhile, anti-Pope Clement VII dies at Avignon on September 16, 1394; and ten days later his cardinals hold a second anti-conclave and elect the Spaniard Peter de Luna as Benedict XIII. In Rome, Boniface IX dies in October 1404. Conclave 23 meets on October 12. The nine cardinals are split by factional feeling for Guelfs, Ghibellines, Colonnas, Orsini, Roman nobles. Every one of the candidates has promised to be willing to resign from the papacy (should he be elected), if this will heal the division in the church. Five days of conclave produce Cosimo dei Migliorati as Innocent VII. When he dies less than two years later, Conclave 24 (fourteen Roman cardinals) elects the eighty-year old Venetian Angelo Corra as Gregory XII, on November 3, 1406.

Then, in March 1409, the cardinals of anti-Pope Benedict XIII and some of Pope Gregory XII's cardinals meet, depose and excommunicate both Gregory XII and Benedict XIII, and choose a new anti-pope, Alexander V. There are now two anti-popes and one pope. Pope Gregory XII flees from Rome for his safety. So anti-Pope Alexander goes to Rome. All three claimants hold synods in March 1410: Gregory XII in Cividale, anti-Pope Alexander in Rome, and anti-Pope Benedict XIII at Perpignan in Spain, at which each one condemned the other two. Alexander V dies (poisoned) on March 17 and is succeeded by anti-Pope John XXIII, Baldassare Cossa, who provides an excellent cameo of the fatal peril into which the Roman Church is falling.

Pick a Pope,
Any Pope

In the lovely castle of Gotleben a few miles from the town and the lake of Constance in Germany, there are three distinguished prisoners, all loaded with chains, all bruised and paining, each in his own cell adjoining the other two. On this morning of May 29, 1415, each of the three stands to lose his life by violent means. One will be burned alive eight days from now. Name: John Hus. Crime: Heresy. A second will be burned alive one year and one day from now. Name: Jerome of Prague. Crime: Heresy. The third also expects to die painfully and soon. Name: Baldassare Cossa, until a few days ago regarded by a large part of the world as the pope of Rome. Crime: "All mortal sins and an endless list of offences. . ." are the words of his judges at the epochal Council of Constance.

As they await their fate before the council, Hus and Jerome often shout at Cossa. They could well have been demanding an account from him of his behavior; for if they were heretics, Cossa surely was a provocateur.

Still, Cossa unknowingly gave the papacy and the Roman Church another huge chance of total reform. Because of Cossa, for three months, ordinary men—politicians, peasants, shopkeepers, kings—made a desperate bid to force churchmen to give up politics and money and to rely solely on the spiritual and moral authority which were the promise of Jesus to Peter and his successors. Those layfolk almost succeeded. But the

187

clerics finally outwitted them, and the chance was lost. (There was only one more such chance before the final breakup of Christian unity. And again the clerics would refuse it.)

But in this year of 1415, the fate of the Roman pontiff and of the Church of Rome are inextricably enmeshed with the details—sometimes sordid, sometimes pathetic, always regrettable—of this one man, Baldassare Cossa. As of this May morning, he claimed to be pope for five years. His papal name: John XXIII. Those have been five years of energetic cunning, twisting and turning, confusing some enemies, liquidating others, buying off still others, parleying, temporizing, compromising, warring, raiding, massacring, lying, perjuring, betraying. Today he has been caught finally in a trap of his own making. A year ago, while he still exercised power as pope, he had summoned a general council of the whole church, thinking he could use it to his own advantage. But he failed. And today he is to be hauled in front of that same council like a common criminal, and be condemned by five nations—by the rulers and the churchmen of those five nations. What will they do to him?

Cossa had started off life in his teens as a corsair, a common pirate. But his family, Neapolitan nobles from Ischia, had bought him a pardon from the king of Naples (who always needed money), let him cool his heels at soldiering for some years, and then sent him to the University of Bologna, where he became renowned for gluttony and lechery, and where eventually he took holy orders. The whole of Europe knows Cossa's background.

Yet Cossa certainly believes that he is truly pope (although the council will decide otherwise), or at least he *must* believe, because he must prepare himself mentally to face his accusers today. Certainly no one could really blame Cossa for his faith in himself, for all was confusion, general confusion, all over Europe. That confusion had the whole world on its head. Nobody seemed to know the truth.

For the last forty years, there have been simultaneously at least two and, much of the time, three men in Europe each of whom claimed to be pope, each condemning the others. Since all order in Europe's political life and all meaning in its religious life came from the pope, the politics and the religious practice and the quality of ordinary life had deteriorated to a stage of vileness.

Cossa was caught in all that confusion. About the time his family sent him to Bologna, there was Pope Clement VII and there was Pope Urban VI. Urban VI had been elected in Rome by sixteen cardinals on April 8, 1378. Clement VII had been elected in Fundi (near Rome) by thirteen cardinals on the following September 20. Urban had merely been archbishop of Bari. Clement had been the lame, squinting, greatly powerful, and mercilessly cruel Cardinal Robert of Geneva, famous for his skill in decapitating a man with a pike, for his leadership of 6,000 cavalry and 4,000 infantry in 1375 when he subdued Florence and Bologna by massive brutality, and still more famous for his massacre of 4,500 citizens of Cesena in 1394 (8,000 others escaped to neighboring towns). So there were two men in Europe claiming to be pope, each with a large number of acknowledged electors in his camp.

This council that will condemn Cossa today will also find that Urban VI was the true pope and that Clement VII was, like Cossa, an antipope.

At the University of Bologna, Cossa and everyone else saw what was going on. Urban VI and his cardinals hated Clement VII and his cardinals. And vice versa. Urban lived in Rome, Clement in France. Urban was supported by the emperor of Germany, by Scandinavia, England, Ireland, Hungary, Poland. Clement was supported by Naples, Savoy, Scotland, Spain, and France, by the powerful University of Paris, by hundreds of bishops all over Europe. Urban excommunicated Clement and all who were with him. Clement excommunicated Urban and all who were with him. Each created his own cardinals, held his own papal court, made his own alliances, issued his own decrees, sold his own indulgences. Both employed spies, assassins, mercenaries, thugs, to cheat, kill, bribe, betray, undo the other side. They made war on each other involving most countries of Europe, and thousands were killed, maimed, burned, tortured. Each kept saying the other was a false pope. Each kept offering to step down if the other would do so first. Each one avoided that ultimate step, hoping to win by war or poison or persuasion or the hand of God. The whole world was divided with them. There were good men and warriors and common people on both sides. No clarity. Just confusion. For all Cossa's young years, the same confusion continued.

Here in his cell at Gotleben, Cossa awaits his arraignment and the

189

opportunity to justify himself. "How could I have chosen between Urban and Clement?" he will ask his accusers. Urban had six cardinals whom he suspected of treachery. He had them lowered into a cistern to be tortured, while he paced above on the roof reading his breviary and shouting encouragement to the torturers. Clement VII, besides corrupting local princes with gold, led his company of murderous Bretons in forays around Rome, finally rode off to France to settle at Avignon, where he hurled fulminations and curses against all who opposed him. Then both died—nobody was sure how, Urban in 1389, Clement in 1394. But the divisiveness continued. Urban's cardinals elected Pope Boniface IX (validly, the council will decide). Clement's cardinals elected (invalidly) a hardy Spaniard, Peter de Luna, who will go down in history as anti-Pope Benedict XIII. Still two rival "popes" in Europe. More excommunications. More edicts. More wars. More killing. More hate. More confusion.

Cossa's career in the church started with the tall, handsome, large-bodied, uneducated, crude (but true pope, says the council) Boniface IX. Pope Boniface needed forthright young men. He met the thirty-five-year-old Cossa, noticed the gleam of ambition in his eyes, made him an archdeacon, and in 1390 brought him to Rome as his papal chamberlain— really, his jack-of-all-trades, his *âme damneé* in Roman affairs. The "pope's procurer," the clear-sighted Romans called him. That same year, Boniface dispatched his agents into the provinces of the church and collected more than 300,000 gold florins in the sale of indulgences for the Jubilee of 1390.

"How could I have said no?" This is what Cossa will ask his accusers today. "What would you have done?" And they will retort: "What about the wealth, the pleasures, the horrors, the plotting, all of which you indulged in? What do you answer to that?" "Yes! But someone had to do something. Besides, I was given responsibility by the pope."

Boniface made Cossa a cardinal when Cossa was forty-seven, then sent him as papal legate to Bologna. When Boniface died in 1404 (his last words: "If I had money, I would be all right"), Boniface's nine cardinals elected another pope, the sixty-five-year-old Innocent VII, who was immediately denounced by Benedict XIII. So there were still two claimants.

"What happened to Innocent VII?" Cossa can already hear his accusers ask. Innocent was healthy as an ox. But he was dethroned, abused, chased out of Rome, and murdered. Again Cossa will answer, "Something had to be done." Innocent encouraged his nephew, who was a known common murderer. As pope he was ineffectual. There was no way out. He had to go. He did, by Cossa's poison—painlessly, of course.

As dominant cardinal, Cossa organized the election of a saintly (he thought) eighty-five-year-old prelate as Gregory XII, succeeding Innocent. Cossa and the others figured Gregory only for a year or two. But Gregory surprised them all. First he exchanged lusty excommunications with the perennial anti-Pope Benedict XIII, who sent a powerful fleet to besiege Rome and drive his new rival, Gregory, out of the city for a time. But Gregory was soon back, and full of mischief. He spent half his day eating and drinking, the other half making money—or spending it. He pawned the papal tiara for 6,000 florins to pay his debts from war and gambling to Paul Orsini of Rome. He sold books from the Vatican library to Cardinal Henry of Tuscany for 500 florins. He sold Rome and the Roman estates of the church to King Ladislas of Naples for a paltry 25,000 florins (could have, should have, received five million at least). And, then, Gregory's wars, his cruelty, his corruption, and finally his death-threats to the cardinals and to Cossa in particular.

Cossa and some other cardinals fled to Pisa. There, as a new council of the church, on June 5, 1409, they made a clean sweep: condemning both Pope Gregory XII and anti-Pope Benedict XIII (still alive, still hating) as heretics and schismatics, declaring them both deposed and excommunicated, and electing a new pope. Cossa's choice (he was the kingmaker) was excellent, or so he thought: an old, gentle, feebleminded, unambitious Italian-born Greek, Peter Filargo, as (this present council will declare) anti-Pope Alexander V (the last Greek elected pope had been John VII in the year 705). Each of the three papal claimants—Gregory, Benedict, and Alexander—immediately loosed on the others the obligatory bombardment of anathemas, excommunications, interdictions, imprecations.

Cossa and the others gave Alexander a maximum of a couple of months of life, but Alexander showed every sign of wanting to live. Again Cossa had no choice—his own time was running out. Poison again; again, pain-

191

less. Alexander died on May 13, 1410. (His last words: "As bishop, I was rich. As cardinal, poor. As pope, a beggar.")

On May 25, Cossa had himself elected (as an anti-pope, the council will rule) by eighteen cardinals, calling himself John XXIII, and again came the elaborate fusilade of excommunications with Benedict XIII and Gregory XII. Gilbert and Sullivan would have had great fun with it all. But for those who lived through it, it wasn't very funny.

There was not one kingdom in Europe which hadn't suffered because of these papal cantrips, not one city-state, not one ruling house, not one major city, not one bishop, whose life was not disrupted. Above all, the governments of Europe finally saw that without a stable papacy—and that means without one universally recognized pope—all governments were doomed. After all, every ruler and every government, from the emperor of the Germans to the smallest dukedom in England and the petty squires of Sicily, all depended on the pope for their legitimacy.

Immediately after Cossa had himself made pope, therefore, the pressure on him was enormous: call a general council! That was the message. Already when Cossa had himself crowned, in Germany and France and England there was a potent body of men—bishops and theologians and rulers—who demanded reform and a new method of electing a pope. So he set out as a fox pursued by hungry fearful hounds to run from covert to covert; his objective was to achieve the security of being the only pope acknowledged universally, and thus the safety of St. Peter's church.

For five years he would promise the general council and promise reform. In the meanwhile, his two rivals—old, feeble, garrulous, gluttonous (but, as the council will decide, validly elected) Gregory XII, and insane, spiteful, perennially Spanish Benedict XIII—could be side-stepped, sidetracked, foiled, perhaps eliminated. Somehow eliminated . . .

But it all became a nightmare, a series of inescapable failures. The other two rivals kept on and on. Cossa set trap after trap for his pursuers, only to fall into each of them himself. Sigismund was elected emperor of the Romans and Germans on September 20, 1410. Cossa as John XXIII immediately supported Sigismund. Sigismund, now very powerful, turned around and insisted on a council. The first trap. Cossa temporized. He then employed the best mercenaries of the day, took Rome from

King Ladislas of Naples, and entered in triumph. Then the mercenaries turned against him, refused a bribe of 36,000 gold florins, and drove Cossa into a fortified Vatican like a refugee. Cossa decided he would bribe Ladislas to save him and to expel Pope Gregory from Naples. Ladislas accepted the bribe, then turned on Cossa and drove him out of Rome with his cardinals (seven of them died of hardship and assassination by mercenaries on the journey). The second trap. Cossa fled to Bologna, seized the city government in February 1414. The Bolognese appealed to Emperor Sigismund, who came to meet Cossa and demanded a general council.

Cossa had to agree, but refused to hold the council in Rome. Anywhere but in Rome was his answer. Cossa had no control in Rome. Very well. In Constance, was the emperor's reply. In Constance, Cossa would be under the emperor's control. In December of next year, Cossa proposed. On October 30 of next year, retorted the emperor. There was nothing for it. The third trap.

Cossa as Pope John XXIII proceeded to Constance and opened the council on October 30. Sigismund arrived after Christmas. Cossa could still have made it his own success, but a last trap awaited him. He knew his own Italianate party had the most individual votes, so he allowed the council to convene and the discussions to begin. But on February 17, 1415, the council decreed that all voting should be, not by individuals, but by nations. So his party was outvoted. And the council demanded that he and Gregory XII and Benedict XIII resign. All three of them. Cossa's last trick had been played. The last trap closed on him with a snap.

Now, he attempted his last recourse: flight. It was late at night on March 20, 1415, in Constance. That was the day when the council demanded his resignation. After midnight, Cossa took off his papal clothes, put on the clothes of a horse-groom, stole out the window, and left Constance in an ox cart carrying only one bag containing his still enormous sums of money, his papal seal, and his engraved papal coat-of-arms. He fled to Schaffhausen, which belonged to his friend Frederick of Austria, the "grim duke." But he did not know that Sigismund had told the duke: "We will insist on Cossa's resignation; and you will give him no sanctuary. Else you will die. You and yours." For a week, Cossa wan-

193

dered around from Laufenburg to Freiburg to Breisach seeking to escape to Italy. Finally, the duke's armed men caught up with him, put him under arrest, confiscated his money and seal and coat-of-arms, and took him here to Gotleben Castle. It was all over.

At the council, Cossa's humiliation is complete. The town's population is swollen with visitors: 24,000 knights-at-arms, 80,000 laymen, 18,000 prelates—among whom are 24 cardinals, 80 bishops, 102 representatives of absent bishops, each one with his retinue of retainers, secretaries, and servants, 300 doctors of theology and philosophy, and representatives from the chief nations of Europe—Italy, France, Germany (including Germans, Hungarians, Poles, and Scandinavians), England, and Spain. The city has attracted 1,500 wandering prostitutes, one of whom will earn 800 gold florins in three months. There are factions and fights. And the gray waters of Lake Constance will disgorge the bodies of 500 men waylaid and assassinated for a variety of reasons, good, bad, and indifferent.

Cossa is paraded through the crowd to reach the council already assembled and waiting. He has to sit—his papal seal, his papal coat-of-arms, his money reserves at his feet—throughout the famous Session 4 and hear this universal council of bishops decree that any such council is superior to any pope—whoever he may be. Cossa is then brought forward. They read his bill of indictment: fifty-five accusations of crimes in all, ranging from criminal simony (buying and selling ecclesiastical offices) to adultery, fornication, murder, perjury, sacrilege, and gluttony. Cossa himself remembers more than his accusers know or even suspect, but they enumerate: "the beheading of seventeen Roman nobles in 1398 and of thirty-one more in 1400," all of which he supervised for Pope Boniface IX . . . the indulgences he sold . . . the bishoprics and benefices and ecclesiastical appointments he bartered for gold, for women . . . the two hundred or so married ladies and widows and girls he kept in his stable of pleasures . . . the clerics and laymen he had seduced by chosen prostitutes . . . and Boniface IX striding up and down on the roof of a fortified Vatican, caged, cursing, killing, warring. He, Cossa, had done all Pope Boniface had demanded and ordered.

194

His accusers recall the "legitimate" popes since 1378; they name Urban VI, Boniface IX, Innocent VII, and Gregory XII; they recapitulate in full what calamities the "anti-popes"—he, Cossa, Clement VII, Benedict XIII, Alexander V—had brought about. They now state that they are reducing the accusations against him to five, but any one of these suffices to send Baldassare Cossa to the stake to be burned alive.

Cossa answers with a meek, "*Ita* (Yes)," to the accusations. He utters no other word. Half in sheer humiliation, half in the sure knowledge that this assembly will not take his life, he submits to the judgments of the council. The directors of the council realize their position. They are also touched by the last gesture of humiliated dignity in Cossa: he looks them all straight in the eye, not arrogantly, not fearfully, not pleadingly, merely realistically. They know: any one of them could be where he is now, today. And they know: Cossa has touched at least near the supreme mystery of Rome's power—he had been once called the vicar of Jesus. And they all depend on that power for the maintainence of their own powers. Finally, they know the weakness of their own position. It is clear to them that Gregory is the legitimate pope. But if so, why are they deposing him? And if Gregory is not legitimate, then Cossa must be. No one is willing to lay his head on the line. All agree that they should wipe the slate clean, beginning with Cossa.

Prudently, they sheer away from the death penalty and declare Cossa deposed and condemned to prison. Before Emperor Sigismund and the other rulers of Europe, in the eyes of all the cardinals and bishops, a goldsmith comes forward in dead silence, takes aim at Cossa's papal seal, and smashes it with one blow of a hammer. There is a small murmur of wonder in the surrounding tiers of onlookers. Then a second goldsmith comes forward and with one swift hammer blow fragments Cossa's engraved papal coat-of-arms.

Pope Gregory XII cannot wait to submit to the council once he hears of Cossa's fate. He renounces his tiara and his cardinals on July 4, is allowed to retain his cardinal's red and to live in a rich ecclesiastical benefice, where he dies in 1417. Anti-Pope Benedict XIII never changes. He refuses all requests to abdicate. He flees to the Pensicola rocky for-

195

tress in Aragon, Spain, locks himself in there with two remaining cardinals, wears his papal tiara, issues letters, insists he is pope, and dies by poison in 1423 after almost thirty years of claimed papacy. After his death, his two cardinals laughingly enter a private room in the fortress, close the door, and hold a two-man conclave, electing as successor to Benedict a certain Canon Mugnosas, known as anti-Pope Clement VIII. Clement VIII is challenged by the sacristan of Rodez, Bernard Gauthier, who calls himself Benedict XIV. But by now the whole of Spain and Europe is laughing at anti-Popes Benedict XIII, Benedict XIV, and Clement VIII.

Now that the three divisive claimants to the papacy are eliminated, the movers and reformers of the council, Chancellor Gerson of the University of Paris, Cardinal d'Ailly, and Sigismund of Germany, press forward: first, they propose, let us reform the church, purify it, rid it of its temporal power, render it purely spiritual; then, let us elect a truly spiritual head of the church.

It was the great chance. It would never return again. For the first time in over one thousand years, Roman churchmen as a group had an opportunity to renounce all worldly power, to escape from the mesh of politics, and to wield only spiritual authority. As yet, there had been no Luther, no Reformation, no breakup. Christianity was still one. And all the nations and all the rulers of Christendom demanded this!

It would have meant giving up ambition, money, temporal authority, family glory, diplomatic might, and panoply. And, in the end, Roman churchmen simply could not do that. They could not believe that the spiritual power given to Peter by Jesus was the only real power they had or needed. They could not. They would not. They did not.

The breakup at Constance starts with the Italians. They know: if the reformers succeed, it is the end of their Vatican, the end of their power. So they start canvasing and buying and blandishing and promising and threatening. They succeed. Every man has his price. First, the English, then the French and the Spaniards, go over to the Italian side and vote against the German proposal. They win and say: First, let us elect a new pope. The ayes have it. A convlave of fifty-three electors—twenty-three cardinals and six co-electors from each of the five nations—meets on November 8, 1417, in the market-house of Constance. Conclave 25. Three days later, on the feast of St. Martin, they elect an Italian, Cardinal Oddo Colonna. He takes the name of Pope Martin V. And Martin V has one sole purpose: head off all further reform efforts, get back to Rome and the Vatican, and assert once more the pope's independence and the pope's power.

They take Cossa to Heidelberg to be a prisoner of Count Palatine Lewis for three years. In the end, he was nobler than the long-living and still hating anti-Pope Benedict XIII, and more courageous and meritorious than old Pope Gregory XII.

Pope Martin V and Baldassare Cossa meet but once. In Florence, in 1418. Martin V has come in all his newfound papal panoply to take possession of this city which had always been a headache for the popes. Cossa has come in pilgrim's clothes to ask the pope for forgiveness and amnesty in his declining years. The dry and cynical Florentines jeer at Martin as an upstart. For Cossa, conversely, they have come to feel extreme compassion. Martin senses the difference and grants Cossa his amnesty, allowing him his cardinal's red and letting him live out his days in peace. Cossa dies one year later in his own bed and with honor. And the great Cosimo de' Medici buries him (out of gratitude for money received) in Florence's ancient Baptistry of St. John, and inscribes as his epitaph: "Here Lies Baldassare Cossa Who Was Once Pope John XXIII."

Even though Pope Martin V refused the chance offered him at the Council of Constance to detach the papacy from the toils of earthly power, there was still to be one more occasion when the papacy and its Vatican were stripped of all worldly power. The sword was snatched from its hands; only spirit was left to it. Again the pope in question, Clement VII, refused the invitation of destiny to abandon all reliance on the sword and on gold.

The blindness of Pope Clement VII to the providential happenings of his pontificate seems all the more obtuse to us when we realize that in his

197

day the revolt of Martin Luther and his fellow reformers was in full swing. It had started under the previous pope, Leo X. Leo, like Clement after him, had no stomach for the truth. Neither he nor Clement realized that papal power in the temporal order had gone beyond all bearable limits. Christians in Europe were finally rising in revolt against the scandalous mixture of religion and politics. By the death of Clement, it was all over. The death of the Christian heartland was on the horizon.

Leo X: Hail and Farewell!

"Magliana! Magliana! Magliana!" The dark-skinned boy singer's voice dwells lovingly on these last long curving syllables of his song. Then with "de' Medici! de' Medici! Forever reign!" he finishes. There is an echoing silence in the hall. Pope Leo X is there with his cardinals. Leo spends all his autumn vacations in lovely Magliana with its lawns and fountains, its woods and streams, its incomparable flower-gardens enameling acres of earth with every color and perfume. "My private heaven," Leo calls it.

His cardinals all are glowing at Leo's success: Milan has been taken; the news has arrived today. His cardinal-legate entered the city five nights ago, on November 19, 1519. Two other of his cardinals, Gonzaga (minister of war) and Sitten (army commissariat) marched from Switzerland in their red robes with their silver crosses carried in front of them at the head of 10,000 Swiss mercenaries (costing Leo 200,000 ducats), crossed the River Po, took the city, and executed all Leo's enemies. Now he needs only Parma, Ferrara, and Piacenza to restore all the papal lands, Leo states. "This victory means more to me than my election as pope," Leo tells the assembly. A true de' Medici, Leo.

It is a little over one hundred years since the amazing Council of Constance when, at the very last moment, the church approached the precipice of reform, and then drew back in fear and trembling. Obviously, it is business as usual again. And the chance for reform is now almost gone.

An obscure German monk named Luther is already at work, on a reform of his own.

Next day they will leave Magliana to return to Rome. Leo reveals a message from his gamekeeper, Giovanni Moroni, warden of the ten square miles of forest and game preserve around Rome where only the pope and his cardinals may hunt. All trespassers have their hands and feet cut off, their homes burned, their children sold as servants. The hunting is marvelous; that is Moroni's message. Leo, born Giovanni de' Medici, loves to hunt, and is a great fun-lover. He is famous for the little jokes he plays on his cardinals.

Just two years ago, a Roman, Lorenzo Strozzi, invited Cardinal Cibo and three other cardinals to a special midnight party—first the guests found themselves in an appalling mortuary chamber full of skulls, naked bodies, blood, pigs' heads, torture instruments; then they were led into a sumptuous hall where the finest food, the loveliest waiters and waitresses, buffoons, clowns, musicians, awaited them. The queen of all Rome's prostitutes, nicknamed Madre Mia, was there with her stable. And the food was brought up from below by machinery. Leo had a report on his desk at 7 A.M. the following morning, even before Cibo had recovered from his hangover. He summoned Cibo and had intense delight in asking him to trace the origin of the Spanish exclamation, "Madre Mia!" "Did it refer to the mother of Jesus?" Leo had asked Cibo archly. That was fun. A valuable man, Cibo, cultivated, refined, and above all, with an entry to all the banks, a vital interest of Leo's.

All and any thought of banks and bankers is painful for Leo right now. He can never forget his present huge debts—200,000 ducats to the Bank of Bini, 37,000 to the House of Goddi, 10,000 to Ricasoli (all three Florentine banks had charged him a usurious 40 percent); then there are individual loans—300,000 from Cardinal Salviati, 150,000 each from cardinals Armellino and Quatro Coronati. Leo sighs. "It would be more possible for a stone to fly into the air by itself than for this pope to keep 1,000 ducats together," the Venetian ambassador had written of him. Just like the miserly Venetian.

Money, money, money. With Leo, it was always money. This year his revenues in ducats are considerable: direct revenue, 420,000; river dues,

60,000; land dues, 37,000; wine and vinegar taxes, 8,000; taxes from Spoleto, the Romagna, and the Coast, 60,000 each; sale dues from Cervia and Ravenna, 70,000–100,000; alum revenues, 40,000. All this over and above his personal benefices, abbeys, and estates in Italy, France, and Sicily. Otherwise, Leo has an unblemished reputation: no lechery, no duels, no shady deals, no gluttony. But even before his election as pope he lost 8,000 ducats a month at cards and another 8,000 on a popular lottery game called *primiera*. As pope, he is the same—only more so.

But Leo knows how to amuse himself. For the spring carnival this year, he organized a play about eight hermits and one virgin, in which the naked woman prayed to Venus and the hermits became lusty lovers whom she seduced and who then killed each other for love of her. He fed his cardinals and friends on refined delicacies and exquisite sauces, tongues of parrots, live fish from Constantinople, apes' meat, marvelously aromatic wines, quail, monkey brains, and fruit from three continents, pheasant, venison—anything money could buy. No man and no pope has been more serious about the riches and the dignity of his family as well as the promotion of scholarship; yet he distracted his cardinals and his court with buffoons, clowns, and vulgar jokes. On his deathbed, he will confess his sins, receive Holy Communion, and die whispering "Gesu! Maria! Gesu! Maria! Gesu! Gesu!" Yet in life, he devoted himself far more earnestly to magnificence than to Maria. He was perforce a nonpareil fundraiser.

Despite inflating the membership, Leo was still able to raise the price of a cardinalate to unprecedented levels. On one day, two years before, cardinals Conti, Valle, and Colonna all paid 25,000 ducats apiece for the Red Hat; Poncetta had paid 30,000, Campeggi 24,000, and Armellini 40,000. The fathers general of the Dominicans, Franciscans, and Augustinians each paid 70,000, and the two young sons of his sister and one son of Lorenzo the Magnificent put up 35,000 each. In all, over 500,000 ducats. Where has it all gone? Somehow, there must be more money. Somehow.

Meanwhile, as Leo often has said to his court, "The mind of the great find sufficient satisfaction in the glory of their achievements"—this when he refused to attend a bacchanalian midsummer's night party at the Villa

Farnese. Leo has many achievements: defeat and death of the duke of Urbino (that war cost him 800,000 ducats); the royal marriage he arranged between Lorenzo de' Medici and Madeleine la Tour d'Auvergne, another between Giuliano de' Medici and Filiberta of Savoy; his two main wars against France and Spain; even now he is playing what will be a successful game of using Emperor Charles against Francis I of France (Leo is negotiating with both secretly; he will finally side with Charles in his hour of victory): his elimination of Duke Alfonso de Ferrara (stiletto) and Giannolo Baglione (beheading). Italy is no longer the plaything of Spain or France. The states of the Church are solid, compact, the northern frontiers are protected with de' Medici holdings. Rome has become a museum of fine arts. For seventy years before his time, it had been known throughout Europe as Cowherds' Village. Now, it is in a flourishing state; the people are not overtaxed. His own statue stands on the capitol for public salutes every day of the week.

Of all his glorious moments, three gave him intense pleasure: his escape from the French, the royal Portuguese mission, and his own coronation as pope. His escape was sheer triumph! In 1512, the French had captured him as the papal legate for Pope Pius III. "I will return on a white Turkish horse in triumph," he told his captors. They just laughed at him in the French way. Taken in chains to Milan, he was being transported at night across the River Po into France and to prison as a hostage. He broke loose, swam the Po, disguised himself as a swineherd, reached Bologna, and before year's end rode back into Ravenna triumphantly on that white Turkish horse! The de' Medicis always took revenge. A year later he was pope.

Leo also loved to talk about the royal Portuguese mission. Those Portuguese and Spanish and their tiny caravels sailed around the world: Columbus to America in 1492, Vasco da Gama to India in 1493; Cabral to Brazil in 1500; Almeida and Albuquerque to Ormuzd in Goa and as far as the straits of Molucca in 1504. The Spanish and the Portuguese will squabble some day. Anyway, in May of 1515, King Emmanuel of Portugal sends a diplomatic mission to Pope Leo, to lay India and all the lands beyond at the feet of His Holiness. Leo remembers the exotic animals and plants, the Arabian horses, the chests of gold and precious stones, the one elephant they brought him (the last time a Roman saw an elephant was over 1,300 years before in the third century before Christ when Hannibal invaded Italy). Leo relished the words in King Emmanuel's greeting: "Your Holiness is the sun among the stars! You rule, as Peter, from the Tiber to the Poles. The kings of Arabia and Saba will bring their gifts to you, as well as all the princes and peoples from Ultima Thule!" Such glory for the de' Medicis and for Peter's successor! A month later, he, Pope Leo, granted Portugal all lands from Cape Non to the Indies.

And as for his coronation, it seemed indeed true, what Cardinal Farnese had said as he placed the papal tiara on Leo's head on March 19, 1513: "Receive the tiara adorned with three crowns and know that you are father of princes and kings, victor of the whole world under the earth, and Vicar of Our Lord Jesus Christ to whom be honor and glory without end." They should have known that a de' Medici always does things in magnificent ways. That one day alone cost 100,000 ducats: the white Turkish horse (the same one) he rode bejeweled and robed in cloth-of-gold; the 2,500 troops, the 4,000 kings, princes, nobles, barons, patriarchs, cardinals, bishops, abbots; the banners and bunting and flags; the marvelous statues of Ganymede, Apollo, Jesus, Caesar, Mary the Virgin, Augustus, Trajan, St. Peter, Marcus Aurelius, St. Paul, Apollo with his lyre, Diana with her faun, Neptune with his trident; the slow cavalcade past the Forum and Coliseum into the Lateran; the evening banquet with its food and fireworks and illuminations turning night into day and then his night in Castel Sant' Angelo spent alone with Cardinal Petrucci. "We begin gloriously. We live gloriously. We die gloriously," a favorite phrase of Leo's.

One matter also troubles Leo besides money—Petrucci. Petrucci is a name Leo never forgets. He used to love that cardinal—and the other conspirators. But they did not understand; and when Leo banished Cardinal Petrucci's brother from Siena, drove Cardinal Piera's brother from Florence, defeated Cardinal Riario in the conclave, and refused the rich archbishopric of Marseilles to Cardinal di Saulis, they plotted against his

203

life. A stupid plan: they employed a surgeon, Battista Vercelli, who, pretending to operate on Leo's hemorrhoids, was supposed to poison him through the rectum.

Cardinals Soderini and Adrian had been in the plot and they are free— at a price. Perhaps they should have shared the fate of Petrucci. Petrucci was given a safe-conduct pass by Leo, on condition he come back to Rome in 1517. Once back, Leo had him thrown, cardinal's robes and all, into the infamous Sammarocco dungeon in Sant' Angelo and tortured daily on the rack. "No faith need be kept with a poisoner," Leo retorted to the Spanish ambassador who was guarantor of Petrucci's safe-conduct. Leo had not got where he was by being predictable. The same day, Cardinal Riario (forty years a cardinal) and cardinals Soderini, Adrian, and di Saulis were also arrested, imprisoned, and tortured. Leo presided at their trials in which Adrian and di Saulis were fined 25,000 ducats apiece, Soderini and Adrian 12,500 ducats each. Cardinal Riario was fined 150,000, to be paid in three monthly payments, and promised a grandniece in marriage to a de' Medici nephew. Cardinal Petrucci was condemned to death and received his sentence with a stream of blasphemies and curses. He kicked a priest in the groin who approached to confess him, and was strangled in prison by Leo's official executioner, Roland the Moor.

For two years after this, Leo lived in fear of assassination; he sought out and liquidated the family and friends of Petrucci; all others remotely connected with any of the conspirators were under constant surveillance. Leo himself said mass daily surrounded by men with drawn swords and hidden archers with arrows at the ready. When meeting in consistory alone with his cardinals, two deaf bowmen were stationed behind his throne. Leo shivered at Petrucci's confession on the rack: "Eight times, I, Cardinal Petrucci, went to a consistory with a stiletto beneath my robes waiting for the opportune moment to kill de' Medici [Leo]."

The ingratitude of it all. After all the banquets Leo gave, the theater he organized, the hunts, the lute music, the dancing, the masked balls, comedies, orations, poetry readings, the beauty he created through the artists. And, if it was not the Genovesi or Milanesi or Veneziani, it was those hulking Germans who hated him.

Now it was some bumpkin monk called Luther, who had denounced Petrucci's trial as a "financial operation." Leo called Luther *"Luder,"* German for carrion, which had been Luther's original name. Leo, the prize falcon hunter of Europe, knew all about carrion. Prince Albert had sent Luther's Theses to Rome, asking Leo "to grasp the seriousness of the situation, so as to meet the error at once." But to Leo, it was a mere squabble between envious monks.

Three weeks ago, he listened to Cardinal Egidio of Viterbo, who pleaded with Leo to reform the church. Francesco Pico della Mirandola also joined in the plea: "The corruption is gone too far, Holiness. We need a council of the whole church."

Not so for Leo. He has no trouble in doctrine or in the solidity of his papal authority. The only trouble is money. This is because of that Luder-Luther character.

Four years ago, Leo negotiated a very delicate, intricate, but mutually profitable agreement with Albert, prince-archbishop of three dioceses, Mainze, Magdeburg, and Halberstag. Actually, it was illegal, a felony violation of church law, to hold three dioceses at one time. But Leo permitted it—for a consideration: 21,000 ducats for being granted the dioceses; 20,000 ducats for being allowed to keep them illegally. Albert, of course, told Leo he was penniless; but he borrowed the money from the Jacob Fugger banking house. Leo allowed Albert to sell a special inventory of indulgences in all three dioceses, in order to pay back the Fuggers. Prices of indulgences went from half a gold florin (for the very poor) to three gold florins (for mendicants), five gold florins (for doctors), and so on to twenty-five gold florins for nobility and royalty.

To enhance his position as source of mercy for the faithful suffering in Purgatory, Prince Albert had something special, his collection of relics (all, of course, fraudulent): a wisp of straw from the manger where the baby Jesus lay on the first Christmas night, four hairs from the Virgin's head, fourteen pieces of her clothing, a strand of Christ's beard, a nail from Christ's cross, a little over 19,093 sacred bone parts of saints and martyrs. For venerating all this and a payment, anyone—prince or pauper—could shorten the stay of any close friend or relative in Purgatory by 1,902,202 years and 270 days. And now, Leo fumes, in a little intellectual cabbage patch called Wittenberg (in Albert's diocese), this Luther fellow has started a revolt against the selling of indulgences. Result: Albert can't pay the Fuggers; he therefore can't pay Leo; and Leo cannot pay for the continuing beautification of Rome.

Leo remembers what his legate, Cardinal Tommaso da Vio learned from a face-to-face confrontation with Luther in Augsburg one year ago. "A peasant, Your Holiness, smelly, vulgar, superstitious, ungodly, ignorant, and obstinate. He must be liquidated. Perhaps the emperor will advise and help." Leo hasn't much use for Emperor Charles. That "nineteen-year-old, pale-faced, blue-eyed, lantern-jawed, taciturn, laconic, defiant, and reserved Spaniard born in a Ghentish street," is how Leo describes him. Anyway, at present he is plotting against Charles with the French, while entrapping the French with Charles. Charles, after all, is "Emperor of Spain, Flanders, Naples, Swiss Germany, King of the Indian Isles and Lord of the Oceanic Isles," as his official title goes.

But there is always Solimando to comfort Leo. The boy singer is one of Leo's prize possessions: the grandson of Sultan Mehmet, the Turk who took Constantinople in 1493. Little Solimando's father, Sultan Djem was driven from Constantinople by Sultan Bajuzet and took refuge in the Vatican of Pope Alexander VI. Bajuzet had sent 40,000 ducats to Pope Alexander, asking him to kill Djem. Alexander waited. When Bajuzet sent another 200,000 ducats, Alexander had Djem quietly poisoned. Pope Julius II had denounced Alexander after his death as "a rapacious hyprocrite," and had forbidden any masses to be said for him.

Once upon a time, Leo would have made Solimando his favorite, if it were not for one horrible memory: Pope Alexander's favorite, Manuele, and how he ended. Alexander's son, Cesare, repeatedly stabbed Manuele through Alexander's white cloak as Manuele hid there. Alexander sobbed impotently as Cesare's dagger scattered blood all over Alexander's white papal clothes. No pope should lay himself open to such indignity.

At Leo's coronation, Cardinal Farnese should have intoned the ritual phrase "*non habebis annos Petri* (you will not have the years of Peter)." These words were said to every new pope, as if to say: you will never be as good as Peter, who reportedly reigned as pope for forty years. But to Leo, Farnese had not said those words.

Leo has exactly two years and twenty-seven days left. His nephew, Cardinal Giulio, who will be pope also, arranges an agreement with Emperor Charles. Martin Luther is declared anathema, is excommunicated, and placed under the ban of the empire (to be killed on sight). Luther escapes death by hiding out in Wartburg, and produces twenty-four publications about his new faith. Giulio gets 10,000 ducats, an archbishopric, and the special protection of the emperor as his reward. Leo makes an alliance with the emperor and crowns him in St. Peter's.

On December 1, 1521, contrary to all expectation, Leo sickens, is anointed and confessed, kisses the crucifix, and dies muttering, "Gesu! Gesu! Gesu!" Cardinal Farnese, kneeling at his bedside, now completes the phrase he omitted eight years ago: "*Non habebis annos Petri!*"

The Last Chance

It is the summer of 1534. Pope Clement VII (Giulio de' Medici) is now sure that he is dying, and he is haunted by the memory of his three great failures.

He never seems to have troubled himself about other fundamental things—his election as pope, for example, in 1523. As a bastard, he was barred from that office by church law. Legalistic foolishness! All hushed up years before by the gold of his uncle, Pope Leo X. Besides, Clement had brazenly bought his election, distributing 60,000 ducats among the conclave cardinals. He had even persuaded Holy Roman Emperor Charles V of Spain to help ("I poured out streams of gold to get de' Medici elected," Charles was later to remark bitterly after Clement had betrayed him). He had bought Cardinal Colonna's vote with a palace and the chancellorship, Cardinal Carnaro's with the Palace of San Marco, and the infamous Cardinal Soderini's with total amnesty for Soderini's heinous crimes, including several murders. So what? That's how it was always done.

Yes, Clement knows all this, and it never soils the innocence of his dreams. None of the de' Medicis ever had scruples about personal behavior. They viewed themselves as being somehow outside the historical process and therefore free from its everday rules. Remember how Clement's uncle and predecessor, Leo X, had had Cardinal Petrucci tortured and strangled after guaranteeing Petrucci's safety? Typical de' Medici behav-

209

ior. Clement was no different. Yet he felt a frightening immobility of his spirit as he waited for death. A faithful Christian would have said that only divine grace could have melted that fearful fixity. Clement would have accepted that notion—he was, believe it or not, a believer—but wouldn't have seen how it applied to him. That was for ordinary folk. He was a de' Medici.

He is deeply troubled, however, by his three failures. He knows he's done wrong, that what he has done has grievously harmed the church, but doesn't see how he could have done differently, and this acid of anxiety corrodes his very soul.

"My sole aim was that the Holy See be independent politically and militarily of Spain and France," he had confided in a memo to his confessor, Father Michele, "so that we could be impartial in our judgments on both. The papal state must be sovereign," he wrote further. And by that it is clear that Clement meant politically sovereign. He had taken the final step of identifying the empire of the spirit with the empire of the world. Also, from Leo X Clement had inherited an almost empty treasury and enormous debts.

Therefore he played the game of wordly power—and he played it with tenacity, with cunning, with endless audacity, with unflagging energy, with boundless appetite and zeal. And he lost.

Banished from Rome

Clement's chief antagonists were France and Spain, both of which he believed—correctly—wanted to take Rome and control the papcy. Clement's court became the arena for an almost literal tug of war between those of his counselors who were partisans of Emperor Charles (von Schönberg, Hurtado, Colonna, de la Roche) and those who championed Francis I of France (Giberti, Saint-Maria, Carpi).

Clement smiled benignly at both Charles and Francis while negotiating secretly with Venice and Milan for an alliance that could withstand them both, neutralizing Switzerland and using it as a buffer against both

France and Spain. As a blind, he sent von Schönberg on two "peace" missions in 1523 to Madrid, Paris, and London. But someone informed Charles of Clement's double-dealing, and the emperor invaded France in July of 1524.

By September, the war had spilled over into northern Italy, and Charles had vowed to revenge himself "on that poltroon, the pope." Clement therefore hastily made a secret alliance with Francis, which included the promise of marriage between the pope's niece, Catherine de' Medici, and Francis's second son. But he had guessed wrong. By May of 1525, Francis had been taken captive by the Spanish and Charles had exacted a fine of 100,000 ducats from Clement. It was either that or have the emperor march into Rome. Charles did leave Clement with the papal monopoly of the salt pits in Milan, and he did let him keep Naples.

But in Charles's court, the message of Martin Luther had already been received. "Reform the church while there's still time," Charles's advisors told him. "You can do it if you do it now. If you don't, Luther will." The popes have a spiritual mission, and spiritual only, they told him. The church was never intended to have temporal power. "Take it away. You can do it, but you've got to act fast."

Receipt of this intelligence galvanized Clement into a frenzy of reaction that eventually led to the formation in 1526 of the Holy League of Cognac, pitting France, Venice, Milan, and the papacy against the emperor. A number of Clement's cardinals, led by Colonna, sided with Charles. Colonna, seeing the chance to depose Clement, who had beaten him in the conclave of 1523, invaded Rome at the head of his own army of 5,000, driving Clement to refuge in the Castel Sant' Angelo.

The Colonnas plundered St. Peter's, stealing the papal tiara, the tapestries by Raphael, the chalices and crosses. They raped the women, killed about 1,700 men, fed their horses on the communion wafers. The damage amounted to about 300,000 ducats, before Colonna and his army withdrew.

Meanwhile, up north, Charles's imperial army was mowing down all resistence. Milan, Siena, Pescaro, Lodi, Cremona, Genoa, Bologna, Florence—all fell to the enemy. Clement sent for help to England and France,

211

but the English king (Henry the Eighth) was too busy changing wives, and Francis of France demanded too high a price. So Clement had to face the emperor alone.

By May 5, the pope was bottled up in Rome: an imperial army of over 40,000 Spaniards, Germans, and Italians was occupying the vineyards behind St. Peter's, advancing across the old Neronian fields. The imperial fleet lay off Ostia. Charles de Lannoy, the fleet commander, said: "It is incredible that the Vicar of Christ should acquire wordly possessions at the cost of a single drop of human blood."

But Clement had been assured that the Roman garrison could hold out. A deep fog enshrouded the whole city from daybreak Monday, while the pope prayed in his private chapel. Perhaps the fog helped the Spanish to make a surprise attack. Anyway, suddenly the pope's historian, Paolo Giovio, burst into the chapel screaming that the Spaniards were in the city. The papal party hurried across the covered passageway to the Castel Sant' Angelo fortress, about 3,000 of them: all the foreign ambassadors and their families, the household, staff, and the loyalist cardinals, thirteen in all. Everyone who could get there before the drawbridge was lifted. Cardinal Pucci was thrown from his horse and trampled on, but succeeded in making it. Cardinal Armellini was lifted up in a basket. Cardinal Deseo was crushed by the drawbridge as it closed. (Imperialist cardinals [della Valle, Cesari, Aracoeli, Siera, Enkevoirt] remained in their palaces quite secure.) Over 2,000 people drowned in the Tiber trying to get in with Clement. The great artists, Benvenuto Cellini and Raphael da Montelupo, manned the cannon. But there was not much fighting in the streets. The garrison of the fortress-castle was tiny—90 Swiss guards, maybe 400 Italians.

All resistance was ended by about midday. The imperial army of 20,000 Spaniards and 20,000 Germans together with 10,000 camp followers—male and female—fell upon the city; and the looting, the pillage, the murder, the suffering which went on for about ten days was indescribable. They went methodically from house to house, killing the men and children and old people, raping the young women, taking all gold and silver and valuables, slaughtering all the orphans and nuns in the eleven orphanages together with all horses, donkeys, and mules in Rome. Every church was plundered and set on fire.

No monk was spared. No nun was not raped several times before being killed. The survivors were sold in the Piazza of St. Peter's as slaves. Any cardinal or bishop they found was stripped naked, dragged through the streets at the end of a rope, then thrown into prison to be ransomed heavily.

The tombs of the popes were opened and rifled—even St. Peter's grave, which was robbed of the silver and gold votive offerings put there by previous popes. Philibert of Orange, commander of the army, stabled his horses in the Sistine Chapel. His officers stabled theirs in the Vatican apartments.

For ten days, the only sounds in Rome were the wailing of women, the crying of children, the scream of men being tortured, the raucous laughter of the Spaniards and the Germans. Every day there were more hangings, floggings, beheadings, burnings, rapes.

The plundering and killing went on until they had inflicted damage amounting to 12 million gold florins; and another 8 million worth was taken in church plate, tapestries, clothes, furniture, pictures, precious stones, jewelry, and hard cash. They burned the Library of San Sabina and destroyed all the papal records in the Capitol and the Holy Office. To say nothing of the dead, the maimed, and the defiled.

But by June 1, the emperor wanted peace: he had just received threatening letters from the English and French kings. Colonna, acting for Charles, and the pope quickly came to terms. Clement agreed to surrender Sant' Angelo, the ports of Ostia and Civita Vecchia, Castellani, Piacenza, Parma, and Modena; to pay a ransom of 40,000 ducats in several installments; to restore Colonna's churchly status (he'd been anathematized); to give seven important hostages over to the Germans; and to retire permanently to Naples with his cardinals.

To produce the first installement of the ransom, the pope put Benvenuto Cellini on top of Sant' Angelo, where he constructed a wind furnace and started melting down all the papal tiaras (the precious stones having been first removed) and chalices, the gold and silver statues of the

213

Madonna and the saints, the gold and silver plate and weapon handles and shields.

It wasn't enough. The pope had to throw in as sweetener the town of Benevento, the church tithes of Naples, and personal valuables worth 30,000 scudi. Bartolomeo Gattinara, the emperor's emissary, personally removed from the pope's finger his diamond ring valued at 150,000 ducats.

Through the long summer as Clement struggled to meet his ransom, a plague hit Rome, killing about 2,500 of the occupying German *landknechts*. The emperor was getting tired of the whole thing anyway. He negotiated again with the pope, and a final bargain was struck. The papal states would be restored on payment of three quick sums, specified as 73,169 ducats, 35,000 ducats, and 14,983½ ducats (that half ducat always bothered the pope). The pope immediately ordered the sale of all cardinals' palaces in Rome and of church property in Naples, in order to pay quickly and on time, and he left Sant' Angelo disguised as a majordomo. The streets of Rome were in shambles: dunghills everywhere; half-eaten corpses (gnawed by the dogs) lying in the doorways; no house that had not been burned; no shop or church that had not been looted and burned; prostitutes and drunken Germans everywhere, copulating in the streets; the stench of burned flesh like a pall over it all. In cleaning up Rome, over 2,000 corpses were thrown into the Tiber.

All the business of Rome had been torched but one: the House of Fugger. The German looters needed this multinational bank to ship home the benefits of their pillage.

A Botched Comeback

No sooner had Clement fled from Rome than he was planning his return—and the punishment of his persecutors. He went first to Orvieto, taking refuge in the dilapidated bishop's palace. He had nothing left. Even the canopy over his bed was borrowed. He was emaciated and wearing a seven-months' beard, swearing that he would not shave until he returned to the Vatican. His will to recoup was unyielding. After nine months of exile and misery, Clement—after one final attempt at unseating him—negotiated with the triumphant emperor and was allowed to return to Rome in October 1528.

The city was still a smoking, fetid ruin. Four-fifths of all houses were abandoned. In the Sistine Chapel and the Vatican apartments and the chancellery were the festering dungheaps and overflowing latrines of Philibert's horses and men. And everywhere it was whispered that the emperor was going to strip the pope of his political power.

Gasfaro Contarini, the Venetian ambassador, spoke to the pope confidentially: "Holiness, the Head of the Church should not pursue, as rulers of secular states do, particular interests only . . . but should fix his eyes on the general welfare of the Church and thereby direct the other princes of Europe away from their private, selfish systems of policy." Contarini got all this out in one breath. He was ashen-faced when he finished and looked like a man expecting a blow across the eyes.

"And what practical steps does this imply?" the pope inquired.

"A repudiation," Contarini answered, warming to the subject, "a repudiation of at least a portion—no, no, Holy Father, better still, of all the Papal States."

"And," Clement asked, still quite evenly, "what about the welfare of the Holy See and the Church?"

Contarini responded with tears in his eyes, passion in his voice: "Let not Your Holiness suppose that the welfare of the Church of Christ stands or falls with those morsels of worldly dominion. Before their acquisition, the Church existed and indeed existed at her best. The Church is the common possession of all Christians, but the Papal States are like any other states of an Italian prince."

"Therefore?" Clement asked.

"Therefore," he went on, "Your Holiness must set in the forefront of your responsibilities the welfare of the entire true Church."

"And that, in your opinion, consists of?"

"Of the peace of Christendom, Holiness. You must allow the interests of the temporal states to fall for a time into the background."

215

"What about this new alliance between England, Florence (which rightfully belongs to us, by the way), Ferrara (a rebellious vassal of ours), and your beloved Venice? You intend to confront Charles V and so keep what you have?"

"We are secular states, Your Holiness. This is the way we subsist."

"Yes, Contarini. You will be allowed to keep what you have got, while I as the good-natured man who has been robbed of all his belongings will be left where I am without a chance of recovering one simple thing."

"But, Holiness, what other course is possible? Christendom is falling apart. All Europe is in revolt against your authority."

"I will presume that you are speaking the truth, Contarini, and that I as one faithful to his trust ought to act as you exhort me. But, then, those on the other side ought to act in a similar way."

"They will have to do so, if Your Holiness leads the way."

"I would rather be the emperor's chaplain or horse-attendant than allow myself to be insulted by rebellious subjects and vassals," the pope responded. "I mean the Florentines. Wasn't it they that put you up to this flamboyant proposal?"

"No, Holiness. No. But, as we are going now, the states of Europe are going to renounce their official attachment to the Church and even to Christianity as the guide of their behavior—or, if they fail there, at least as the ultimate criterion of their history."

"Leave history to us, the successors of Peter, Contarini. We have lived more history than any state existent today." Contarini bowed and left. The interview was over, and with it, Christendom.

From that January onward, the pope worked speedily and efficiently to reestablish his power. He negotiated peace with the emperor in the Treaty of Barcelona of June 29, 1529, which allowed him to reoccupy the papal states in exchange for enormous indemnities. He would be allowed, even helped, to retake Florence. The greatest concession of all: the emperor would come to Bologna and accept his coronation from Clement, thus acknowledging the 119th successor of St. Peter as the source of all power on earth and in heaven. Charlemagne and Leo all over again!

Perhaps, perhaps once the killing and the looting had died down, and all had acquired enough booty; once the kings had got the women they currently lusted after; then German princes, Dutch merchants, English kings and barons, and those dour Swiss confederates would need confession and church blessings. As for those squabbling theologians in France and Germany, the Inquisitors had effective methods of silencing them.

But, Clement must ask himself, where did I fail with Contarini? The church would cease to be visible if it lost its power. Luther means nothing. Even the emperor thinks so. How could the church subsist in a secular world if it could not defend itself and had no economic sinews of its own? What would ensure the spiritual health of nations, of Europe? Obviously, Clement thought he'd found the answer.

A New Golden Age?

The coronation of Charles V of Spain as new Holy Roman emperor was set for November 1529. Clement made his triumphal entry into the city of Bologna on October 20.

The governor had prepared it all magnificently. Along the road leading to the Church of San Petronio, he had erected arches and pillars covered with draperies and green garlands around hundreds of shields bearing the de' Medici coat of arms. Everywhere there were triumphal arches supported by Doric columns plated with allegorical reliefs, paintings, and stucco groups of figures from ancient Greece and Rome. "The names of Leo X, of Sixtus IV, of Julius II are reborn again," the pope remarked.

On November 5, Emperor Charles arrived. During the two prior weeks, the pope had had a magnificent decor created. About 300 architects, sculptors, plumbers, painters, carpenters, masons, and engineers produced an ephemeral facade for all of Bologna's main streets that evoked exactly, but exactly, the magnificence and the color and the majesty of Rome it self. Bologna became ancient Rome for a week. To the eye. Every street was covered with an awning. Garlands of green boughs

217

stretched around every arch making Bologna a city of luscious green arcades.

Charles rode a white Arabian charger. He wore flashing armor inlaid with burnished gold. He was surrounded by cardinals and bishops, preceded by his own courtiers and knights, followed by all his foreign envoys, guarded by his elite Flemish and German troops. He entered Bologna by the Porta San Felice, where the pope had erected an archway decorated with two classical scenes. On one side: the Triumph of Neptune (was not the emperor the new Neptune of all the seas?) with his tritons, his mermaids, his sirens, his dolphins, his sea horses. On the other: the glory of Bacchus (did the emperor not promise to inaugurate a new era of happiness?) surrounded by flute-playing satyrs, by Diana with her beautiful virgin fauns, and the woodland nymphs carrying the phallic power of Dionysus. Over the gate: the papal keys and the imperial eagle of Spain. Along the streets there were huge plaques and shields with the portraits of ancient heroes and great men: Caesar, Augustus, Titus, Alexander, Trajan, Diocletian, Cicero, Pericles, Aristotle, Plato, Sophocles, and so on. It was unending glory.

Through the crowds, the emperor proceeded in grave dignity, everywhere provoking a delirium of joy. Papal treasurers scattered gold and silver coins among the people. Bells pealed. Cannons thundered. Trumpets blew fanfares. When he reached San Petronio, Charles dismounted before the raised platform where the pope sat enthroned. He came forward, knelt and kissed Clement's ring and foot. Just as Charlemagne had done to Leo III in the year 800. Then both men retired to their apartments in the Palazzo Pubblico. The pope had arranged adjoining apartments with one private communicating door between. They could come to each other in complete privacy, and thus could do all the talking needed without being spied upon or interrupted. The French were in the city seeking to disrupt the affair. And the Lutherans were at the same business.

Luther they both dismissed as a pinprick. The pope would condemn him for doctrine. Charles would liquidate him and his supporters. It was the status of Milan, Florence, Ferrara, and Venice that interested the pope. Apparently Charles had concluded in previous months that the best guarantee of Italy and of his Europe was a strong papacy, so all the papal states were to be guaranteed by imperial power. Of England (King Henry was a boor, they agreed), of France (Francis was finished, they concluded), of the Turk (they could deal with him), there were conclusive discussions. On December 23, the twenty-nine-year-old emperor, under the guidance of the fifty-one-year-old pontiff, signed a treaty linking the papal states, Spain, the Netherlands, Austria, Hungary, Bohemia, Milan, Mantua, Venice, Montserrat, Savoy, Urbino, Siena, Lucca, and Florence in a new league.

"The new Holy Roman Empire!" the pope said to Charles upon the signing. The emperor paused, then said: "Sufficient if we have the Holy Roman Church and a Holy Empire, Holiness." Charles could be imperious when he wanted. They agreed to wait until February of 1530 for his coronation. Meanwhile, the pope would organize the capture of Florence, and both he and the emperor would assemble the new league's members and get their sigggatures. Huge amounts of money had to be transported in security over land and sea.

The original idea had been that the coronation take place in the same spot in St. Peter's where Pope Leo III had crowned Charlemagne. But they were in Bologna. Very well! They would create in Bologna's San Petronio an exact replica (in reduced size) of that sacred spot in St. Peter's. They did just that.

On February 4, the coronation took place. French spies and Lutheran provocateurs were in the city. So the wooden bridge from the Palazzo Pubblico to the church was guarded by 400 German *landsknechts,* 2,000 Spanish infantry, and ten pieces of heavy artillery. But as the emperor stepped onto the bridge, it shivered and collapsed slightly, throwing him to the ground. (The Inquisition questioned several Lutheran and French agents later and concluded that sabotage had been done.)

But the emperor was not hurt and the ceremony went on. Charles already wore the iron crown of Lombardy. In San Petronio, he swore on the Gospels to defend the Holy Roman Catholic Church. In a private chapel he was anointed with sacred oil. After a reading from St. Paul's letters, they put the imperial sword on him. The pope placed in his hands the golden orb representing the world, the silver scepter symbolizing all

219

power in the world, and on his head the diadem of emperor. The Vatican castrati choir filled the air with the purest music, and the Benedictine monks sang a glorious Te Deum.

Then the great triumphal procession began. Emperor and pope rode solemnly through an almost delirious crowd, following the flowing banners of the Crusade, of the church of the de' Medici, of the city of Rome, of Germany, of Spain, of the New World, of Naples, and of Bologna. As they passed, the papal treasurers threw handfuls of gold and silver into the crowds.

That evening there was an immense banquet peopled with glittering personalities—everybody worth anything in the world at that time. Oceans of tiaras, crowns, jewelry, beautiful clothes, handsome men, majestic women, loyal and princely and noble figures, all of them. The tables were replete with delicacies from four continents; and all food was washed down with forty-five choicest wines from Spain, France, Germany, and Italy. The feasting went on for three days.

Then the pope left for Florence. By September of 1530, Florence had been regained, the whole expedition costing 2 million ducats. He immediately punished the rebels, some by exile, some by beheading, some by imprisonment and torture (although those who could ransom their bodies and their crimes were allowed to depart in safety). Florence became once more the citadel and glory of the de' Medici.

As to the doctrinal difficulties up north in the German principalities, in Switzerland and the Netherlands, the pope ignored them. He brusquely dismissed all talk of a council as "only a cloak for trying to reduce the power of the Holy See." Instead, he immediately began again to play France and Spain off against each other, with England and Switzerland in between as cat's-paws. He saw his coronation of Charles as inaugurating a new period of glory for Rome and therefore for the church. But somehow it didn't seem to be working. Why?

"No effort," he wrote, "has been spared by us to vindicate the royal dominion of the Roman Pontiff over all princes and kingdoms. For, with our predecessor of holy memory, Boniface VIII, we hold and teach and lay down that the Roman bishop possesses two swords, the spiritual sword of spirit, and the temporal sword of political power. Like Leo,

220

we have conferred the temporal sword on Charles V of Spain."
It was the spiritual sword, however, that turned in his heart as he waited to die. No de' Medici had as miserable an end to such a failure-ridden life as Pope Clement VII. From June through September of 1534, the fifty-six-year-old pope was continuously and alternately trying to live and trying to die. The unhealthy air of Rome in the summer did not help him. Many of his symptoms could be explained by a stomach malignancy. But some could not—the violent fluctuations, for instance. So it was taken for granted that he had been poisoned. Anyway, his was a three-month struggle against some deadly enemy eating away silently at his stomach. At times, Clement fought to live, joking, laughing, eating, even planning for the future. At times, he whimpered for death to release him from the needles of pain piercing his bowels, and perhaps from the dark memories of all those he had ruined by his ambition.

In mid-June, he was mortally ill. In July, he recovered but then relapsed again, so low this time that he drew up his will (leaving the city of Florence to nephew Cardinal Alessandro and all the rest of his possessions to nephew Cardinal Ippolito). In the beginning of August, he recovered, only to relapse so dangerously by the 24th that they administered the last rites to him. On September 1, he felt fine enough to dictate his spiritual testament to Father Michele. He relapsed immediately, but recovered again by the 8th. On September 21, he developed a high fever, writhing with such nerve-shattering cramps and in such pain that by the 23rd he was exhausted—not too exhausted, however, to dictate and sign a letter in the middle of his agony to Emperor Charles of Spain recommending nephews Ippolito and Alessandro to Charles's good favor. Delirium set in that night and raged all day on the 24th.

Clement could take no more of it. His death was near. The physical sufferings of those three months had been accentuated by bitter toubles: Cardinal Ippolito's degrading way of life and his murderous plots against Cardinal Alessandro (Clement always referred affectionately to Ippolito as "my foolish devil"); the horrific raids by Moorish corsairs on the coasts near Rome; the persistent and contrary claims of French King Francis and Spanish Emperor Charles, tearing him apart between them mercilessly; his huge personal debts; the faces and the tears of thousands whose

221

pain and death he had encompassed; and, above all, the recurring feeling of certainty that, while he spent all his years in vainglory, a mortal blow had been dealt to the Christian church and he had done nothing to ward it off. Rather, he had facilitated it.

But he ended as a believer, convinced that he had to face Jesus and answer for everything. Clement had started off as pope in perfect health, a tall and graceful cleric, expert politician and statesman, efficient administrator, cagey dialectician, fluent speaker and cultured man, friend of kings and princes, and the most powerful man in Europe. He was truly what he has been called by one historian, "the unluckiest of popes." But in promoting the church, he was also a worse than useless pope. On September 25, at 3 P.M., they saw his body go limp after one terrible spasm of pain. He uttered one word only—"Florence!"—and then was silent.

DECLINE
AND
FALL

Going . . .
Going . . .

Following hard upon Clement VII's death—and precipitated by his triple failure—the furious rain of the Reformation fell upon Western Europe, in torrents often of blood. All things were changed. Christian unity under the spiritual leadership of church and pope was washed away like straw. Luther, whom Leo X dismissed as stinking carrion and Clement VII despised as a pinprick, was the final winner. All Leo's preoccupation with family glory and his personal advantage, and all Clement's maneuvering for political supremacy, were wide of the mark. Neither of them took the time or had the interest to understand what was happening.

Christian unity, the ancient patrimony of Rome and its popes, was breaking up. And the popes in that crucial period were busy about everything but the disappearance of a 1,500-year-old hegemony. Within one hundred and twenty years of Clement's death, the rulers of Europe definitively decided to go their separate ways and never again allow the factor of religious unity under Rome to decide national or international politics. Since those days, it never has.

This debacle of Roman power went in two long jogging leaps marked by bloody wars, treachery, curious alliances, greed, and personal ambition, until the final break at the Treaty of Westphalia in 1648. Luther may have started it all by arguing about mysterious things called "grace" and "justification by faith alone." But the German and Dutch and English and French nobles, merchants, and burghers who took up the cause

225

of his rebellion against Rome and its allies, were fighting for freedom from the political control which Rome's religion ultimately exercised over their lives. And once they had enriched themselves at Rome's expense, no religious claim was going to get them to return that wealth and that freedom.

The first series of wars between Catholics and Protestants ended with the interim Peace of Augsburg in 1555. It was a nerve-wracking event for Rome, for it established the first legal basis for the existence of Protestants. Rome's prime enemies, hitherto outlaws, were now respectable and protected. Protestants not only had a right now to church lands they had seized by arms and bloodletting; the religion of any particular region or territory was to be the religion of the ruler and the people living there. The old principle of the unique supremacy of Roman Catholicism had been undermined.

Just as ominous was another decision at Augsburg: no signatory member of the peace would ever again wage war against another member on religious grounds. Religion—in other words, the Catholic cause—was removed as a justification for war. It was taken out of contention. Rome could promote no more religious wars.

The Treaty of Westphalia in 1648 completed the process. Catholics and Protestants were given equal rights. The decision not to wage war for the religious motive was again reasserted. The sovereignty and independence of the individual states in Europe were declared inviolable. None would ever again be fiefs or subjects in any way to a central religious authority in Rome or elsewhere. The old medieval idea of the Christian republic, the Christian heartland, with the Holy Roman emperor and the Roman pope as its temporal and spiritual heads, was abandoned in favor of a community of independent nations equal in status with regard to religion and form of government. The Rome of imperial supremacy and international domination in politics had passed away forever.

By the end of the seventeenth century, there were already at least a dozen Christian churches with highly specific differences among them, and the centrifugal process was only beginning. It continued exponentially right down through the Victorian era, and when its energies at last were spent, well over a hundred denominations defined themselves as

Christian, although many of their adherents had no belief in Christ whatsoever and almost all of these institutions were dying.

The effects of this tremendous psychic shock of the Reformation permeated all areas of life. Without ecclesiastical encouragement—even in defiance of ecclesiastical ban—the natural sciences flourished and forever after changed the way human beings looked at the world and at themselves. As John Donne, the Anglican dean of St. Paul's Cathedral, wrote in seventeenth-century London about Copernican cosmology:

> The new philosophy calls all in doubt.
> The element of fire is quite put out.
> The sun's lost, and the earth, and no man's wit
> Can well direct him where to look for it.

The Church of Rome did not die then. It bent, but didn't break. Its roots were 1,500 years deep, after all. But from the days of Luther and Clement VII its history has been a 400-year decline and fall. Through vicissitudes of exile, war, persecution, and bankruptcy, the popes continued into our day, until at the beginning of the eighties in this century, the most definitive signs of inner and irreversible decay appeared in the church which Emperor Constantine made possible. In that 400 years, on three occasions, it looked as if external forces would level that church. They never did.

Yet the ecclesiastics in charge of the Roman structure never for an instant reflected on the long past of their churchly structure in such a way as to appreciate the fateful lesson of history: when churchmen tried to foment and propagate the Catholic faith by means of politics and money and worldly prestige, the condition of their church always deteriorated. No one ever reversed that single but complex decision of Pope Silvester I to accept the temporal power and influence Emperor Constantine offered him. It would have taken a pope who was at once a saint and a genius. For his belief in his faith and his trust in God would need to be gargantuan. Such a pope never arose. Hence right down to the end of the twentieth century, the Church of Rome labored on burdened to the point of decay and death by what one ancient emperor and one ancient pope

227

decided—in the face of the message which the Man of Galilee had come to preach.

In the town of Valence, France, there is a three-storied government-owned building. The roof is intact but the chimneys have collapsed, the fireplaces are blocked, the plumbing is clogged, the water pipes are broken. Most of its rooms have no doors; most windows are mere gaping holes. The plaster downstairs is broken. Upstairs, the wallpaper is yellowed and torn. Since it was built about thirty-seven years ago, the house has been successively a family residence, an orphanage, a nunnery, a military barracks, an inn, a grain storehouse, an arsenal, a sheep-pen, and then a deserted shell, full of echoes and the peculiar emptiness of places now abandoned that were once frequented by people, once warmed by their love.

It is July 1799. From now until the end of August, this building will be the prison and death-place of a man described in official French documents as "Citizen Pope" and addressed merely as "Citizen" by his French jailers and guards.

Citizen Pope, the eighty-two-year-old Pope Pius VI, born Giannangelo Braschi, is suffering from partial paralysis, recurrent dysentery, and phlebitis; he is subject to sporadic convulsions and comas. For the last twenty-three years he has been pope in Rome, where he fought unsuccessfully to defend the temporal and the spiritual power of the papacy. He was ordered out of Rome under armed arrest by the French government on February 20, 1798, allowed to bring two attendants and one doctor with him, but no food, no money, no extra clothes.

He spent one year and five months being dragged from place to place in Italy—Monterosi, Viterbo, Bolsena, Siena, Florence, Certosa, Parma, Bologna. At Bologna, on April 10, 1799, ten minutes after his arrival, he is ordered to leave in two hours for France. He had a sudden and frightening convulsion all over his body, then went rigid and paralyzed and icy cold. "Citizen Pope is dying" was the laconic dispatch sent to Paris. But Citizen Pope did not. On May 30, 1799, they lifted him into a carriage and drove him over the Alps—up one side of snow-capped Mont-Genèvres to the top and down the other side to Briançon, France, thence to

Grenoble, and finally to this Valence house in the late afternoon of Bastille Day, July 14. He will die at 1:20 A.M. in the small morning hours of August 29. Meantime, he will live suspended, swinging unpredictably between memories of failure and the anticipation of death.

Citizen Pope is already dying when they carry him into the Valence house. His iron constitution is broken. He can eat next to nothing and spends most of his days and nights shaking and speechless. He is still wearing his white robe and his Fisherman's Ring. Swiss General Haller tried to take it from him when he was leaving but got only Pius's other, personal ring. Something in the old man's stare froze Haller's fingers as he laid hold of the Fisherman's Ring. "It belongs, not to you, Citizen, but to our successor," was all Pius had said. A week after his arrival at Valence, a Saturday, a French official enters the room, clicks his heels, salutes, bends down over the bed, and shouts into his right ear: "Citizen Pope! By order of the government, you are to proceed to Dijon tonight! Prepare yourself!" But they let him stay. A government doctor examines Citizen Pope and writes his report: "In some days, you will be rid of this carrion. Long live the Republic!"

But Citizen Pope does not die. He remains alive, shuddering, moving his head from side to side, now and again touching the Fisherman's Ring to make sure it is still there. Some say: He doesn't know if he is alive or dead. But Citizen Pope knows he is still alive. He has not yet seen Jesus on his cross, and this, he knows, is the only sure sign a pope has of his own imminent death. Besides, for over ten days until about August 3, he is talking in short phrases ("fundamental rights," "privilege of Peter," "go to them," "hoped in him," and so on) and single words ("school," "Austria," "Naples," "danger," "priest," "Portugal," "Russia," "Ricci," "Napoleon," "Naples," "Mass," "Charlemagne"). And sometimes, in a moment of extreme quietude, his eyes open wide and large tears fall down his cheeks. But the single recurring phrase (and Pius's single recurring memory) is "without our power in our own house." For this, he is weeping and aching.

This is the fire of his pain—uncontrollable regret. For between 1776 (he was made pope in 1775) and 1798, he lost it all. The household: the

Catholic nations and powers of Naples, Austria, Spain, Portugal, Holland, Belgium, Hungary, Italy, Poland. The power: in some cases (Naples, for example), feudal tribute; in all places, the pope's direct and privileged possession of vast properties and his exclusive right to make, unmake, and change bishops, bishoprics, parishes, priests, schools, universities, seminaries, printing presses. And each government turned around and condemned a public protest which Pius made in August of 1794. He became the international pariah. Something secret had been eating away at the whole papal household, like a dry rot set in for years through the timbers and rafters, behind the wallpapered plaster, above the stuccoed ceilings, beneath the deep-carpeted floors. Suddenly the whole house collapses.

It really started in Naples, Citizen Pope remembers, although in 1775 the apostate Andreas Zamoisky had tried to abolish all his papal jurisdiction in Poland. That danger was avoided, but Poland was swallowed up by Russia and lost to the papacy anyway. Then the king of Naples refused to pay the annual tribute of 7,000 ducats to the Holy See. (Pius condemned this as late as June 1795, in a solemn document.) Not only that. The government of Naples arrogated all ecclesiastical power to itself—dissolving seventy-eight monasteries in Sicily and two-thirds of all those in Naples, appointing bishops and priests, deciding what was to be taught in schools and seminaries and what preached from the pulpits, and denying the primacy of Peter's 251st successor, Pius VI, and all his jurisdiction. By 1788, a complete collapse of all papal power.

In Portugal the same thing happened: all his jurisdiction over bishops, priests, cardinals, seminaries, schools, was taken away from him. By 1792, the same was true in France, Italy, Austria, the Netherlands, and elsewhere. All over, a destruction of papal jurisdiction. "National churches"—this was the cry. Pius's day fevers and nightmares go over and over and over all this interminably. So complete a collapse . . . Only by touching that Fisherman's Ring is he reassured that he is still pope, still Peter's successor.

By August 2, he is sitting up in bed, taking a little nourishment, talking. "We saw the handwriting on the wall," he says to a visitor, Cardinal Bathhyany, primate of Hungary (who brings much needed funds to

230

Pius). "If Emperor Joseph had not done it, none of this would have happened." The real villain was Emperor Joseph II of Austria ("the Emperor-Sacristan" he was nicknamed for his attempts to interfere in church matters). Pius has the bitterest recollection. Joseph's master plan, simple but devastating: create a centralized ecclesiastical government for all the empire (Austria, Hungary, the Netherlands, Lombardy); wipe out all differences between Catholics and Protestants ("only ability qualifies for any post," decreed Joseph); create all bishops and give them power to dissolve mariages; organizes all schools and seminaries and universities on a uniform plan of instruction which does not include religion as a subject; appoint all eccesiastical posts from parish assistant to cardinal; and create one supreme spiritual head of all religions—a pope just for the Austrian Empire. "We saw it coming," repeats Pius.

It was the last straw, when Emperor Joseph declared in December 1781: "Christian religion is only to be measured by the needs of the sovereign power, so that the Pope in Rome is entitled only to the guardianship of the *principles of faith*; the State is entitled to everything about the Church that is not of divine but of human invention and institution."

"Yes," repeats Pius to Bathhyany, "we saw it coming." Pius feels guilty about what he did in this emperor's cause. In 1781, he went to Vienna, he himself, the successor of Peter, the vicar of Jesus. At the cost of 80,000 thalers to the Vatican treasury, and unaccompanied by any of his cardinals, he went to see the emperor, talked with Joseph for one month, was acclaimed by hundreds of thousands, made concession after concession to Joseph, attended banquets, gave audiences, preached, gave his blessing, created new cardinals at the emperor's request, put up with the public abuse poured over him in printed pamphlets written by that frivolous Freemason Blumauer and that bitter Protestant Sonnenfels (both published with Joseph's permission—"freedom of expression," Joseph called it), and returned exhausted to Rome only to find that things became worse. "He has a mountain of sorrow and dismay. It is killing him slowly," Bathhyanya whispers to Spina, the pope's faithful servant.

The slow killing went on. As Pius regained some strength, the full impact of his position pressed on him. Where did he go wrong? What did

231

he do wrong? By 1783, the emperor's hand was in everything: regulating prayers said at Mass, abolishing Latin (in favor of the vernacular!), making marriage a civil contract, supressing all 413 religious houses and all 116 religious societies in Austria, fusing all into one single pious organization ("for the practical love of one's neighbor in respect of the helpless poor" was Joseph's definition of its aim).

"We went as far as we could with him," Spina hears Pius repeat to himself when he thinks he is alone. When Emperor Joseph came to Rome in 1784, Pius even gave his chief duke the power of nominating bishops and all heads of institutions—"so long as our fundamental rights remain intact," Pius stated to Joseph. Joseph had smiled patiently. Pius recollects that smile and now he understands it. "*Il sorriso imperiale*" became a catchphrase of his during his last weeks on earth. Emperor Joseph's two successors, Leopold (1790) and Francis (1797) wore that same supercilious smile and did exactly as Joseph had done. (For good measure, Leopold destroyed all private alters, closed all private chapels, and destroyed all relics of the saints and statues of the Madonna.)

In the afternoon of August 10, while he is sitting in the garden of the Valence house, Citizen Pope is told that an emissary of Napoleon Bonaparte, ruler of France, will be with him in an hour. The previous day, the pope had sent a message to England for help. "Holiness," said the faithful Spina, "we cannot trust anything the French will say. Remember Tolentino." Citizen Pope nods and tears fill his eyes. He remembers.

First, France, "eldest daughter of the church" he used to call it, abolished all religion, beheaded its king, enthroned Reason officially as supreme deity, massacred over 17,000 priests and over 30,000 nuns as well as forty-seven bishops, abolished all seminaries, schools, religious orders, burned all churches and libraries, then sent the Corsican Bonaparte to "liberate Italy and Rome." "Just as you please," wrote the Paris government to the Corsican. "Destroy Rome and the papacy utterly." "We are the friends of the descendants of Brutus and the Scipios. . . . Our intention is to restore the Capitol, to free the Roman people from their long slavery," the Corsican declared in May 1796, just before taking Rome.

Then the capture, and the humiliation of the Peace of Tolentino

232

between the papacy and the Corsican: a ransom of 46,000 scudi in three installments (Pius melted down all available silver and gold ornaments); 100 objets d'art and 500 rare manuscripts from the Vatican; the opening of all papal harbors to the French fleet; renunciation of all papal property in Italy and France and Naples and Sicily—everywhere. "They made us their prisoner, Spina," mutters Pius. "Peace treaty! Bah!" The vatican and Quirinal were occupied by French troops. They deposed Pius, and created the republic of Rome. As Pius had remarked the day the French entered Rome: "Oh, yes, we are alive. But that's about it!"

"Citizen Pope!" The Paris emissary's sharp disrespectul tones hit Pius's ears. "Yes, Citizen. What is it?" General Bonaparte, explains the emissary, staring Pius in the eyes, is preoccupied with reports that the prisoner is in negotiation with the enemies of France. The gaze of Pius does not waver. Not for nothing has he been in diplomacy for over fifty years. He lifts his hand deprecatingly, as if to say, "reports, rumors, all false."

In addition, the emissary continues, Citizen Pope is behind in his payments of the ransom. Pius, even in his weakness, fixes the emissary with a sudden blaze of disgust in his eyes. When will they have enough loot and booty? Between March and July 1793, the French had taken out of Rome gold and silver and precious stones to the value of 15,000 scudi (including 386 diamonds, 338 emeralds, 692 rubies, 203 sapphires from the tiaras of Popes Julius II, Paul III, Clement VIII, and Urban VIII), 2 million scudi from the Holy Office and 260,000 scudi from the German-Hungarian College, besides a herd of 1,600 horses. A convoy of 500 horse-drawn vehicles left Rome for France loaded with works of art and furniture and arms—all booty. Will they ever have enough?

Spina intervenes: "Citizen Pope will make up the deficit by August 30, Citizen." The emissary bows, then in a sharp staccato: "Citizen Pope! You will leave Valence for Paris in September." Pius looks at the emissary. Spina hears the pope laughing for the first time in about fifteen months. "You have kept the good wine until the very end, Citizen. I am ready for a long journey in September." In spite of himself, the emissary turns white—something in the pope's tone chills him. He leaves abruptly.

For the next ten days, Citizen Pope is busy on his only remaining hope. Yes, he answers Spina, he still hopes: for release, for restoration of all papal power—temporal and spiritual, military and political, economic and intellectual. But, curiously enough, he does not hope in any traditionally and substantially Catholic power or nation. Only in anti-papist and Protestant England, in anti-papist and schismatic Russia, in anti-papist and Lutheran Prussia and Lutheran Sweden. "The throw of the dice of history makes strange bedfellows," Pope Alexander VI had said once. No one could have known better than he. "Above all, the English, Spina," Citizen Pope murmurs. "The English and their fleet." Pius had always loved the English and permanent English residents in Rome used to visit him frequently—Lord Bristol, the art-dealer Jenkins, archaeologist Gavin Hamilton, sculptor John Flaxman.

"Do not forget," Spina reminds the pope, "all those who visited Your Holiness in Rome and loved Your Holiness." Citizen Pope recalls them all, all non-Catholics: the duke of Ost Gothland in October 1776; the Landgrave Friedrich of Hesse-Kassel and the duchess of Kingston in 1777; Prince Heinrich of Reuss in 1779; Russian Grand Duke Paul and his wife, Sophie Dorothea of Brunswick, and Louis Phillipe Orleans in 1782; King Gustavus of Sweden in 1783; the Duchess Maria Amalia of Parma, daughter of Empress Maria Theresa of Austria in 1784; the duke of Cumberland, and the duke of Gloucester in 1786; the Dowager Duchess Amalie of Weimar in 1788; the duke of Sussex in 1791. Yes, Citizen Pope reflects, our strength lies in the constitutional houses that rule Europe and keep it together. Without them and without us, only chaos stares us all in the face.

But all Citizen Pope's negotiations and hopes come to a standstill on August 18. The previous day, a visitor stayed late. It was an emissary of Cardinal Antonelli, his old secretary of state. Antonelli's message was brief and fateful, but it provoked an all-day discussion with loud, almost apoplectic protests from the pope. "The older order is going," wrote Antonelli. "Better renounce all temporal power. Let us fight only with weapons of spirit. Soon, only these—if we still have them—will be sufficient to preserve us." But the pope will have none of it. He vomits continuously that night and the following day. On the 19th, he has fearful

234

convulsions and shudderings, vomiting blood continuously. By evening he has a high fever.

On the 27th, it is clear Citizen Pope is definitely dying. He receives the last rites on that day; and, before going into a calm sleep, tells Spina: "I forgive Haller and Cervani." French General Cervani and Swiss General Haller brutalized Pius in February 1798, trying to get him to renounce his power. After that, Pius sleeps calmly. On the 28th, Spina, under duress, summons the French officer in charge and tells him, "Citizen Pope is dying." All day on the 29th, Citizen Pope passes continually from gentle consciousness into a troubled sleep punctured by horrors only he knows, and then back again to consciousness. Toward midnight, the seven people around him recite the rosary. Pius has a few words with Spina, ending: "Something bigger than church or state is upon us all. We were blind to it." The pope sleeps after that. About 1:15 A.M. he wakes up muttering hoarsely. "*Dio! Non ci vedo!* (God! I can't see!)" But Spina cleans away the film of sweat and powder that clogs his eyes. Now his eyes seem luminous, brightened by a light only he sees. They place a crucifix in his right hand. He raises it and gives the triple papal blessing. The eyes close. A final gentle shudder. He stops breathing at 1:20 A.M.

The French officer leaves the death room and scribbles a short dispatch for the Paris messenger: "This morning, at 1:20, Citizen Pope died. Long live the Republic!" Next morning the biggest newspaper in Valence carries an article saying that "the death of Pius VI placed a seal, as it were, on the glory of philosophy and modern times." They embalm his body (the heart and entrails are put in an urn), enclose his remains in a lead coffin within a black walnut coffin, and bury it in unconsecrated ground outside Valence. Spina writes to Cardinal Antonelli: "If what His Holiness said is true, what is going to remain? What is upon us all?" On February 17, 1802, with Napoleon's permission, the coffin is disinterred and brought to Rome and buried there with honor. The urn remains at Valence to this day.

A Brainwashing and
a Last Hurrah

At two o'clock in the morning of July 6, 1809, the sixty-seven-year-old
Pope Pius VII is sitting at his table in his study at the Quirinal Palace in
Rome. He is fully clothed. But, in addition to his ordinary clothes, he has
put on the velvet cape and stole which he uses on special occasions and for
important visitors. The visitors: French General Radet and a company of
soldiers. The occasion: on the order of Emperor Napoleon, Pius is going
to be taken prisoner and deported to France. Since early June 10, the
French tricolor has flown from Sant' Angelo Fortress, and French heavy
artillery is aimed at the pope's windows.

In May, Napoleon had annexed all the papal states to the French
Empire, declaring Rome a free imperial city and the pope free only in his
spiritual functions. Pius VII, like Pius VI, could not even imagine the
papacy without its papal states, its own military and economic power, its
own chancellery, its own status as a European power. Pius VII, like Pius
VI, is going to be given a choice to get rid of it all. But he also will refuse.
Pius has already retaliated: since two o'clock this afternoon of the 10th,
Emperor Napoleon has been excommunicated "as a violator of the patrimony of St. Peter." When they told Napoleon about that, he said: "The
Pope is a wild fool who must be interned." Indeed, as Napoleon knows,
Pius is negotiating with the English in secret. That, Napoleon knows, is
why the pope refused to fight with him against England. And England

237

must be suppressed. Napoleon has sent a special officer, Radet, to take the pope prisoner.

The Quirinal Palace stands on a hill. Radet and his men surround it, scale the walls with long ladders, smash in the gates, rush through the gardens, break in the main doors, and take possession of the huge Court of Honor—the main lobby. The attack has taken them less than three minutes. All well timed and on target. Then, with drawn swords and carbines, Radet, followed by two officers, leaps up the wide staircase several steps at a time. On the first landing, they stop and shoot the locks of the door to pieces; the way to the pope's apartments is open. Led by a servant, they stride through the reception rooms and toward the pope's study. Without breaking their speed, Radet and his officers crash into the door of the pope's study and send it splintering off its hinges and flat on the floor. They halt just inside among the splinters and silence with their swords in hand. Sitting at his table, Pius is facing the doorway and Radet.

In his autobiography, Radet will write later: "Finding myself with armed soldiers in front of the revered head of the Church, an oppressive and spontaneous weakness ran through all my limbs. A holy respect filled my whole being. At that moment, my first Communion came to my mind." But still, a good soldier of the emperor, he stretches out his hand, dropping a document on the table in front of the pope.

"Your Holiness will sign this document annulling the excommunication of the emperor."

"We acted only after consulting the Holy Spirit. You may tear us in pieces. We will not retract what we have done." There is silence. Then Pius again: "We cannot. We ought not. We will not."

Radet takes a deep breath: "In that case, I have orders to conduct you far from Rome."

Pius gives no answer. He stands up, takes his prayer book, goes to the door. Radet bows, kisses the Pope's ring. Pius moves out through the outer room, past the broken locks, out to the landing, down the great staircase into the Court of Honor. The detachment presents arms as he steps over the debris of the main doors into the driveway. Already a carriage with four horses is waiting. He gets in along with Cardinal Pacca. The crack of a whip, and they are off.

In the next forty-one days, they will travel up Italy through Florence, Alessandria, Murdoni, and over the Alps to Grenoble in France, then through Avignon, past Nice, until they reach Savona on the Gulf of Genoa giving onto the Mediterranean. And here Pius will remain for two years.

In early June 1811, the emperor's spies learn that the English fleet is going to rescue the pope from Savona and take him to England. So, in the dead of night, on June 19, 1811, at a time when he is very ill and doubled up with stomach cramps, Pius is thrown into a carriage, the door is padlocked, and he is driven posthaste to the chateau of Fontainebleau. Here he remains for another three years.

From the time of his arrival at Fontainebleau, Pius's memories are disjointed, partial, disturbing. And there is a good reason for his condition. He is confined to two rooms in the huge chateau. He is allowed no correspondence; he has no attendants and no court functionaries; he receives no accurate news of the outside world, possesses no funds of his own; he is constantly watched, his laundry and personal belongings constantly searched. His health and spirits decline, and with them his grasp of reality. Pius now actually undergoes a brainwashing at Napoleon's hands—the only successful brainwashing of one world personality by another world personality we know of in the last 800 years.

As the treatment progresses, Pius's memory of any political or diplomatic strength he used to have is slowly dimmed. The blows fall one after another on Pius. He is told—and it is true—that a French ecclesiastical court has declared Napoleon's marriage with the Empress Josephine null and void. He is told—and it is true—that fourteen cardinals (the "Red Cardinals") assisted at Napoleon's second marriage (to Maria Theresa of Austria), and that the thirteen cardinals who refused to attend have been deprived of their cardinalate by Napoleon—that they are now called the "Black Cardinals" (they are forbidden to wear their scarlet robes). The emperor has appointed three archbishops and five bishops on his own initiative. The emperor has called a church council of thirty-five bishops,

239

and all are in favor of allowing the emperor (not the pope) to nominate all future bishops in France, Italy, Austria, and the whole French Empire.

Then the brainwashing technique is varied. One day an emissary of the emperor arrives merely to inform Pius of all the good the emperor is doing. Napoleon is supporting 30,000 chapels, financing seminary studies for 24,000 students. He is publishing a new journal—*The Parish Priests Journal*—in place of all former church publications. He has issued a new catechism for teaching Christian doctrine in schools (first teaching: "Every Christian owes to Napoleon love, respect, obedience, fidelity, and military service"). He has authorized two new feast days (August 15, the Feast of St. Napoleon; December 2, the Feast of the Emperor's Coronation), and three religious orders (Holy Ghost Fathers, Lazarists, Foreign Missions). He has restored the Trappist monks. "As the Emperor once said," concludes the emissary politely, "I will make a present of thirty million Catholics to the Holy Father." Pius's memory is more confused than ever. The emissary kisses his ring before leaving.

Within two weeks of that visit, pressure of another kind is applied. Pius is visited by the fourteen Red Cardinals in all their scarlet glory and pomp. They are very firm. Does His Holiness want the French church impoverished? The emperor will cut off all its revenues unless the pope signs a concordat.

"Charlemagne gave the Pope his temporal power," the Red Cardinals tell Pius now. "The Emperor is Charlemagne's succeesor."

They leave, having asked for Pius's blessing.

Still, the next week, Pius is visited by a group of Napoleon's retinue who assisted at the emperor's coronation ceremony in 1804 in Paris. They rhapsodize over His Holiness's presence at that ceremony. "Without legitimate royalty, there can be no Catholicism in France"—they quote Bishop Nicolai of Bezier to Pius. Ever since Charlemagne, the church has lacked a strong right arm to defend it. This the emperor now offers the pope. And they have a message from the emperor: "For the court of Rome," says the emperor, "I shall always be Charlemagne."

All these vagaries of treatment are crowned by Napoleon's own visit to Pius at Fontainebleau on January 19, 1813. The emperor takes the sick, seventy-one-year-old pope in his arms, kisses his face, and his ring. Pius is so relieved that he embraces and kisses Napoleon. The two men talk. Napoleon's voice rises with army profanity. Those listening outside the pope's door hear the pope's querulous voice. There is a sound of a hand striking flesh, the smack of a slap against the pope's cheek. The shouting goes on, interspersed with cajoling, for five hours. When Napoleon leaves, they find a very shaken and dazed pope sobbing quietly.

Six days later, four of the Red Cardinals return, grim, solemn, refusing to sit down, refusing to kiss Pius's ring. They carry the text of an agreement.

His Holiness must sign it. Otherwise . . . Pius weeps as he reads it. He must renounce forever for himself and for all his successors all temporal power; there will be no more papal states, no army, no police, no finances, no diplomatic corps; the Vatican must be transferred to France; all the mechanics of church government are to be in the hands of Napoleon or his deputies; the pope will have an annual revenue of 2 million francs. If the pope does not sign, the emperor will imprison him for life, appoint his own bishops, secularize all the schools and colleges in France and throughout the empire, and deprive the church of all its property anyway—monasteries, convents, printing presses, abbeys, all—in France, Italy, Austria, and everywhere else the emperor rules. The "terror" of the French Revolution will be reenacted, but this time to the complete obliteration of the church.

Pius looks up at the cardinals' faces. But neither Doria, nor Dugnani, nor Ruffo, nor Bayone give any sign. Not a word of advice. No expression. Passively, they each watch him.

Pius remembers the "terror": 17,000 priests killed, twice that number of nuns, all religious houses closed, apostasies by bishops and priests and lay people. It is too much. All his memories are bitter and painful; all his alternatives are extremes; there is no way out.

"Just in order that we survive," the cardinals hear Pius mutter. They put a pen in his hand and hold his wrist while he signs. They kiss his ring now, and impassively bow themselves out of his presence. It is all over. The brainwashing of this pope has taken Napoleon 4 years, 7 months, and 14 days.

Napoleon practiced—without benefit of prior training—the loathesome art which has been put forward as a peculiarly twentieth-century discovery by the subtly pitiless teams of German, Japanese, Russian, and Chinese keepers throughout their "rehabilitation" centers in Europe and Asia. It is an art that recognizes and then preys on one human fact, namely, a man's weakest point is usually where his most confirmed desires lie. Napoleon knew that Pius's whole life—piety, religious belief, education, personal commitment, eternal hope—all centered on the pope's power as a temporal prince. And the emperor's mailed fist—now in velvet, now bare—struck again and again on this weak spot until it gave way. Pius VII collapsed, in spite of all his preparation as pope, his anticipation as a politician, and his intentions as a prisoner of his greatest enemy. The only saving grace is that, like Hungary's Cardinal Mindzenty in the twentieth century, and unlike Clement VII in the sixteenth century, this Citizen Pope realized what he had done and repented.

Within ten days of the signing, an invitation arrives: "The Emperor awaits the Bishop of Rome in Paris."

On February 13, Pius is taken there. There is a public meeting attended by scores of thousands. Pope and emperor embrace while military trumpets sound out triumphantly and the bells of Notre Dame Cathedral peal joyously. Then, and only then, is Pius allowed a first reunion with his two advisors, Cardinal Consalvi (his secretary of state) and Pacca (general manager of the papal household).

Pius is returned to Fontainebleau with Consalvi and Pacca. As they bid him good night on the evening of their return to his prison, Pius cannot remember why they went to Paris. He keeps referring to "Empress Josephine" and to the British Prince Regent. "He sent me his own portrait as a token of respect," Pius is mumbling as they close his door.

Napoleon publishes the concordat on February 13 of this year.

About February 15, the thirteen Black Cardinals are allowed to visit the pope. He remembers some of their names, but cannot understand why they are not wearing their scarlet robes. These thirteen men with stolidly sad, anguished faces stay with Pius, spending hours every day going over each event in the last twelve years, recalling all that has been done to them and to him, and showing him what his signature on the concordat has done to the church and to his position as pope.

Bit by bit, day by day, Pius emerges from the haze and numbness. Besides, Consalvi tells him, the English will finish off the emperor.

Slowly, Pius remembers his function as supreme pastor, as successor to Peter, as regent of all princes and powers in this world, and as sovereign ruler of the papal states.

He reaches a firm resolution. In a letter of March 12, 1813, he writes to the emperor repudiating the agreement expressed in the concordat. He takes back his concessions, all of them.

But at that moment the emperor could not care less about the bishop of Rome and his scratchy letter. His hands are full with war. When England is humbled and Europe is pacified, he will deal with that "old bag of papal bones in Fontainebleau."

But after one more year's imprisonment for the pope, Napoleon surlily grants Pius permission to return to Rome in May 1814. Now all the pope's memories are of what he had possessed and the power that had been invested in Rome.

Within a year, Napoleon is in exile. The nations of Europe gather in the Congress of Vienna. Here, Consalvi petitions the powers to restore the papal states and to get the French to return all the art and manuscripts they had looted in Rome.

Cardinal Consalvi is a diplomatic genius in all this. Metternich of Austria, Castlereagh of England, all the other kings and diplomats recognize the papacy as part of this world. The powers recognize the value of a solid papacy. And so the Protestant king of Prussia, the Protestant king of England, the Eastern Orthodox czar of Russia, and the Catholic emperor of Austria agree: they return Pope Pius's papal states and all the art treasures stolen by the French. King George III of England spends 200,000 francs of his own monies buying back some of the looted Vatican treasure and sending it on to the pope. Everyone has conspired to reload the church with the burden of temporal power.

Pius now has a healed memory. The patrimony of St. Peter is intact. True, he has to take huge loans from Duke Torlonia and from Napoleon's mother, Madame Letitia, now a renowned and accepted resident in

Rome. The hostess *par excellence* and a financial wizard, she and Napoleon's uncle, Cardinal Fesch, are knee-deep in postwar investment financing. But Pius will build new monuments: the Pinacotheca Gallery, the Chiaramonti Museum (in honor of his family), and the Museum of Inscriptions. A papal army, police, and civil administration are set up again. New and stiffer laws are enacted. Political suspects are put under strict surveillance.

And there is still more to delight the heart of the supreme pastor: agreements and concordats, a whole network of concordats thrown over Western Europe—with Bavaria in 1817, with Russia and with Naples in 1818, with England, with Switzerland, with Austria, with France. Pius generously allows King Louis Philippe to keep as a souvenir the famous porphyry chair he uses at the signing.

And the crowning piece of diplomatic and papal achievement: Consalvi has successfully formed the Holy Alliance. In it, Pius VII can see the beginning of a new hegemony for Rome. Pius reads again and again the important words of that agreement: "Being intimately convinced that the powers must base their advance on the sublime truths taught us by the eternal religion of God and Saviour, we proclaim before the whole world our unshakeable determination to take as the rule of our conduct only the principles of that holy religion, precepts of justice, charity, and peace. We will regard each other henceforward as brothers and compatriots, will remain united by bonds of a loving and indissoluble brotherhood and offer each other on every occasion and in all places, assistance, aid, and succor."

The alliance is the brainchild of a deeply religious Emperor Alexander of all the Russias and of the mystic and mysterious Baroness von Krüdner. The declaration could be signed by Buddhists, Muslims, Jews, even by Rousseau and every French atheist of the eighteenth century. But Pius sees it in a different light—the light of Roman memories and of papal significance. Prince Metternich of Austria is wildly enthusiastic for it. The Bourbon kings are all back on their thrones. The ruling elite must stay together. Of all European powers, only Saxony and England refuse to sign the declaration: Saxony because of local politics; England because of "the balance of power."

244

But Pius is enchanted. He recalls for Consalvi the words used by the sons of King Louis the Pious of Mersen in A.D. 847: "We proclaim the ideal of living in concord and union as wished by the order of God and true brotherhood." Memories! Memories! Holy memories gild Pius's restored situation.

Even in his last months of life, from July 7 to August 3, of 1823, as he lies in severe pain from a broken hip, Pius's memories are fond ones. In his death delirium, "Savona" and "Fontainebleau" are the key words on his lips. They frame his Calvary. After a pontificate of 23 years, 5 months, and 6 days, he has saved the patrimony of St. Peter. And he dies in peace.

This was Pius VII's satisfaction, when perhaps it might better have been his sorrow, because he left the church as he had found it: mired in power politics, chiefly reliant on wealth and prestige, and in association with an establishment of kings and royalty already overripe and about to fall.

The Last Pope-King

On the morning of August 19, 1870, seventy-year-old Pope Pius IX gets up two hours earlier than usual in his Vatican apartments. The sun is barely above the horizon, reddening and gilding the blue of a cloudless sky. His valet throws open the central window. Rome is still asleep. Across the way, Pius can see the papal flag fluttering over the Quirinal Palace. In between and all around, the steady sunlight, silent and peaceful, is creating a pastel of brown, ochre, cream, gray, white, and maroon, as walls, tiles, roofs, marble monuments reflect the new day's smile.

This day and tomorrow are going to be very busy days for him. And he knows exactly what is going to happen. Today and tomorrow, as sovereign pontiff, ruler of the papal states, regent of all princes and powers and governments on earth, he is going to enact a drama of political suicide. In two acts. This Monday will witness the first act.

Pius IX and his chief advisor, Leonardo Cardinal Antonelli, are dominated and directed by that rugged, granite-hard, weather-beaten Roman memory of an authority that has outlived all its enemies. But both Pius and Antonelli realize what is happening: this day will witness the last act of Pius as pope-king. Since the first pope-king, Leo in the fifth century, there have been 210 pope-kings. After more than 1,420 years of successful survival, who better than they could know that their long reign is about to end? Besides, this last of the pope-kings has already played his trump card. The world at large will take at least one hundred years, perhaps two, perhaps more, to understand the significance of that trump. Pius together with 535 bishops from all over the world played that card one year and one month ago, on July 18, 1869.

Before this century, whenever an external and secular power threatened the papacy, popes regularly had recourse to some other secular power as the right arm of their defense—Silvester I in the fourth century, Leo III in the eighth century, Gregory VII in the eleventh century, Clement VII in the sixteenth century. They sought help from this world below. Now, in this supreme hour, in 1869, there was no more help from any secular quarter, no temporal power to turn to. All the major powers and many lesser powers of Pius's day have decided the papacy must go. The authoritative *London Times* has already written its lugubrious obit in which it will shed crocodile tears over "the final passing of this venerable institution." Pius knows this. Antonelli knows it. Everybody knows it.

So Pius and his bishops sought help from above. If the secular world would strip the papacy of its temporal power as a prelude to suppressing it totally, then the papacy would reach for a power the secular world could never touch. The power of the spirit. The power Jesus guaranteed to Peter the Apostle. On that July 18, 1869, the bishops declared that the pope was infallible and that he was the titular head of all and any Christianity that might exist on the face of this earth—what Catholics call the pope's primacy. Infallibility and primacy: the trump card.

Papal infallibility means that a pope, when teaching matters of faith and morals for all the faithful, cannot err and is to be obeyed. Papal primacy means that no other bishop in all Christianity and no gathering of bishops or theologians—much less of layfolk—can supersede or set aside the teaching authority and jurisdiction of a pope.

No one should forget in what frame of mind and with what intention Pius and his bishops chose this particular moment to define papal infallibility and papal primacy. Cardinal Manning of England, leading light at the First Vatican Council, clearly expressed that frame of mind and that intention.

"European powers," Manning wrote, "are dissolving the temporal power of the Vicar of Christ . . . because they are no longer Christian . . . and, in so doing, they are striking out the keystone of the arch which hangs over their own heads. This done, the natural society of the world will still subsist, but the Christian world will be no more."

As to that intention, it was clear. The peace of Europe is broken: never again, it may be, to be restored, till the scourges of war have gone their circuits among the nations. . . . The head of the Church, be he in Rome or in exile, free or in bondage, will be all that the Vatican Council has defined: supreme in jurisdiction, infallible in faith."

Now, on this August morning of 1870, with this irrevocable step taken, Pius and his advisors are ready for what is to follow. After his private Mass and a light breakfast, Pius is at his desk. He puts the finishing touches on a speech, composes a letter to be sent to all governments, reads some documents left for him the previous evening. At 7:30 A.M., Antonelli enters Pius's study, a sheaf of papers, some books, and the morning edition of *Osservatore Romano* in his hand. Tall, bony, distinguished-looking, Cardinal Antonelli has always refused, for personal reasons, to be ordained a priest. He is a lay cardinal. Antonelli gives Pius a summary of all foreign dispatches and telegrams and letters. Minor details such as the death of novelist Charles Dickens, an announcement that Tchaikovsky's *Romeo and Juliet* would have a first Roman playing in the coming September—these Pius puts aside.

It is the war between Prussia and France which occupies him. The German armies are besieging Metz and Chalons. The French armies are falling back everywhere. It looks like a Prussian victory before the end of the year. All French troops are leaving Rome today. Finally, the latest figures on foreign investments, the condition of Rome's municipal financing, and of food supplies in the city are discussed. Pius and Antonelli pore over the latest messages from Bleichröder. Bleichröder, Bismarck's financial advisor, takes care of Vatican investments in one sector. Then the two men turn to the day's program.

"How many men have we?" Pius asks.

"Barely four thousand. Badly led. Badly armed," is Antonelli's answer, and he adds: "General Kanzler is a pessimist."

One dispatch informs them that General Raffaele Cadorna, commander of the Italian national army, is advancing on Rome with 60,000 troops. One day's march from Rome's walls! They are going to attack within thirty-six hours.

"Tell Kanzler to make only a show of resistance. One breach of the walls, and we surrender." These are Pius's instructions.

Antonelli reads a last series of dispatches from Austria, Russia, Spain, Portugal, England—reactions to what he had told the assembled diplomatic corps in Rome two days ago, namely that their governments had an obligation "to cooperate by their intervention to reestablish his Holiness in his See and in the capital of his dominions guaranteed by all the treaties which form the basis of European public law." Now, all the answering dispatches are negative: no help, no intervention. Pius is alone.

Antonelli pauses, then cautiously: "Should we not read the king's letter again?" A shadow crosses Pius's face as he remembers. In late July, King Victor Emmanuel of the new, utterly new Italian republic, sent Count Ponza di San Martino to Pius with that letter. "Acquiesce in the occupation of Rome. Your Holiness," the letter said. "Italians are one now, are a nation. Rome is their capital." The letter went on to describe the conditions. A *quid pro quo*: Pius and his successors would be confirmed as owners of the Vatican, of the surrounding buildings and streets. The pope's summer residence at Castel Gandolfo, and a narrow strip of land running down to the Adriatic Sea would be theirs. The pope would receive cash indemnity for the loss of land and property and an annual income of not less than 2 million lire. Pius remembers the letter well and bitterly. "A beggar's remnant" . . . "salaried servant of the state" . . . "make the Pope a penurious *campesino* (dirt-farmer)" . . . "our dignity and sovereignty" . . . "never" . . . "never". . . . He again mutters all the phrases with which he assaulted Count Ponza. Then to Antonelli: "No! No!" He does not need to read the letter again.

"*Ebbene, Santità* (Antonelli's favorite way of ending an unpleasant interlude), please glance at the translation of Karl Marx."

Pius stares a moment, then puts his hand on one of the books Antonelli had brought him. They had been over this ground before. Secretly, Pius
250

felt Antonelli may have been right all along. One day in 1848, Antonelli had come to him with a document just published: *The Communist Manifesto*, composed by this Karl Marx and a fellow-German, Friedrich Engels.

"I fear, Your Holiness," Antonelli had said, "I fear this is what is going to happen. The old order, our order of things is finished. It may take one year. It may take one hundred, two hundred. But I fear it is ended. All of it."

Pius now looks at the cover of *Das Kapital*. It is only Volume One. "Let's wait until the second one appears. Then we can make a proper assessment of the whole thing." Pius turns away and begins writing.

At 11 A.M., Pope Pius is escorted to the Basilica of St. John Lateran. He gets out of his carriage, kneels for a few moments at the bottom of the Scala Sancta, a staircase of twenty-four steps. Christians believe that these were the original steps up which Jesus climbed, all bloodied from his scourging, to be judged by Pontius Pilate. They had been brought to Rome in the fourth century.

Pius then commences to climb the staircase in the traditional way of a penitent—on his knees, knee by knee, step by step. At the top, after a few more moments of prayer in the basilica, he is helped down to his carriage and returns to the Vatican. The crowds are sullen. There are few cheers.

Time was in his first year as pope, in 1846, that the crowds in Rome used to unharness the horses and themselves draw his carriage in joy and triumph through the streets. And he had played up to them: demolished the ghetto, expelled the Jesuits, granted a general amnesty, allowed the people to publish a newspaper, permitted the first railway in the papal states, allowed the mob's popular orator and leader, Angelo Brunetti (whom the Romans wittily nicknamed *Ciceruacchio* because when he opened his mouth to speak you thought Cicero was about to speak divinely but he sounded just like a quacking duck), to harangue him in the Trastevere district: and he even proclaimed a civil constitution. *The Fundamental Statute.* But all to no purpose. They hate him now. They want to belong to the newly born Italian nation. He, the pope who owns them and Rome, has refused to cede. Hence their hate. Hence Cadorna's army advancing on Rome to liberate it. The hate is on all the faces on either side of his carriage as he proceeds home.

Beneath the Quirinal Palace is the last painful stop before entering the Vatican courtyard. A small cluster of Italians block the way. No weapons, of course. No tricolor flags. No violence. Just silence. Those sullen reproachful faces. Each man's hand is raised and pointing to the Quirinal steps. And in a flash their message is clear to Pius and Antonelli: "There," they are saying silently and significantly, in their dreadful mime, "there, as Rossi went, so you too." The silence is deafening.

Rossi was the last of the pope's prime ministers, the only successful one after the failures of Bofondi, Antonelli, Ciocchi, Monriani, Gallietti. Pius can recall how Rossi went: Rossi the aristocrat with nerves of granite stepping out the main doors of the palace, casting one sharp experienced eye down those steps at the knot of surly young men leaning nonchalantly on their canes, each left hand inside each frock coat holding something, all the eyes staring expressionlessly. Then, shoulders squared, head up, hat in hand, Rossi stepping down dignifiedly, his lips moving in death-prayers taught him by his mother fifty-three years before. Halfway down, a sudden halt. A young man leans forward; as quick and sure as the fangs of a serpent, the stiletto severs the carotid artery in Rossi's neck. Rossi falling, tumbling, falling, leaving little pools of red blood, glistening living blood. And, then, for the first time that low roar, the soul of the mob as a beast, growling and threatening with one animal beat. Pius had seen it all from the windows of his study above.

They drive his carriage past those steps at breakneck speed back to the Vatican. Pius remains closeted, receives Antonelli's reports on the approaching army, prays, composes letters of protest, paces to and fro, finally goes to bed.

Act 2 of this last drama of the last pope-king opens one month later on September 19. At 7 P.M., Antonelli comes with two members of Pius's court and Marcantonio Pacelli, the undersecretary of state. "Holy Father, we think you should leave the city. We cannot guarantee your safety. We must leave immediately. One hour more and all exits are blocked."

"No!" Pius fairly shouts the word. "You both know what happened the last time. We very nearly never got back here again!"

On November 24, 1843, that year of revolutions, the mob had taken over in Rome. Pius remembers how, a week after Rossi's assassination, he put off his papal clothes, donned the garb of a stableman, and fled with Marcantonio Pacelli and Cardinal Antonelli by night in the open carriage of the Bavarian minister, Count de Spaur and his countess, all the way to Naples, staying at Gaeta for nine months, then Pontici for a few more months, while the Romans established a republic, declared him deposed, desecrated the churches, killed priests and nuns, and he, Pius, futilely launched excommunications, petitioned France, Austria, Spain, and Sicily for help to repossess his domains; finally to be humiliatingly restored to Rome on April 12, 1850. A French army took Rome and sent Garibaldi scurrying to the mountains, and Mazzini yelping into Switzerland.

"No," Pius says again, this time more quietly. They all retire for the night. Before they are asleep, the Italian army is camped around the walls of Rome. Escape is now impossible.

On the morrow, the 20th, at 5:30 A.M., the Italian cannons send a first hail of destruction at the walls of Rome. Kanzler's troops respond with a weak volley—a token resistance. The Italian cannons speak again and again and again. Pius says a special Mass at eight o-clock for the diplomatic corps and preaches a sermon holding "the King (Victor Emmanuel) and the Republican Government and ultimately the Great Powers of Europe responsible for this unworthy and sacriligious spoliation of the patrimony of St. Peter. "As for us," Pius concludes, "we will be a prisoner in St. Peter's until this desecration is over."

At 10 A.M., back in the Vatican, behind barred doors and gates, Pius gets the news: the Italians have breached the Aurelian wall at the Porta Pia; they are pouring into Rome. "It is finished," Pius says, crossing himself. He orders the white flag to be hoisted on the cupola of St. Peter's Basilica. There is a sudden silence as no cannon speaks anymore. Then, imperceptibly at first, but growing more audible, Pius and Antonelli and Marcantonio Pacelli standing on the central balcony of St. Peter's hear that five-syllable cry growing rhythmically as the repeated beats on the syllables grow nearer. "*Roma o Morte!* (Rome or Death) *Roma o Morte!*" Garibaldi's war-cry repeated by thousands of throats. Within minutes, they see the first ranks of the invaders running and shouting and waving the Italian tricolor. The three men retire within St. Peter's.

They spend the next ten days just waiting. On all sides, the armies of the republic have them hemmed in. "Antonelli, what do we do?" is Pius's repeated question. "We wait, Holiness. We wait. We both have made our last confession. We wait." Then another repeated question: "Antonelli, where did we act wrongly?" Antonelli wants to explain that this is only the beginning of some profound ending in the old order of things: but he unfortunately mentions Pius's former popularity with the mobs. And this sets Pius off in a regretful reverie. What did all that give him? he wants to know. He always had bad advisors. The very cardinals who elected him pope wanted him to be liberal. So he was. And look what has happened!

"Remember, Holiness," Antonelli breaks in, "long before you became Pope, the damage was done."

Pius was not yet a cardinal on the death of Pius VI. But he remembers the three popes after Pius VII (Leo XII, Pius VIII, and Gregory XVI); they had done the damage. The legacy of Pius VII was a terrible one: oppression, surveillance, a dictatorship. Between 1823 (death of Pius VII) and 1846 (when Pius IX was elected), almost 200,000 citizens of the papal states were severely punished (death, life imprisonment, exile, galleys) for political offences; another 1.5 million were subject to constant police surveillance and harassment.

There was a gallows permanently in the square of every town and city and village. Railways, meetings of more than three people, and all newspapers were forbidden. All books were censored. A special tribunal sat permanently in each place to try, condemn, and execute the accused. All trials were conducted in Latin. Ninety-nine percent of the accused did not understand the accusations against them. Every pope tore up the stream of petitions that came constantly asking for justice, for the franchise, for reform of the police and prison system. When revolts occurred in Bologna, in the Romagna, and elsewhere, they were put down with wholesale executions, sentences to lifelong hard labor in the state penitentiary, to exile, to torture. Austrian troops were always being called in to suppress the revolts. Secret societies abounded. Assassinations, robberies, crime in general increased.

Pope Leo XII kept cats, about three-score cats, as his pets and rebuilt St. Paul's Church with 60,000 francs from King Charles of France. He also forbade the selling of wine and any woman's dress that went above the ankles. He restored the Inquisition and its torture chambers, hated France and all Frenchmen. Pope Pius VIII was pope for twenty months, suffered from violent torticollis, took long placid walks with members of the diplomatic corps, and literally dropped dead on hearing that Charles X of France had died. Pope Gregory XVI published one book, *Triumph of the Church Against the Assaults of Innovators*, took two extended tours through the papal states, each costing 400,000 gold crowns, was a renowned epicurean, created the Egyptian and Etruscan museums in the Vatican, put down a revolution in Rome by wholesale butchery of the rebels, and died suddenly and unaccountably in 1846. Pius IX remembers that he got a full account of it all from Marcantonio Pacelli, who had been head of Gregory XVI's finance department.

"Where did we go wrong, Antonelli?" Pius asks again and again, as he goes over all this. "Give them what they ask, and the papacy is ruined. Refuse it, and they will ruin us. What to do?" Neither today nor on the succeeding days have they any real answer.

Then on October 2, the victors held a plebiscite: Did the inhabitants of the papal states want to join the Italian republic? There are 46,785 yeas to 47 nays in Rome alone; and, in the whole papal states, there are 132,681 yeas to 1,505 nays. When Pius gets the news, he breaks down.

Eight months later, the Italian parliament passes the Law of Guarantees: the pope is an independent sovereign, the parliament acknowledges; he has personal inviolability and immunity, and liberty to come and go, to hold conclaves, councils, consistories, as he wills. He owns the Vatican, the Lateran, the papal offices, and Castel Gandolfo. He will have an annual revenue of 3,225,000 lire.

Pius tore up the copy of the law saying: "We will be a prisoner." He keeps repeating it for years to all and sundry, to Antonelli, to public audiences, to foreign powers, to visiting ambassadors, to the Lord at Mass, to himself in bed at night. He remains shut up in the Vatican. He relies on Pacelli and Antonelli exclusively. Pacelli fulminates about Pius's imprisonment on the editorial page of every edition of the *Osser-*

vatore Romano which he, Pacelli, founded in 1861. It is Pius's only way to speak to the world.

In 1876, Antonelli falls sick and is dying. Pius IX comes to give him the last rites.

"When, Holiness," asks Antonelli, "when did Your Holiness first know that the Holy See was in trouble?"

"After Pius VIII became Pope," is Pius's answer.

How? Simple: from the diplomatic corps, from the type of useless careerists who replaced the energetic and formidable envoys of previous times. Pius IX has the dying Antonelli even chuckling gently as he runs over the principal envoys to the Holy See in 1829: the bearded Prussian, Baron de Bunsen, dabbling in scientific research and nearly killing himself: the Russian Prince Gagarin perpetually talking of his conquests among the ladies of Rome; the gloomy Spanish misanthrope, Marquis de Salvador, solemn, taciturn, taking long walks by himself, always discoursing with the ghosts of Ferdinand and Isabella about their conquests of the Moors in Spain in the thirteenth century, the Neapolitan Fuscaldo, swarthy and suspicious and tortured by a perpetual fear of being assassinated by some secret society; the Portuguese Funchal, as ugly as a chimpanzee ("as ugly as Cavour," Pius quips; Cavour was prime minister of the new Italian republic, nearsighted, stout, balding, low-sized, with a commonplace appearance), lost in his music day and night. And so on down the line of the diplomats.

"When they sent such idiots, we knew we no longer had any value or dignity for them," Pius conludes.

Only one event before his own death gives Pius IX a moment of enthusiasm. On January 9, 1878, the first king of Italy, Pius's archenemy, King Victor Emmanuel, dies in the Quirinal Palace. And Emmanuel's minister, Crispi, who had vowed an implacable hatred for Pius and the papacy, had to read the official announcement: "His Highness, King Victor Emmanuel, died today fortified by the Sacraments of the Church." The king had asked for a priest before he died. "They have to come back. They have to ask for forgiveness," Pius remarks, as he is reminded of all the other times in history when rebellious Christians had to return. His Roman memory has not given an inch. He still hopes he can recover Rome and the papal states.

But it is not to be. Three weeks after King Victor, the eighty-six-year-old Pius IX, who has been sickening over two months, dies. He receives Filippo Pacelli, son of Marcantonio, for the last time, asks him how things are going at the Consistorial College of which Filippo is dean, and asks how Filippo's two-year-old son, Eugenio, is doing. "He will serve the Holy See well, Filippo. Teach him well," are Pius's parting words.

Just before he dies, Pius says simply: "Let us go into the house of the Lord." It is February 7, and thirty-one years since they made him pope. Over on the Via degli Orsini, the little Eugenio Pacelli notices the tears in his father's eyes and asks: "Why are you sad, Papa? Isn't the Pope gone home to Heaven?"

The real pathos and enduring tragedy of this last of the pope-kings was not his final loss of political power and territory. Rather it was the legacy of bitterness he left in the papacy and the church. He left the whole church repeating, "We've been robbed," for over sixty years.

After Pius IX died, three more popes remained '-prisoner" in the Vatican. In 1928, the up-and-coming dictator of Italy, Benito Mussolini, decided for the sake of national unity that the "Vatican question-' should be solved amicably. After protracted negotiations, in 1929, Mussolini's government and the Vatican of Pope Pius XI signed the Lateran Pacts, thus ending the sixty-year-old official enmity between the Vatican and Italy. Young Eugenio Pacelli, now an archbishop and the highest ranking diplomat in the Vatican, was deeply involved in the process. Mussolini could point to the pacts as proof that he was as Catholic as the pope (this was meant as much for foreign consumption in Spain, France, Germany, and the U.S.A., as for the Italians). The Vatican could now move more freely in the Italian political arena: and immediately it would launch into a new career in the world of international finance.

The Vatican was guaranteed sovereign territorial integrity within the Vatican state, an area equal in size to a substantial golf course and englobing St. Peter's Basilica and Square, the Apostolic Palace with its famed gardens, and other adjoining buildings. Included in that sovereign integrity were extraterritorial possessions—about fifty of them, such as the papal summer villa at Castel Gandolfo, a mountain on which stands

257

the antennae of Radio Vatican, institutes in the city of Rome and elsewhere. Indemnities of over 90 million were paid for the material losses incurred by the Vatican because of the nationalist takeover in 1870.

The successor of the popes today lives in the Apostolic Palace flanking St. Peter's Square, with its 10,000 halls, suites, rooms, and passages, its 12,532 windows, its 997 flights of stairs. Within his city-state, he has thirty squares and streets, two churches, one parish, a railroad station, four post offices, a court of law, two jails, his own coinage and postage stamps, and at least four newspapers and periodicals. The normal population of his state is about 2,000, the vast majority being clergymen. He has a tiny army, the Swiss Guards, and his own police and security forces who work in close collaboration with Italian police and state security. The official colors of his state are white and yellow, the national anthem a piece composed by Gounod. Vatican automobiles carry license plates marked with SCV (State of Vatican City). Within his city-state, the pope has all the offices of his administration, religious, financial, political, diplomatic. And from here he governs the religious life of over 740 million adherents. Over on the Quirinal Hill is the seat of the Italian government with which the Vatican maintains diplomatic relations, as it does with over 110 other sovereign nations.

This then is the visible worldly status of the Roman pope, after all the vicissitudes of greatness and misery, of holiness and unworthiness, of empire and of poverty, over a period of nearly two millennia.

Between the death of Pius IX and our day there have been nine popes. Two of these stand out. Eugenio Pacelli as Pius XII (1939–1958) was the last of the great Roman popes. He was succeeded by Angelo Roncalli as John XXIII (1958–1963), "Good Pope John," as his contemporaries knew him. The surprising aspect of Pope John is that in a short five-year period he undid what every pope since the fourth century had sought and fought to maintain and foment. John's successor, Pope Paul VI, merely completed Pope John's destruction of the old church. And the present pope, John Paul II, is left with a shattered institution waiting at the crossroads of history with only the gravest of doubts and the deepest of problems as his constant companions.

The Last Great Roman

Eugenio Pacelli's bedroom has two windows overlooking St. Peter's Square. Other than the brass bedstead, there is little else in the room: a plain rug, a chest of drawers, a mirror, a mahogany desk, a painting of the Virgin on the wall, white window curtains. The bedroom leads onto a small dining room where there is a carved walnut table with some chairs, two closets, white curtains, a statue of Jesus, a cruciix. For the past twenty years, most of Pacelli's life has been spent between these two rooms, his private study, the audience hall, his private chapel, and St. Peter's Basilica.

Now he is lying in bed, exhausted, but sleepless as yet. His housekeeper, Sister Pasqualina, puts away Pacelli's robes, makes sure the bell-button is near the pope's hand, and goes to close the curtains. "Leave them as they are, tonight, Sister," Pacelli tells her. Outside in the dining room his doctors are holding a consultation in hushed voices with Pacelli's officials. Their conclusion: Pope Pius XII, 261st successor to St. Peter, is dying.

It is December 1, 1954, and the doctors are medically sure that Pacelli will not spend the coming Christmas on earth. Pius has outreached his strength. He has always said: "A pope must work until he dies," but it is not work that has laid Pacelli low. Some other strain is breaking down his resistance. Pacelli's secretary and Cardinal Maglione, Pacelli's chief executive, exchange rueful nods. The dying time of a pope is crammed with important preparations for the next pope. They both know what they have to do. The last to leave is the secretary. A glance at the bedroom door, a swift jab of memory (Pacelli's parting remark a few moments ago: "After tonight, all will be clear"), and he too retires.

Inside the bedroom, Pacelli is waiting. He is not even trying to sleep. Occasional sounds of distant traffic from outside St. Peter's Square reach his ears. Among themselves, the doctors agree on one thing: physically, the pope is in rapid decline; death should be in a couple of days. Pacelli feels that they are right. But that is not enough. He has to *know*, as he has always known. He looks quietly out through the parted curtains at the starry night. All the past autumn he has watched the shortening daylight hours and the darkness of every dusk deepening more quickly and earlier—he has seen it as an image of the quickening pace of his own mortal decay. That's what he said to himself again and again all this autumn. Not morbidly or avidly or sadly. Nor with resignation. Rather as an anticipated homecoming from voluntary exile in service to a beloved master.

But tonight he would like to know for sure, as he has always been sure in the past in moments of mortal crisis—the two or three occasions in Munich, Rome, and elsewhere when death brushed his cheek. On those occasions, Pacelli has reported, he felt everything around him become transparent and the light of Jesus shine through, reassuring him that it was not yet finished, that he had to go on.

The first time was thirty-five years before, in April 1919, in Munich, when German Communists had proclaimed the short-lived Bavarian Socialist Republic as part of greater Soviet Germany, when all government buildings in the city were in German Soviet hands, and when the streets of the city were governed by the party's bully-boys.

Pacelli, then archbishop and papal nuncio, came home one evening to find that the front of his residence in Briennerstrasse had been sprayed with machine-gun fire. He telephoned his protest to the German Communist high command and was told curtly: "Leave the city tonight or you will die." Already, six prominent citizens had been assassinated. It was no idle threat.

The next day, at 5 P.M., they came for him, seven of them, with daggers, revolvers, rifles, bandoliers, and red armbands adorned with the hammer and sickle.

"Open in the name of the people!" they screamed, then broke down the door and rushed up the stairs to his second floor study. They found Pacelli standing at his desk, wearing his full robes and fingering the crucifix around his neck. He just looked at them. Already he knew: not this time.

"Why have you come here armed? This is a house of peace, not a den of murderers." The men stopped in their tracks. "This is not German territory but the property of the Holy See."

The leader of the group started to bluster. "Give us the food and money hoarded in this building or we will kill you." But Pacelli does not feel threatened by the muzzles of the rifles, the heavy jackboots, the hard faces. They were not the masters of the situation.

"Under international law, this house is inviolate. I demand you leave at once."

They left. But it was the same sort of thing ten days later. A mob of a few hundred was waiting for his car as it swung onto the main thoroughfare.

"Get out!" they screamed engulfing his car. "Get out, so we can kill you here in public!"

Pacelli stood up in the open car and looked. Again, the weapons pointed at him, the blazing faces, and the screams—all lost any substance. Again, Pacelli knew.

"I, too, have a weapon I always carry with me, my friends. This"—he held up the crucifix. "Nor am I an ordinary man. I represent the Vicar of Christ here in your Germany." He had presence, all right, this Pacelli.

Pacelli still remembers the stillness, the lowered weapons, the whispered confusion as he publicly blessed them all. The crowd melted, opening a way for his car; and he passed on in the strange silence that followed his words.

That day, he had been hurt and held by only one thing: the stabbing, impotent hate in the eyes of the mob's commissar, a stocky German who stood apart, watching the entire proceeding. Something more than hatred for his function as papal nuncio, Pacelli felt. Something more personal, as

261

if they knew each other, as if they were ancient enemies. But on the essential point, he knew on each occasion: I am not to die here. Even when a grenade shattered his study window the next day and showered glass on his desk and person. Even when the independent socialist party received 4,896,095 votes and eighty-one seats in the Reichstag in June 1920, and Pacelli was again in danger, he knew no ultimate harm would come to him.

It was the same in Rome of 1943, when the Allied bombs fell. With tears in his eyes, Pacelli watched and saw the smoke billowing up. Then he rushed off in his car carrying bandages, food, and 2 million lire. That evening, when he had finished walking among the injured, the dying, and the dead, his white cassock was bloodstained.

And on August 13 of the same year, when bombs fell near the Basilica of St. John Lateran; again on November 4 when four fragmentation bombs fell on Vatican City; and, again, on March 1 of 1944 when one bomb fell in the courtyard of San Damaso some yards away from Pacelli's apartments. Always he knew. The gutted buildings, the bomb craters, the rubble, the broken bodies, the cries of the wounded, the angry drone of the planes, the explosions. Many died, but somehow Pacelli knew that none of it was ever a solid threat to him.

But, this evening in bed, there is a strange quiet in him and around him. He does not understand.

A gentle sound distracts him. Sister Pasqualina stands in the doorway. "Your Holiness rang?" Yes, he must have rung. He wanted to, anyway.

"Call Father Bea." And while he waits for the Jesuit, his former confessor and perpetual confidant, Pacelli goes over the little details again and again. Bea knows so much, knows also what has overshadowed Pacelli's waking hours for over thirty years: the Soviet threat. Not just Soviet Russia. But sovietization, the possibility of a Western European Soviet. Not an armed Soviet takeover, but a slow peaceful corrosion of the Christian West by Marxism. A diplomatic Marxism. An unthreatening Marxism. A Marxism posing as fellow-sufferer with Christianity.

In the darkness of his night-thoughts, Pacelli could still see the eyes of that Munich commissar staring at him like a very old enemy, saying: "We *do* know each other, don't we? We *always* have."

Bea never hurries, either in walking or talking or thinking or feeling. Never ceases to present an urbane face, wrinkleless forehead (except when he laughs), eyes seeing all but never staring and never furtive. Bea is invaluable to Pacelli as a reflective mirror and as intellect. He could understand Pacelli's support of the Marshall Plan and of NATO, could help him with a prohibition for Catholics against joining the Communist Party; and when Pacelli became deeply saddened about Catholic Lithuanians, Belorussians, Volga Germans, Ukrainians, Armenians, Hungarians, Slovaks, Croats, Germans—all swallowed up in the Soviet Empire—Bea could console him.

They greet each other now with looks and smiles. Pacelli begins. Does Father John Baptist Janssens, Jesuit general, realize that his French and Belgian theologians are flirting with Marxism? Yes, he does, Bea answers. Yes. And Janssens wants to heal them with the love of Christ, not cut them off. And Torres, Father Torres, the Chilean Jesuit? Torres had come to Rome from Chile some six years before, had talked with Pacelli and Janssens, had got their blessing for a "new social order."

"They will try and kill you, Father," Pacelli had warned him bluntly— "but only if you refuse to compromise with the devil of Marxism."

Torres's response was laconic: "We have, all of us, for so long compromised with Satan himself, Holy Father," and left the sentence unfinished.

"We expect you, as a son of Ignatius Loyola, to be faithful to Peter," Janssens had said to Torres.

Pacelli the aristocrat had never liked Janssens, a plebeian, blamed him for not controlling the northern European Jesuit theologians. Once, in a fit of sputtering rage, Pacelli reportedly had quoted to his private secretary what King Herod said in the Bible to his private executioner: "Give me the head of John Baptist [Janssens] on a dish!"

In any event, Torres had gone back and was now said to be with the guerrillias—a Christian Marxist, the fatal compromise.

No, Bea answers. No more news of Torres.

263

Pacelli stirs uneasily. If Jesus takes him home now, he asks Bea, has he done all he could to avoid that fatal compromise throughout the church? Could there be more like Torres? Has he been wrong in his assessment of Marxism, not just Russian Marxism?

"Yes," Bea answers to the first two questions. "No" to the third.

Pacelli now wants to tell Bea something he has never really spoken about to anyone. Each month he spent as nuncio in the old nunciature in the Briennerstrasse in Munich from 1919 to 1925, Pacelli had gathered information about Marxism and about Marx. Everything he learned stirred some deep fear in him. By the end of his stay in Munich, he knew the life of Marx backward, had visited his birthplace in Trier, and the University of Bonn, where Marx studied for one year (1835–36). He had even talked with surviving relatives of Marx and of Jerry von Westphalen, Marx's wife.

Things became still clearer for Pacelli when he was posted to Berlin in 1925. His official mission: negotiate a concordat with Prussia. It took Pacelli four years to bring it to fruition; even then it was only initialed, never signed. He could have got it sooner. He did not want to do so. On the horizon of Germany, he could see two specters: sovietization and National Socialism. One was going to take over Germany.

His procrastination was not so much the self-serving action of an aspiring diplomat rounding off a mission. Pacelli was far too sure of his future to indulge in such petty personal plays. Rather, the decision was the result of his personal mission in Berlin: to find out about Marx and his Marxism, and to gauge who would win: Marx or Hitler. Pacelli read a Hitler victory and a defeat for German Soviets. In spite of Communist political victories (they polled one million votes in Berlin alone just before Hitler came to power), Pacelli foresaw correctly. But he also saw the struggle with Marxism going far beyond that one election. During his Berlin stay, he read the records of Marx's studies at Berlin University, visited Marx's lodging house at No. 1 Old Leipzigerstrasse, even went out to the suburb of Stralau where Marx had joined the famous *Doktor-Klub*.

"I found," Pacelli recounts to Bea, "that, as of that year, Marx's nineteenth, the year he became a member of the *Klub* and began meeting with

264

the *Young Hegelians*—Bruno Bauer, Karl Friedrich Koppen, Theodor Echetenmeyer, David Strauss, Arnold Ruge—and the Young Germany group—Heine, Boerne, and others—a profound change came over him."

For instance, in his first youthful composition called *The Union of the Faithful with Christ*, Marx had written that "through the love of Christ, we turn our hearts to our brethren for whom He gave Himself as sacrifice." And this kind of theme runs through all his early writing. Then suddenly all that changes. His poems are now to Oulanem, one favorite name used in Black Masses and Satanic hymns to denote the Devil. Marx's poems suddenly show a delight in the destruction of men and women. He repeats over and over again the words of Mephistopheles in Goethe's *Faust*, "Everything in existence is worth being destroyed." He writes words and sentences that are intelligible only on the lips of a dedicated and consecrated Satanist.

A couplet from Marx's poem *Oulanem* fascinated Pacelli for weeks: "Till I go mad and my heart is utterly changed/See this sword, the Prince of Darkness sold it to me."

Before he left for Rome in 1929, Pacelli pursued his search even into police records. Yes, there were reports, unconfirmed, of occult ceremonies by members of the *Doktor-Klub*. Long before his departure, Pacelli had become convinced that behind Marxism and its Soviet version there was a modern Stanism. In forty out of forty-four addresses as papal nuncio, Pacelli inveighed against Antichrist and warned of a gigantic struggle about to begin between Satan and Jesus for the soul of Europe and the souls of all men.

Bea nods. This is old hat for him. He has seen the materials Pacelli is talking about. He also knows that Bakunin and Proudhon, both erstwhile friends of Marx, were self-confessed Satanists. "I never forget, Holiness," he says, "that Generalissimo Stalin's first chosen pseudonym was *demonoshile* (the demoniacal)".

"Have we done all we could?" Pacelli asks again.

Bea knows what is bothering the pope. In 1941–42, under pressure from U.S. President Roosevelt among others, Pacelli had collaborated in soothing religious objections to the Western alliance with Soviet Russia against Hitler. He had yielded to the argument that Hitler was the greater of two evils.

But what if he had chosen neither? Now Pacelli is afraid that he had thereby helped Marxism in taking over Europe and the whole world. Bea consoles him. Who could have known that the Anglo-Saxons would let the Russians go that far?

"We should have known," Pacelli keeps saying. "We should have known. Our Lady told us all at Fatima."

He is referring to a Roman Catholic belief that the Virgin herself appeared to three children near the village of Fatima in Portugal during the year 1917, and that her appearance was certified by the miraculous reversal of the sun in the sky, as attested by many witnesses, Catholic and non-Catholic. The children said that the Virgin had told them three secrets, to be told only to the pope. In 1951, Pacelli received all three secrets, and immediately found that he no longer could operate on his old guiding principle in diplomacy and geopolitics. He used to maintain that the church needed political power and even the protection of a military alliance. Now he knows that was an illusion. A strong Europe was a dead myth. The Anglo-Saxons had let Soviet Marxism get away with it. The future was a gray-black threat.

Pacelli was shattered. His guiding vision of Europe and the world had been incorrect, according to the Fatima secrets. There was, it appeared, very little danger of generalized war in the near future. The danger really was the fatal compromise: the acceptance of Marxism, the penetration of Marxism into European culture, thought, politics, and economics. Nothing he did, it now seemed to him, nothing he can recall now looks like an adequate response. He had consecrated the Russian people to the Virgin in 1952. In the year 1950 he honored her by proclaiming her special privilege: that she has been in Heaven body and soul since the moment of her death. He has written a letter to all Christians about Our Lady of Fatima, and in November he started a basilica in her honor at Fatima.

Has he, however, toyed with generalities and diplomatic niceties for too long? We should have known, he keeps repeating to Bea, if not in 1948 when a massive persecution of Catholics started throughout Stalin's prison-camp empire, then at least in 1952 when the Americans had not driven home their advantage in Korea and when the moles planted by the Soviet within the upper echelons of the Vatican were rooted out.

Bea is tired and disheartened, but he reminds Pacelli of the reassurances that the pope himself has reported occurring to him—the vision in the Vatican Gardens for instance, when the pope says he saw a replica of the very vision the Portuguese children had seen in October 1917 at Fatima: the orb of the sun rolling from west to east, from zenith to horizon; and then the pope said he had seen the Virgin with St. Joseph and with her son, Jesus, consoling, enlightening, encouraging.

"We saw it," Pacelli answers. "And we saw her, Our Lady."

Bea rises. He notices the weariness in Pacelli's eyes. "Holiness, she will obtain her son's protection. Your Holiness has fought the good fight."

Bea kisses Pacelli's ring and bows his way out. Outside the room, he turns to Pasqualina: "Call me, Sister. Call me, if things get worse."

They both look back: Pacelli's eyes are closed. He is breathing regularly. Sister Pasqualina says, characteristically: "Men always bother about the future. The Lord will protect His Holiness. The Church still needs him. And you, Father, go home to bed."

About five minutes after they leave, Pacelli is still awake, his mind drifting over the past, but drifting toward sleep as well when he hears a sound. Instinctively, he says "*Avanti!* (Come in!)" as he always does to visitors. Then, without surprising him or puzzling him, but as if it has been sounding in his ears already, a voice he knows says gently: "There will be a vision." After a pause, again: "There will be a vision." Now he can sleep.

He awakens at about 6:15 A.M. on December 2, 1954. It is still dark. The sky is still cloudless and starry. Pacelli lies there remembering the voice of the previous night as he fell asleep: "There will be a vision."

He still feels his doubts, but peace is now his. He hears an early monastery bell tolling over on the Janiculum, calling to prayer. When is he going to die? Is it now? Is it today? He starts to recite slowly the old prayer of St. Ignatius Loyola, the *Anima Cristi*. "Soul of Christ, Sanctify me! . . . Body of Christ, Save me!" savoring each word and thought.

But he does not finish the prayer. As he recalls it later for Bea, he had

267

the sensation that the walls, the ceiling, the furniture, even the bed he is lying on are all flooded with a light that does not dazzle or frighten or surprise, does not merely surround him but rather engulfs him, volatilizing the resistant face of things, the colors, the opaque depth of all material things in the room, animating all with a pure white translucence everebbing around him and through him and flowing away upon space too infinite for four walls and too profound for ceiling or floor or street or city or the very earth itself.

Now, like pain forgotten, remembering is no more for Pacelli. And all anticipation of the future as a looming unknown has come to a gentle standstill. The very present, like a clock that has ceased ticking, no longer has passing seconds. All Pacelli's world is the presence of his Lord and master, the utter serenity of infinitely secure and boundless power governing all, holding all, in all love, all tenderness. He is in that state of rapture Paul of Tarsus described as a moment in the Seventh Heaven, and John of the Cross celebrated as the only ecstasy our being could be satisfied with, when all tears are dried by God's hand and all the painful fragments of life are made whole again.

It was encouragement. "My faithful servant: Eugenio." It was endorsement: "My vicar, my representative." It was confirmation: "My strength is yours." It was counsel: "Believe in me above all and always . . . no fear. Ever." It was reassurance about those faces that had always haunted Pacelli, all the faces of those he might have saved, but did not.

Now they ceased to be haunting. They were made whole from the sufferings which he had not been able to spare them or had failed to spare them: now smiling eyes in the once bloodstained eyeless sockets of that simple priest whom Pope Pius XI had sent to him, Pacelli, in Munich to be consecrated bishop secretly and then sent into Soviet Russia where Stalin's secret police had caught him and tortured him; the now smiling and living children who had been eviscerated by the bombs at San Lorenzo; the Spaniard, Jose Antonio Primo de Rivera, his friend, whole and healed from the dumdum bullets pumped into his body in 1936; the millions he had not saved during World War II; the tens of millions he had never known who nevertheless needed saving. This is what he saw. And

268

much, much more that Pacelli did not, could not, would not tell Bea or Pasqualina until three years later.

At 6:25 A.M., a knock on Pacelli's door. Sister Pasqualina is there to prepare him for his doctors. They, on arrival, find no dying man. "Good morning, gentlemen! I am glad to see you," is Pacelli's firm greeting. He recovers. He lives for almost four more years.

In June of 1958 (he died in October), when he did tell Bea of his morning vision, Bea just nodded. And then Pacelli went on to tell Bea that everything would be all right. The Marxist revolution was dangerous. It would sap Western Europe, would strain the U.S.A. to the last point of its strength, by snapping the waistline of Central America and isolating Canada and the U.S.A. from South America. But everything would be all right. "If Satan has a plan, Our Lord Jesus can work through it."

This time, Bea realizes, the old pope really is dying. His doctors know it. Pacelli himself knows it. Already, the search for a successor has begun; and Bea, as an intimate Vatican advisor, is involved. He does not load Pacelli's mind with any further remarks about the real revolution and the real difficulty. For, as Bea saw it, Marxism was only a temporary thing and the real revolution lay deeper in the souls of nations. How could he disturb the last months of this, the last of the great Roman popes, telling him that the whole idea of Roman hegemony and grandeur was outmoded? Once Pacelli saw the face of Jesus in Heaven, Bea later remarked, the pope would understand it all in a full peace of holiness. But to Pacelli's credit let it be said that, as the last of the Romans, he was the first of them to realize that the revolution was at hand—even though he only partially understood it.

Decline and Fall

All the popes from Silvester I in A.D. 316 down to and including Pius XII thought of themselves as kings and of the church as their kingdom. So they ruled. So they taught—rightly or wrongly. The break came in 1958 with the election of Angelo Roncalli as Pope John XXIII, succeeding Pius XII. Roncalli was to die within the short space of five years, yet the change he inaugurated was as great as the one Silvester I had brought about by accepting the apparently generous offer of Emperor Constantine that established the church as a worldly power, eventually as *the* worldly power. In his five years, John created the circumstances in which the authority and unity of his church were destroyed. This was not his intent. This was, however, what he achieved. The most popular of modern popes was to prove the most dangerous of them all.

This is all the more surprising because Roncalli had been nourished and shaped exclusively within that Roman kingdom, and had never been considered a threat to it except once in a minor way during his early years as a professor of theology in Rome. He was then once found too inclined to empathize with thinkers characterized as "modernist" and therefore dangerous. But a long subsequent life of rather humble and obscure service in the Vatican diplomatic corps convinced Roncalli's superiors that he was as safe as, well, as the church. Besides, he was "popular" and "pastoral" and—on account of huge girth, thanks to a huge appetite for good food, and his ability to make wisecracks—somewhat amusing. He took ribbing, even acrid criticism, then and later with great grace. "We did not stoop to pick up the stones that were thrown at us," he said once with his customary gentleness, "and we did not throw them back at anyone."

Any reader of Roncalli's personal diary, published posthumously as *The Journal of a Soul*, will realize that he was capable of understanding the world only in the shadow of Christ's cross and in the light of Christ's resurrection, and that he had no vision of nor interest in a new social order. He was, as Cardinal John Heenan of England wrote of him in 1964, a year after his death, "the old-fashioned 'garden-of-the-soul' type of Catholic. . . . He was responsible for no great reform. His great achievement was to teach the world . . . how small is hatred and how great is love."

Yet already before he became pope, Roncalli had sensed a mysterious drumming tension in the world around him, although he seems never to have expressed any understanding of its causes or its nature, nor any sympathy with commentators who saw it as the outgrowth of the political and economic deline of the West. His now-famous *Peace on Earth* letter that seemed to spring from a conviction of the need for social change was largely the work of his collaborators, and it is doubtful that Roncalli ever really understood its proposals.

More deadly by far, however, was his ignorance of the internal condition of his church. He understood layfolk and their minds quite deeply as a pastor; but, after his early brush with "modernism," he had shown no interest in, nor understanding of, the theologian, the philosopher, or the ideologue. He never realized that for thirty years already a new theology was aborning, a theology which rejected age-old teachings of Rome. He therefore knew nothing of the conditions in Catholic universities and seminaries in northern Europe, in the U.S.A., and in Latin America, where a whole generation reared on the new theology were merely waiting for a signal to rush out to join their contemporaries in the theater of the absurd—modern man's quest for himself. So John spoke amiably about opening windows in his church while, actually and unwittingly, he was leveling the walls.

He was aware of the political and economic dissatisfaction of the

272

masses, and identified with it, misreading it for religious ferment. In undertaking his work as pope, he could have echoed Chairman Mao in saying: "I am alone with the masses," and he had undeniably a mass appeal, not only to Catholics but to human beings everywhere, in whom he thought he discerned the Holy Spirit moving. He could not get away from his feeling that some strange disruptive dynamism was abroad in his world. In response to it, he aimed at producing one exalted Pentecostal moment of near-mystical experience on a large scale in the sight of all men. And Roncalli meant *all* men. It was his solution of the age-old difficulty the popes in Rome and their Vatican had incurred because of Emperor Constantine's gift of power.

He chose, he said, to be called Pope John XXIII, in order to atone for the bad aroma that Baldassare (the "Corsair") Cossa—the man who was once called Pope John XXIII—had given that name. But Roncalli was really a new Peter Murrone—the hermit who was briefly Pope Celestine V. Like Murrone, Roncalli believed that the Holy Spirit was about to create a new Pentecost and renew all things human. Unlike Murrone, he chose to accept the burden of the papacy so as to help the new Pentecost along.

This was why he summoned the Ecumenical Council of Vatican II (1962-65), hoping that it would create an opening in the thick-woven texture of ordinary lives, displaying the mystery and the complexity of human existence within the Christian plan of salvation by Jesus. This one quick flash of refreshed belief, he hoped, would dispel the apparent meaninglessness and despair of modern life. And Roncalli aimed at something far wider than a mere "Roman Catholic" event. He wrote:

> Now more than ever, certainly more than in past centuries, our intention is to serve man as such and not only Catholics; to defend above all and everywhere the rights of the human person, and not only those of the Catholic Church.

He wished, therefore, to establish solid contacts with the U.S.S.R. and Communist China; but, in aid of this, he chose not to denounce Soviet imprisonment and torture. Thus the Ayatollah's reproach fitted Pope John XXIII.

273

He told the opening session of his council on October 11, 1962, that "false doctrines and opinions still abound," but that "today men spontaneously reject" them. This was no longer the voice of the ancient Roman Catholic kingdom talking. It was much closer to the accents of modern democracy in its suggestion that humanity in concert is in the long run incapable of error, will in fact spontaneously reject error.

Those who formulated this doctrine for Roncalli never pointed out to him that it inevitably led to rejection of both the Christian doctrine of original sin as the cause of human susceptibility to evil, and of the existence of a personal principle of moral evil that Christians always called the Devil or Satan. Both these fundamental doctrines Roncalli had sworn to uphold, and any of his predecessors would have condemned him for not doing so.

But if Roncalli did not see where his new teaching was leading, hundreds of theologians and bishops did. In the sixties and the seventies after Roncalli's death, they drew these conclusions and abandoned belief in original sin, in the Devil, and in many other fundamental doctrines.

But Roncalli changed his mind before the end. Already in the spring of 1963, when an inoperable and incurable carcinoma was slowly killing him, he came to the conviction that it all had been a mistake, but by then it was too late to hold back the deluge that would sweep away all that he revered. "Yes," he told Cardinal Ottaviani some days before his death, "my dying now must be the hand of God."

Before he died on June 3, he saw that his council was in the hands of those who would destroy what he loved. What he had hoped for, never took place; there was no communal experience of the spirit, no new Pentecost, no shining moment of renewal. Instead, something diametrically contrary happened: revolution within the government and membership of his church, led by his successor, Paul VI, Giovanni Battista Montini, whom Roncalli had first put forward as prime papal candidate but from whom Roncalli in the end recoiled because of Montini's identification with the hated revolution.

For the first time in its long history, the Roman Catholic Church under Paul VI decided, without the agreement of a majority of its bishops in the council, to change the way in which it thought about itself, wor-

274

shiped, trained its priests and scholars, and presented itself to the world.

Paul VI and his followers replaced the idea of the church as a kingdom with the idea of an institution destined to serve not the "kingdom of God," but the "people of God." and by "people" Pope Paul and his collaborators meant exactly what the writers of the U.S. Constitution meant, that the people were the source of all sovereignty and order and power, with equality of rights for all, and with no one privileged in precedence. Paul was trying to follow through with Roncalli's solution—as he, Paul, understood it.

Paul went so far once as to state that a pope—to be truly pope—must be acknowledged by the whole human race. One century before this, a French philosopher named Lamennais had been condemned as a heretic for saying just that. And every one of Paul's predecessors, including Roncalli, would have unhesitatingly condemned Paul VI for saying so.

Paul's new view meant recognizing the autonomy of the individual person and therefore accommodating all possible views. It meant that anyone had a right to be wrong. It meant the Catholic Church was no longer "the one true church of Christ." It meant embracing the concept of religious pluralism, and abstention from all "missionary activity." It meant that the people would decide for themselves what to believe and how to behave. Meanwhile, the church was there to minister to their social and physical needs.

Paul consented, further, to abandon the age-old Catholic belief that the Mass was a sacrifice. It was, he propounded in an official document, a sacred memorial meal presided over by a "priest"; and only threats by the powerful cardinals, Ottaviani and Bacci, saved Paul from proclaiming what would have been this formal heresy.

Still, despite this stumbling and confusion, Paul thought he could hold the church together. Yet he was almost totally defeated and humiliated in all that he set out to achieve. He started off with Roncalli's intuition of that rumbling tension in his world. Only, Paul thought he knew how to march safely through it all. Here was his error of judgment. Nothing in his past fitted him for the task.

His own life had always been lived within a dense social space in the arenas of Vatican diplomacy and power politics. He knew no others. But Vatican participation in both arenas underwent a fatal eclipse in his days. His sympathy for Third World causes made him suspect to Western democracies.

He gave moral support to terrorists in Spain and left-wing parties in Latin America. He allowed himself and his office to be used by the Communist government of North Vietnam in order to make the Tet offensive of 1968 possible. He favored Castro's Cuba, and gave free rein to Marxist bishops and priests and nuns in his church of the Americas and Europe and Africa. But Paul never uttered one syllable to protest the crucifixion of Lithuanian Catholics by the Soviets, the persecution of all believers in Hungary, Romania, Czechoslovakia, the tortured prisoners of Castro's Cuba; no more than he did about the planned destruction of the faith he was elected to protect and spread.

Paul's confidants, such as the Frenchmen Jean Danielou, Jean Guitton, and Jacques Maritain, and his outside contacts like Metropolitan Nikodim of the U.S.S.R. and the Anglican canons of Canterbury, could not explain that tension in Paul's world, or offer any workable alternative for church policy other than seconding what they felt was the movement of the "people." In spite of his "democratic" outlook, Paul therefore began to fall back on a power which by now was decried as "imperialistic"; but he found he had no such power.

Paul's own personal limitations also hemmed him in. He was the first pope to walk the earth in Asia, Africa, the Near East, and both the Americas. But in his spirit he was Roman first, then Italian. And he never became more than a European. He could not span a century or possess a continent or understand a fanatic, except in terms of the way of life that had made him what he had become. The crises he faced—Communism, contraception, abortion, theological revolt in Germany and the Americas, the strife in the Middle East—called for vigorous action. But Paul could not walk alone on the peaks of decision. He lacked the ruthlessness of greatness isolated.

Elected as pope to rule universally, he could never cease to be particular. Brought up within the mentality of the kingdom, he took as his own the mentality of the "people." But when he encountered the rude shocks from the new world to which he exposed himself, his initiatives slowed down to a stop; and, in his panic, he fell into an ambiguity and equivocation that nettled his friends and angered his enemies. They called him Hamletic. Time and time again, he forbade something, then permitted it, then proceeded to add restrictions and contradictory instructions. Contraception was a case in point. Paul inherited from John XXIII a blue-ribbon commission that was to study the problem of contraception together with other moral questions. John XXIII had hand-picked the commissioners—men and women. Paul knew their views. When their conclusions did not please him, he rejected them and published contrary views in his now-famous letter *On Human Life*. When a huge galaxy of seminary professors, bishops, priests, and layfolk rejected *On Human Life*, he did nothing about it. The enemies of contraception and those for contraception were both enraged at him. Paul wept and pleaded and scolded both sides.

But nothing he did could stem the onslaught on him—for had he not espoused a "people's church" where all had equal voice?—women who wanted to be priests, priests who wanted to be married, bishops who wanted to be regional popes, theologians who claimed absolute teaching authority, Protestants who claimed equality and identity, homosexuals and divorced people who called for acceptance of their status on their terms, Marxist priests and bishops and nuns and layfolk who claimed his approval to destroy the social order in which Paul and all Catholics lived, traditional-minded Catholics who bitterly reproached him with being Antichrist. It was a cruel time. It was the new "people" let loose on the old kingdom, and Paul had no defense against them. Increasingly he reacted with tears.

Without his being able to do anything about them, the "people" set about changing the church. Irreconcilable varieties in belief and practice arose because of Paul's refusal or inability to exercise papal authority. And because Paul gave up the teaching authority and power traditionally lodged with him and the Vatican, the centrality and unity of the church were in jeopardy.

As Paul VI neared death and the papal electors pondered who his successor would be, his reflections were distressingly sad, almost morose,

277

according to those around him. The power that was bought and sold, and sometimes betrayed, but was always the condition of action in the old Vatican, had vanished, just when the real face of danger became clear.

Paul realized in his last two years that something unimaginably ominous had been moving inexorably toward them, was already in their midst, and that it had nothing to do with the Holy Spirit. "The smoke of Satan has entered the church, is around the altar," he remarked somberly and helplessly. By 1978 and in the last few weeks of his own life, Paul knew that the rumbling tension of his world had grown to a roaring, and that around him there was a conflagration feeding on the dry wood and the underbrush of the centuries-old kingdom. That kingdom, as Gregory the Great, Leo III, Clement VII, Pius IX, and Pius XII had known it, was going—probably forever. Perhaps it was already dead; but Paul, as Roncalli before him, had dug its grave. And now there was no one left to lead the "people."

It was far too late for Paul to start all over again. He had been no greater than any of the children of his troubled age. He, like them, had contributed to the decay of his civilization by allowing the evisceration of his church by the same forces that were choking the art, the literature, the hope of that civilization. He had been merely another child of his time, a pigmy among pigmies. No more.

Still, it was not too late for him to pray and acknowledge that, because he had been neither very good nor very gentle nor very brave, the world had not had to kill him in order to break him—as the world must indeed break all great men. There was no special hurry in his case. Now and again, at crucial moments between 1965 and 1978—the years of profound liquidation of Roman authority and the Catholic tradition—just when Paul seemed to be on the verge of reacting, of reasserting his authority, of repairing the damage done under his eyes and across his signature, he would be visited and talked with. Afterward, his close personal aides would find him weeping, helpless. He could not act, and would speak vaguely about the lesser of two evils.

But sometimes when Paul gave his blessing from the balcony of his study window to the crowds watching below in St. Peter's Square, the telephoto lens picked up on his face that stark look of the imperial mind at

278

bay before a threat it recognized as lethal. Paul preached the "people," but he never ceased to be of the kingdom. And he feared for his own faith, feared also the accounting of his stewardship he believed he would have to deliver to Christ after he died. In the last days of his life, those who passed by his bedroom could hear him repeating endlessly (he apparently thought he was praying silently): *"Credo in unam sanctam catholicam ecclesiam . . . credo in unam . . .* (I believe in one holy Catholic Church . . . I believe in one . . .)" on and on, in a hoarse whisper.

When his death was announced on August 6, 1978, he left behind him a church torn and disoriented. The forces of the kingdom had been destroyed in most places, and were under siege in their remaining bastions. The forces of the "people" were attacking everywhere and gaining new ground every day. The ferocity between the contending forces in the post-Pauline church can be measured by the very short pontificate of Paul's immediate successor, Albino Luciani, who took the name of John Paul I.

In the meager thirty-four days allowed him as pope, John Paul I made quite clear his intention to repel the "people," especially on ground where he judged they were doing mortal damage. He intended to restore the traditional Latin Mass and orthodox theology. He intended to make it quite clear to non-Catholic Christians that huge differences separated them from his church. On divorce, abortion, contraception, priestly celibacy, priesthood of women, the activities of nuns, the political activism of cardinals, bishops, and priests, he was intent on bringing the church back to traditional rules and behavior. On top of all that, John Paul I had fixed his sights on the complex issues of Vatican involvement in the worlds of finance and commerce. There, he knew, lay an acquired and capital weakness of his church.

But John Paul I was not allowed the time he needed. His enemies had disparate aims but one unifying trait: both those whose vital interests lay in completing the dismantling of Roman authority and those whose lives and fortunes were tied to Vatican material interests found John Paul II unacceptable. "They are all starting to kill each other," he remarked, before turning in on the night of September 23, 1978. He was referring to the current assassinations by the Red Brigades. None of the factions

279

opposing him were displeased when, on September 24, at 5:30 A.M., John Paul I was found dead in his bed.

The conclave to elect his successor gathered on the following October 14 and, on the 22nd, chose Karol Wojtyla, the fifty-eight-year-old cardinal archibishop of Cracow, Poland, as pope. He took the name John Paul II. "His own name (*Wojt*) means 'bailiff' or 'person in charge,' you know," one Polish monsignor quipped to his companions, as Wojtyla appeared on the balcony of St. Peter's after the election. To those who stood with the forces of the "people," John Paul II very quickly made it plain that he fully intended to take charge.

This veteran of Communist wars and Nazi oppressions inherited a bedraggled church pushed to the brink by Paul VI's huge betrayal and neglect, a church with depopulated seminaries, politico bishops, lipsticked and miniskirted nuns, bewildered lay people, plus a Vatican that housed Communist "moles," clerical financial wizards, career diplomats, Marxist prelates, a brothel, overworked exorcists, hostile bureaucrats, some silent good people, and a hard-core 37 percent of clerics and people who yearned for the church Paul VI had smothered.

It is very late for the church of John Paul II. From the start, he set out to see and listen. He traveled to Mexico, to Poland, to Latin America, to the U.S.A., to France and Germany and Britain and the Philippines. He heard the same story everywhere. From everyone. And he himself came to the same conclusion. It is late. Late for control of his bishops. Late for control of theologians. Late for any real unity with the Protestant churches. Late for any "democratic" solution in Latin America with its impoverished hundreds of millions of Catholics. Late, above all, for any credibility. The Roman Catholic Church in its organization, its finances, its political alignments, gives little testimony of being the church of Jesus, the poor man of Galilee, the savior who was above all politics and "isms." Already the populations of Western Europe and the Americas have lost faith in the organization as a sign of salvation from oppression. And there is no reasonable hope of making even a dent in the burgeoning populations of India, China, Japan, and the Middle East.

No one understands more clearly than Wojtyla the inherent danger in the policies of Roncalli and Montini. But these policies have brought John Paul's church to a historical crossroads. For good or ill, the kingdom has been overthrown, and the "people" are breaking up into even tinier factions, increasingly chaotic. And John Paul now has the agonizing problem of what to do.

Waiting at the Crossroads

When Pope John Paul II traveled to Puebla, Mexico, in January of 1979, his mind was quite clear about the internal geography of his church, and he condemned "the separation that some set up between the church and the Kingdom of God." He could hardly have spoken more clearly to some of the foremost champions of the "people" concept of the Roman Church who were there listening to him. John Paul did not hesitate to affirm a hierarchic church organized around bishops and priests under direct obedience to the pope.

Neither friend nor foe of the present pope has by now any illusion on this point. For him, "the people of God" will always be a part of the traditional "kingdom of God." By word and action, before Puebla and after, John Paul has been saying over and over again that, as he sees it, the church was never, is not, and shall never be a democracy. It now has many traits having nothing to do with its spiritual mission; but its founder established a hierarchy, and it is his business as the founder's vicar to keep it that way—whatever else may have to be jettisoned.

And Wojtyla is not sparing his directness of language. "We do not need or want," he said trenchantly at Puebla, Mexico, "any politicking priests or priests who take up arms in revolutionary movements." When someone remarked on the widespread popularity of the rebellious theologian, Hans Küng, Wojtyla rejoined patiently: "Maybe. But I am pope."

"Nobody can make of theology," he wrote in March 1979, with one

283

eye on some Dutch and French theologians, "a simple collection of his own personal ideas." And in the hearing of certain professors at the Catholic University of Washington he lashed out that "it is the right of the faithful not to be disturbed by theories and hypotheses they are not expert in judging."

There have been strong reactions to John Paul II. For many conservatives he is "sympathetic" but "way off" on matters such as marital love, contraception, abortion, homosexuality. For many traditionalists he is too much of a "showman" and not quick enough to undo the ills Paul VI wreaked on the church. For progressives and liberals in the Western world he is a demagogue, a species of Polish outlander who made his way into the Vatican and surely to be followed by a band of Polish carpetbaggers; a Slav who could not understand the advanced state of Western intellectualism, and who is dead set on imposing the "crude and primitive Catholicism" of backwater Poland on an already highly evolved Western religious mind.

One progressive French daily sensed in the Pope's flamboyant personal style "a renaissance of Roman triumphalism" and "excessive personalization" of the papacy. The writer, with an obviously "democratic" approach to pope and church, argued that no one should invite or allow anything like the personal acclaim John Paul II has received every time he makes a trip.

None of these epithets and descriptions of Karol Wojtyla as Pope John Paul II really fits the man. One could spend a long time establishing his status as an intellectual, as a humanist, as an administrator, as a theorist, as a world-traveled hierarch, a multilinguist, a street-fighter, a very progressive political thinker, a hard-nosed negotiator. Very few if any of his critics could match him precisely under the headings of their own, sometimes sneering, almost always acrid, criticisms.

At issue here is the fundamental reason he is the object of such criticism. But before examining that reason, we should place Karol Wojtyla in his actual circumstances.

He became pope in October of 1978, the titular head of a world organization structured essentially around priests and bishops, and centered in the Vatican with its subordinated ministries (congregations). Both as regards that worldwide clerical structure and his Vatican government, John Paul II is a man at bay.

During the previous fifteen years, while Pope Paul VI reigned, generations of young priests in their twenties (they are graduated and ordained each year) were being turned out by Catholic seminaries all over the world. They had been trained by professors who minimized or rejected outright the dogmas and formulas of Catholic belief and morality that John Paul considers essential, the infallibility of the pope and his jurisdiction over all other bishops being two of them. On these two, the ancient idea of the Roman Church as a monarchic institution rests. Without them, it is all over for the Church of Rome.

Gradually, the new priests filled the ranks of Roman clergy, some becoming bishops, others becoming professors, others missionaries in Africa, Asia, and Latin America, others still taking up positions in parishes, universities, institutes, the Catholic media, and Vatican ministries, and throughout the multifarious activities that occupy Catholic clergy throughout the world—scientific institutes, local legislatures, social relief services. The overall effect of this new generation had become apparent by the time John Paul II was elected: the traditional Roman Catholic notion of a worldwide hierarchy of bishops under the centralized control of the pope, who has the last deciding word in all matters concerning faith and moral practice, is in high jeopardy.

A survey of Roman Catholic bishops and theology professors in Western Europe and Latin America shows that probably two-thirds of them do not feel any religious or ecclesiastical need to conform to the ideas and principles of John Paul as regards the beliefs and the moral rules he proclaims. In a place like Holland, a majority of the bishops together with its sole cardinal, Jan Willebrands, its priests and layfolk, are in outspoken and declared revolt against papal authority. The bishops of Ireland and Spain, once bastions of Roman authority, are also pervaded by a spirit of total independence from the Vatican. The majority of U.S. bishops pay lip-service to John Paul's directives, but make it quite clear by their actions that they do not expect either their seminary professors, their parish priests, or their laity to take the pope seriously Throughout Latin American countries, in the matter of Communism, John Paul has failed—even by two personal visits—to win the allegiance of most cardinals, as well as over two-thirds of the resident bishops and priests and nuns. They cannot see any alternative to a form of Communist government and Marxist system of economics which euphemistically they call "democratic socialism." The alienation from John Paul's Rome is extensive and growing.

There is now installed in seminaries, universities, dioceses, a new generation of young bishops, priests, and nuns all of whom exhibit the same alienation, and who are engaged in turning out new generations of their own kind yearly. Whether you survey diocesan papers, weekly parish sermons, magazines, periodicals, the reading lists of books recommended by Catholic clergy, everywhere you find reflected a new theology which is distrustful of Roman authority and imbued with the spirit of experimentation. John Paul's trips abroad to Europe and Latin America have only served to underline this alienation. Everywhere, he received tumultuous acclaim, but everywhere he preached doctrines that had been abandoned or emasculated by the priests and bishops who were his hosts.

At home in his Vatican bureaucracy, John Paul is faced with entrenched employees who in the normal course of events would have ten to twenty more years of guaranteed employment in front of them before retiring. They were appointed under Pope Paul VI. They are not sympathetic to the "Pole" and his ideas, and they share many of the beliefs that took hold of the church during the time of Paul VI. John Paul cannot even control his own Vatican bureaucracy. This then is the Roman Catholic institution whose hierarchic structure John Paul defends.

Down on this fractured institution are descending dissonant forces heralding a new civilization based uniquely on the technology of science. The old civilization which the church created and fashioned for itself, is dead; and there is no probability that this church can flourish in this technological era, whose first and most potent effects are being felt already where it hurts Catholicism most.

All over the world, on an increasing scale, men and women are accepting new developments as normal and natural: abortion, contraception, divorce, freedom of conscience in religious matters, a secular (read: nonreligious) education, homosexuality, are among the more obvious. But the
286

near future promises things like euthanasia and genetic engineering. And, at least in the U.S.A. and Holland, it is safe to predict that within John Paul's lifetime there will be Roman Catholic women priests and married priests acting in total disregard of John Paul and his Vatican. There is no way that John Paul can stop these developments. A frank assessment of bishops in Ireland, England, and the U.S.A., as examples, leads to the conclusion that they see these events as inevitable and are seeking an accommodation. For the time being they are not contradicting John Paul's traditionalist Romanism, but there is no doubt that they are preparing for what comes after. They want to survive.

To turn this situation around, to appoint bishops and seminary professors who share his mind, to replace the middle-level bureaucrats in his Vatican ministries, to turn out a substantial generation of priests who uphold the traditional doctrines, to remove those who won't, will keep John Paul busy for the rest of his life. If he can do it at all.

In fact, John Paul's deepest view—although he spontaneously shrinks from it—is that within ten, or at most twenty, years religion as he understands it will have no effect whatever on public affairs. What he is doing to bolster the hierarchy of the church is done in response to this conviction.

For, stripped of its political influence and financial power, all the church will have left will be spiritual authority, which, of course, is all that its founder ever promised it. It is quite a long time, Wojtyla and everyone else knows, since Christians relied solely and exclusively on spiritual authority. Since the time of Silvester I, in fact. Since then, the history of Christianity is one in which its spiritual message has either been muffled in ermine or skewered by its own golden sword. This is true even of so-called reforms. Luther's effort in the sixteenth century, for instance, relied on political and even military means. In this case, therefore, the pope sees that the only way to go forward is to go back. It is such a long time since human beings have seen an exercise of purely spiritual power, however, that many quite likely would not readily recognize it— Roman Catholics included, indeed foremost. Public manifestations of spirit in the twentieth century have been mainly sociological, like "born-again" rallies; fanatical Islamic risings; the political agitation of pro-life organizations or of American Judaism or of the Southern Christian Leadership Conference or of Moonies; or the repellent exclusionism of particular sects like the Rastafarians or the Jonestown community in Guyana.

Whatever true spiritual quickening exists in such movements is soon adulterated if not utterly soured by the politicking. One direct result of this is the genuine fear that religion and religious groups in general are subversive of the ordinary civil and political process.

The opposition between John Paul II and the vast majority of his bishops as well as the intellectuals and theologians of his church arises from a fundamental difference in approach. For quite a long time now, it has become fashionable and acceptable among this pope's opponents to regard as serious and enlightened only that knowledge acquired from the purely secular sciences of our age. They therefore make every effort to bring Christianity in general and Catholicism specifically up to date by modifying the data of Christian and Catholic teaching so that they conform to that purely secular knowledge. They have never considered it even possible that Christianity (and Catholicism) has its own specific way of thinking about man and his world.

Wojtyla, as thinker and as pope, occupies a radically different vantage point. To seek religious enlightenment from secular sources is, for him, to subject man to this material universe. In Wojtyla's view, man has been created by God to be master of, not subject to, the material universe. He must, therefore, have a scale of values, a spirituality, that transcends the universe.

Hence, Wojtyla will condemn a Hans Küng for subjecting Christian revelation to contemporary anthropology and psychology; a Raymond Brown for subjecting the Gospels to the findings of linguistics and archaeology; the defenders of birth control an homosexuality and sexual permissiveness for subjecting men and women to utility values; any Marxist for subjecting man to merely material and economic factors; any capitalist as such for subjecting man to the imperious demands of the market, of production, of consumerism, of the accumulation of riches.

Wojtyla insists that traditional Catholic teaching has an ethical structure and content all its own. And from that emerges his answer to the

288

underlying question behind the sneering reproaches of the Ayatollah Khomeini. And in that answer lies his commentary on the past checkered career of the Church of Rome in the field of politics.

There is nothing against Christian involvement in politics and the social field, provided that its terms of reference are purely religious, provided that it does not adopt the categories of any secular ideology. In that one stroke, Wojtyla denies any validity to the "liberation theologians" who have adopted the theory and practice of "democratic socialism," as well as to the bishops who side with capitalist-supported juntas, as well as to the intellectuals who seek to explain Christian revelation in conformity with secular sciences, as well as to the ethical theorists who wish to "modernize" Christian morality by making it conform to the "sexual liberation" of these decades. He also passes a harsh, if silent, judgment on many of his illustrious predecessors on the chair of Peter. They, in their day drew on secular categories for church government and behavior.

Such a downright viewpoint places Wojtyla in direct clash with the most widespread views of his own churchmen. It also explains the almost vertiginous quality of his papal trips. He is endeavoring to reach over the heads of entrenched clerical bureaucracies and the congealed mentalities of intellectuals, out to the people at large, Christian and non-Christian. His message is clear.

We have gone so far down the road of conformity to the age and subjection to secular values, he is saying, that today there is no obvious or compelling reason for the men and women of our world to recognize in the church's visible appearance and activity any definite sign of God's divinity or the salvation of Jesus Christ, which remain the church's essential teaching for men and women of this age and every age. Such examples as the selflessness of a Mother Teresa of Calcutta, the humanitarian work of church relief services, the scholarly and scientific contributions of single members—all this is willingly and gratefully acknowledged and accepted by mankind in general. None of them are taken as any sign of the supernatural, rather merely as a human commitment to alleviate human misery. But nothing, really nothing substantial, of the Roman Church's core teaching about belief or morality is acceptable to the mass of its contemporaries.

And, as things now are, even if some sign appeared as equally impressive as the cross that Emperor Constantine believed he saw across the setting sun on the eve of a decisive battle some sixteen hundred years ago, it would not do the trick. The twentieth-century human being would be vitally interested, awestruck perhaps, certainly questioning, possibly inspired. But, of itself, such a sign would not point uniquely, unequivocally, to the Roman Church as the institution with a guaranteed salvation for the human race. For, apart from isolated individuals and small scattered communities, neither in the hierarchy nor the general membership of the church, nor in its public organs, can a nonbeliever read an unequivocal message about the value of Christian sacrifice, the principle of Christian poverty, or the promise of Christian hope. In fact, a majority of humans alive today would describe most of the Catholic clergy they know as career men living more or less like everyone else, acting more or less on the same principles, buffeted by the same confusions, threatened by the same dangers, as resourceless as the rest of their fellow-men.

This becomes all the more clear, when one points to the rather impressive number of Roman Catholics (clergy and layfolk) working in Third World areas and in urban ghettoes, selflessly throwing their lot in with local populations. It is noticeable that their contributions do not differ in kind from those made by their nonbelieving contemporaries. Dental clinics, powdered milk, farming methods, cooperatives, technical schools, sanitary plumbing, clothing, medical assistance, political education, trade unionism, all such things are neutral as far as religion goes. There is no distinctly Catholic or Christian sense delivered by these to the miserable, the poor, the oppressed. On the contrary, in many areas, Catholic workers have identified themselves with popular causes, with "democratic socialism," with Communism, even with guerrilla warfare and armed revolution. The suggestion is that no spiritual mission can be accomplished until the material level associated with human dignity is attained. More and more, higher churchmen are turning against capitalism. "The practices of multinational corporations bring famine and destitution to the people of this continent (Africa) and the rest of the Third World," said Cardinal Paul Zoungrana, archbishop of Ouagadougou, Upper Volta, on October 7, 1980.

290

That may be so, yet the conclusion reached by many moderns is that the bishops and theologians and intellectuals of the Roman Catholic Church have no answers exclusively Catholic and specifically religious for the questions torturing the world; that, when the church did intervene in the past in social and political affairs, it did so with basically secular solutions; and that today, having lost most of its power in secular matters, a goodly section of its members is becoming addicted to some form of socialism, while the Vatican and its scattered supporters promote capitalism and right-wing causes.

The cruel fact of life for Pope John Paul II is that in all probability he will not have the time to formulate any adequate answers to the burning question: What is the role of the Roman Church in political and social affairs? He will not have the time for two reasons: because of the condition in which he now finds his church, the institution he believes he was divinely appointed to govern and lead; and because of a vortex of forceful circumstances hurtling down upon it and upon the late twentieth-century world, with demands that will not be satisfied by any reflex solutions, and with a speed that allows him no time to refurbish his shattered institution.

Within less than three years as pope, John Paul has placed himself as pope and the Vatican as his administration, on a new dimension which makes both of them the prime target of those forces that aim at nothing less than the destruction of the political and religious institutions vital for the survival of the way of life enjoyed by the Western world. In this context, we are not necessarily talking about the oft-named "revolutionary" or "terrorist" organizations that claim authorship of frequent *attentats* and destructive actions within the last decade. John Paul's predecessor, Paul VI, had bent over backwards to effect just the opposite, i.e. to make pope and Vatican and the Roman Church acceptable elements in the world order Paul VI and his advisors saw as inevitable. John Paul II does not see it as inevitable, and thus he has labored to undo that dubious achievement of Pope Paul VI.

John Paul effected this as much by his actions as by the very force of his personality. Beginning in November of 1978, some short days after his installation as pope, he created genuine reactions of respect, even admiraton, in the diplomats dispatched by governments to interview him, and in the principal members of those governments who came to see him. The new instructions that went out to all seventy-eight papal diplomatic missions around the globe also produced the same reactions. For the first time in close on twenty years, the conviction arose in government offices and diplomatic chancelleries around the world. that thee Vatican was headed by a churchman who had all the diplomatic skills and acumen of a Pope Pius XII, the almost "show-biz" appeal of a Pope John XXIII, and some added personal quality that forced those with whom he came in contact to revise their most fixed judgements about the role of the official church and its Vatican in the coming crises of the eighties. (John Paul's own judgments went the round of the chancelleries. After an official visit by the U.S.S.R.'s Andrei Gromyko, in December 1978, John Paul was asked how the Russian diplomat compared to the other diplomats he had met. "Gromyko," he said, using a Polish expression, "is the only horse shod on all four feet."

Within the ramifications of international relationships and communications between governments, the attainment of such personal prestige by a statesman constitutes of itself a powerfully decisive force. For, at the very least, it means that the attitudes, the convictions, and the intentions of such a statesman must and will be taken into account, and will necessarily modify and affect the behavior of governments. In that short space of time, John Paul II and his Vatican administration have come to be regarded as one of the important pillars within the Western world, one of the institutions necessary for the survival of that world.

The success of his papal journeys, measured by the reactions of the ordinary people everywhere he went, only confirmed this prestige and its profound influence on the minds and hearts of contemporary men and women. In actual fact, he is the only world leader who can travel to any continent and evoke an almost frighteningly emotional reaction from Christians and non-Christians.

His role and behavior in the Polish "crisis" of late 1980 and early 1981 belong to a particular case in point. The factual history of this "crisis" has yet to be written. From its beginning, John Paul knew what was happening: that the shortages of basic foods were deliberately provoked; that the U.S.S.R. would never need to send troops across the borders into

Poland, since it had already stationed within Polish borders enough Russian troops to control any civil or political outbreak; and that any real crisis in Poland at this time issued from the ranks of the Marxist party in Poland itself.

Already in November and December of 1980, when people connected with the U.S. State Department and other American and Western European agencies were spreading the word to their sympathizers within Poland that a Soviet army invasion was imminent and that they, the sympathizers, should flee into concealment, John Paul knew an invasion of Poland was a very unlikely event. He also knew that the promotion of a Polish-Soviet conflict would serve the short-term interests of certain centers in the Western world. It was clear to him that the emergence of Solidarity, the Polish workers' organization headed by Lech Walesa, was made possible by the organizing ability and intentions of the *Komitet Obrony Robotnikow*, better know in the West as KOR, the Trotskyite inspired Committee for the Defense of the Workers, headed by Poland's Adam Michnick, a devoted member of the Polish Communist Party.

The dream of Michnick and his KOR was to forge an alliance between the Polish left and the Polish Catholic Church, provoke a Soviet invasion or military take-over, and thus achieve the thorough evisceration of the Catholic Church in Poland.

That the Soviets did not panic in the initial weeks of the "crisis," that the machinations of KOR behind the facade of Solidarity were condemned publicly by the Polish Catholic hierarchy, that Western governments were informed of John Paul's resolve to denounce publicly those in the West interested in promoting a Polish-Soviet conflict, that no blood was shed in Poland, these are some of the items in John Paul's list of achievements during the early months of 1981.

But his efforts and role, besides doing a disservice to those who would make money off a Polish crisis, also foiled a very well-planned strategy of promotiong revolution. And thus as a person, he became by the spring of 1981, a very undesirable element of international life. Added to his actions during the Polish "crisis" were his firmness regarding the Basque terrorist movement (ETA) in Spain, the IRA in Northern Ireland, the blunt language he used in responding to the PLO, and his administrative

293

decisions regarding those priests, nuns, and bishops in Latin America whose Marxist and revolutionary sympathies could no longer be excused.

Thus the first overt attempt to eliminate him by public assassination in May of 1981 by means of Turkey's Mehmet Ali Agca, a professional "hitman" employed for this purpose by unknown masters, was schocking (one of its purposes was to demoralize, in much the same way as John F. Kennedy's assassination did) but entirely predictable, indeed inevitable, as will be all succeeding attempts. For those who are intent on promoting social and political unrest in Spain, Ireland, Italy, Latin America, the Middle East, and elsewhere are aware of John Paul's intentions to muster his personal prestige and the prodigious influence of his Vatican and Church against the privileged forces intent on disrupting all the vital institutions in the Western world that make possible the present way of life in that world.

But John Paul's achievement to date as far as international stature goes, when taken together with that first attempt on his life, graphically sums up the dilemma in which this pope and his church are caught. For no attempt would have been made to cut him down so early in his pontificate, if indeed as spiritual leader he represented no political threat to those who ordered his assassination. The present Dalai Lama, the Archbishop of Canterbury, or Billy Graham are not likely to undergo a like fate. They don't matter, as John Paul matters.

By any measure at our disposal, the influence of this pope and his vatican exceeds that of most middle-class powers in our world of today (say, France or Germany or Brazil), and it modifies—sometimes offsets, even upsets—the policies and influence of the two superpowers. Even the innately inimical Communist Politburo in Peking is beginning to feel his influence and the need to be in contact with him. In this context of power, it is relevant to underline the solidly ensconced position of John Paul's Vatican within the privileged membership of international finance. For the sinews of war are made of money; and diplomacy is a somewhat peaceful pursuit of the same aims for which war is waged. Any power engaged to any important degree in the international markets is inevitably drawn into that diplomacy. It is true, in principle, that the final responsibility for the directions in which Vatican financial influence is thrown must lie beneath the signature of John Paul and his papal blessing. Yet, as affairs have proceeded for quite a time now in the Vatican, precise control of Vatican finanacial sinews is not always or principally his.

True, John Paul's Vatican no longer possesses that huge swathe of land and properties, the former papal states, running across the waist of Italy. It and its central government in the Quirinal Palace of Rome were snatched from the papacy in 1870. The armies, fleets, arsenals, fortresses, artillery, and police force the Vatican possessed one hundred and ten years ago are no longer there. It no longer has offensive and defensive alliances with any powerful governments. Nor is there any ruler today who owes his rule and authority to the nod and agreement of the pope—not so long ago, most of Europe's rulers did.

Yet, in point of real estate, the Vatican's holdings throughout the world outside Italy yield far more revenue than the papal states ever did. Its liquid assets and investments have leaped beyond any sum attained by the classical papacy of bygone times. And, now at the beginning of the eighties, the Vatican has a pope who knows how to wield that material power of his Vatican—as well as its intangible but nonetheless real spiritual power. Karol Wojtyla, as Pope John Paul II, seems to have been born for this hour. He sits at the pinnacle of this dual power, material and spiritual, and he has known how to use it in order to attain a position of privileged influence on the most important power centers of our time.

Yet he—and with him, his Vatican and church—has been caught in the automatic dilemma that, as cameo after cameo of past popes show, has always led to a diminution of the spiritual stature of pope and church. Their greatest ills, in fact, sprang from such privileged influence that relied on the twin base of the material and the spiritual. For, on account of the material influence, at least some of their major actions were necessarily political and therefore represented a compromise of the spiritual as well as an exercise of political activity.

Some of John Paul's own actions fall into this category: his role in the Polish "crisis"; his sending of papal secretary Magee to visit the hunger-striking IRA fighter, Bobby Sands, followed immediately by a visit to the

295

British autorities in Ulster; his warning to Spain's prime minister Adolfo Suarez last year that, if a pro-abortion bill became law, there would be no papal trip to Spain (Suarez' resignation in January 1981 was at least partially casused by John Paul's attitude); his agreement to mediate between Chile and Argentina in the Beagle Channel dispute (at least bloodshed has been avoided); his avoidance of what was politically unacceptable to the governments of France and Mexico as a condition of his being welcome to visit each country; even his appointing of the very progressive and theologically "liberationist-minded" Dom Geraldo Majela Reis as archibishop of Diamantina in central Brazil. And was there any way John Paul could not declare, as his papal conscience told him he had to declare, during the heated national abortion debate in Italy this year, that "all legislation favorable to abortion is a very grave offense to the rights of man and the divine commandments"? The Italian lawmakers, the Demochristian Party, and the Italian voter had to be influenced by his voice, as they engaged in what was formally a political act.

The facts of life, therefore, have placed John Paul II in a position where he cannot exercise his spiritual authority and carry out his papal mission without automatically stepping onto the plane of civic affairs, national politics, and international interests. The wheel has turned full circle. The dangers that overshadowed all former popes in the exericse of their supreme office now beset John Paul II. The kind of world he inhabits is the source of this difficulty. The central issue racking that world is not any territorial claim or any greed for natural resources or any religious dogma. It is, rather, what sort of a human society will evolve from present circumstances. And on that basic issue, any pope must continually take a stand. John Paul's world at present is polarized between two contending economic systems, communist and capitalist, based on mutually exclusive ideologies, capitalism and Marxism, each side bolstered by superpower armaments. His church organization is breaking up. His bishops and clergy and followers throughout the world are similarly polarized. For over half his 740 million Roman Catholics belong to the have-nots of this world.

John Paul, then, is and can be nothing more than a pope of transition, a pope caught betweeen the end of the era and the edgy beginnings of another. He belongs in neither. He suits neither. He cannot return to the era ending. He cannot fit into the new era. He must preside over the decline and fall of his churchly organization, but make sure that the basic doctrines of his faith are handed on intact into that new era when human society everywhere on earth will be neither communist nor capitalist, but enveloped in a managerial system of government inspired by no ideology or philosophy, but organized on the basis of a universal technology.

He has no real choice from day to day: he cannot back Marxist communism; when he does act politically, he must opt for a modified capitalism as a temporary measure, knowing he cannot reform that capitalism in its depths, cannot therefore stop its slow decay, and knowing that at certain points along the way he will have to oppose the deadening influence of consumerist capitalism as it attempts to subject men and women to purely materialist values. Whether by natural causes or by an assassin's bullet, he will have left the human scene when human affairs—the civic interests of small towns as well as the national issues of nations—are decided within tiers of supranational bureaucracies carefully guided in their orbits around this human cosmos by a still higher tier of managers. He will not have to contend with this state of affairs, nor match all the wisdom of his oldest of chancelleries as well as his own cunning against the one one who will finally dominate that last tier, the ultimate dictator, the Man of Destiny.

Within his short span, he can only keep on reminding his followers and his contemporaries, as he wrote to the Brazilian bishops on December 10, 1980:

> We have an essentially religious mission which is not in the first place the construction of a better material world, but the building up of the kingdom which starts here and will be fully realized in heaven. . . .

The tenseness of Wojtyla's policy arises because is is racing, not so much against time, as against an ever-deepening twilight in human affairs, in which governments in panic, with the passive connivance of their peoples, are embracing a survival policy founded almost exclusively on technology, according as human society everywhere is trasformed into a world managerial system. This will effectively banish Christianity (and any religion) from the councils of power and the conduct of human affairs. John Paul does not expect to outlive that twilight nor to be alive to enter the ensuing night darkness eveloping the daily lives of all men and women. But, he hopes, there will be a fresh beginning among men in favor of moral authority and spiritual authority, in that long night. He foresees a world in which the surface is frozen over with the hard-stone pavements of birth by decree, life by computer, electronic happiness, conditioned behavior, and death according to actuarial tables. He calls up against this Orwellian future the oldest layer of the Roman Christian memory: It is in giving that we receive, in pardoning we are pardoned, and in dying that we are born in to eternal life. "If I am not ready to die, I am not worthy to live," he has said repeatedly.

John Paul and his church have reached the same crossroads of history as all other human beings today. Neither he nor anyone else can accurately predict which branch of the road the family of nations will take. He does not need to know that much. But he and his church must keep on remembering those farewell words of Christ on the night before he died, when he underlined the two conditions necessary for success . . . . "if you love you will obey my commandments . . . . and I will not leave you without protection . . . My Father and I will give you the life-giving Spirit . . . he will be continually by your side . . . he will be in you all . . . because I live on, and you too will have life." The safety and continuance of John Paul's church depend, finally and only, on that obedience and that belief. All else, in the perspective of religion, does not matter.

LIST OF ROMAN POPES AND CONCLAVES

The Roman Popes
and Conclaves

Number	Name	A.D.
1	Peter	29-64/67
2	Linus	67-76
3	Cletus	76-88
4	Clement I	88-97
5	Evaristus	97-105
6	Alexander I	105-115
7	Sixtus I	115-125
8	Telesphorus	125-136
9	Hyginus	136-140
10	Pius I	140-155
11	Anicetus	155-166
12	Soter	166-175
13	Eleutherius	175-189
14	Victor I	189-199
15	Zephyrinus	199-217
16	Callistus	217-222
17	Urban I	222-230
18	Pontianus	230-235
19	Anterus	235-236
20	Fabian	236-250

Number	Name	A.D.
21	Cornelius	251-253
22	Lucius I	253-254
23	Stephen I	254-257
24	Sixtus II	257-258
25	Dionysius	259-268
26	Felix I	269-274
27	Eutychianus	275-283
28	Caius	283-296
29	Marcellinus	296-304
30	Marcellus I	308-309
31	Eusebius	309-310
32	Miltiades	311-314
33	Silvester I	314-335
34	Mark	336
35	Julius I	337-352
36	Liberius	352-366
37	Damasus I	366-384
38	Siricius	384-399
39	Anastasius I	399-401
40	Innocent I	401-417
41	Zozimus	417-418
42	Boniface I	418-422
43	Celestine I	422-432
44	Sixtus III	432-440
45	Leo I	440-461
46	Hilarus	461-468
47	Simplicius	468-483
48	Felix III	483-492
49	Gelasius I	492-496
50	Anastasius II	496-498
51	Symmachus	498-514
52	Hormisdas	514-523
53	John I	523-526

Number	*Name*	*A.D.*
54	Felix IV	526-530
55	Boniface II	530-532
56	John II	533-535
57	Agapitus	535-536
58	Silverius	536-537
59	Vigilius	537-555
60	Pelagius I	556-560
61	John III	561-578
62	Benedict I	575-579
63	Pelagius II	579-590
64	Gregory I	590-604
65	Sabinianus	604-606
66	Boniface III	607
67	Boniface IV	608-615
68	Deusdedit	615-618
69	Boniface V	619-625
70	Honorius I	625-638
71	Severinus	640
72	John IV	640-642
73	Theodore I	642-649
74	Martin I	649-655
75	Eugene I	654-657
76	Vitalian	657-672
77	Adeodatus	672-676
78	Donus	676-678
79	Agatho	678-681
80	Leo II	682-683
81	Benedict II	684-685
82	John V	685-686
83	Conon	686-687
84	Sergius I	687-701
85	John VI	701-705
86	John VII	705-707

Number	Name	A.D.
87	Sisinnius	708
88	Constantine I	708-715
89	Gregory II	715-731
90	Gregory III	731-741
91	Zachary	741-752
92	Stephen II	752
93	Stephen III	752-757
94	Paul I	757-767
95	Stephen IV	768-772
96	Adrian I	772-795
97	Leo III	795-816
98	Stephen V	816-817
99	Paschal I	817-824
100	Eugene II	824-827
101	Valentine	827
102	Gregory IV	827-844
103	Sergius II	844-847
104	Leo IV	847-855
105	Benedict III	855-858
106	Nicholas I	858-867
107	Adrian II	867-872
108	John VIII	872-882
109	Marinus	882-884
110	Adrian III	884-885
111	Stephen VI	885-891
112	Formosus	891-896
113	Boniface VI	896
114	Stephen VII	896-897
115	Romanus	897
116	Theodore II	898
117	John IX	898-900
118	Benedict IV	900-903
119	Leo V	903

Number	Name	A.D.
120	Sergius III	904-911
121	Anastasius III	911-913
122	Lando	913-914
123	John X	914-929
124	Leo VI	929
125	Stephen VIII	929-931
126	John XI	931-936
127	Leo VII	936-939
128	Stephen IX	939-942
129	Marinus II	942-946
130	Agapitus II	946-955
131	John XII	955-963
132	Leo VIII	963-964
133	Benedict V	964
134	John XIII	965-972
135	Benedict VI	973-974
136	Benedict VII	974-983
137	John XIV	983-984
138	John XV	985-996
139	Gregory V	996-999
140	Silvester II	999-1003
141	John XVII	1003
142	John XVIII	1003-1009
143	Sergius IV	1009-1012
144	Benedict VIII	1012-1024
145	John XIX	1024-1033
146	Benedict IX	1033-1044
147	Silvester III	1045
148	Benedict IX	1045
149	Gregory VI	1045-1046
150	Clement II	1046-1047
151	Benedict IX	1047-1048
152	Damascus II	1048

Number	Name		A.D.
153	Leo IX		1049-1054
154	Victor II		1055-1057
155	Stephen X		1057-1058
156	Nicholas II		1059-1061
157	Alexander II		1061-1073
158	Gregory VII		1073-1085
159	Victor III		1086-1087
160	Urban II		1088-1099
161	Paschal II		1099-1118
162	Gelasius II		1118-1119
163	Callistus II		1119-1124
164	Honorius II		1124-1130
165	Innocent II		1130-1143
166	Celestine II		1143-1144
167	Lucius II		1144-1145
168	Eugene III		1145-1153
169	Anastasius IV		1153-1154
170	Adrian IV		1154-1159
171	Alexander III		1159-1181
172	Lucius III		1181-1185
173	Urban III		1185-1187
174	Gregory VIII		1187
175	Clement III		1187-1191
176	Celestine III		1191-1198
177	Innocent III		1198-1216
178	Honorius III		1216-1227
179	Gregory IX		1227-1241
180	Celestine IV	[Conclave 1]	1241
181	Innocent IV		1243-1254
182	Alexander IV	[Conclave 2]	1254-1261
183	Urban IV		1261-1264
184	Clement IV		1265-1268
185	Gregory X	[Conclave 3]	1271-1276

Number	Name		A.D.
186	Innocent V	[Conclave 4]	1276
187	Adrian V	[Conclave 5]	1276
188	John XXI	[Conclave 6]	1276-1277
189	Nicholas III	[Conclave 7]	1277-1280
190	Martin IV	[Conclave 8]	1281-1285
191	Honorius IV	[Conclave 9]	1285-1287
192	Nicholas IV	[Conclave 10]	1288-1292
193	Celestine V	[Conclave 11]	1294
194	Boniface VIII	[Conclave 12]	1294-1303
195	Benedict XI	[Conclave 13]	1303-1304
196	Clement V	[Conclave 14]	1305-1314
197	John XXII	[Conclave 15]	1316-1334
198	Benedict XII	[Conclave 16]	1334-1342
199	Clement VI	[Conclave 17]	1342-1352
200	Innocent VI	[Conclave 18]	1352-1362
201	Urban V	[Conclave 19]	1362-1370
202	Gregory XI	[Conclave 20]	1370-1378
203	Urban VI	[Conclave 21]	1378-1389
204	Boniface IX	[Conclave 22]	1389-1404
205	Innocent VII	[Conclave 23]	1404-1406
206	Gregory XII	[Conclave 24]	1406-1415
207	Martin V	[Conclave 25]	1417-1431
208	Eugene IV	[Conclave 26]	1431-1447
209	Nicholas V	[Conclave 27]	1447-1455
210	Callistus III	[Conclave 28]	1455-1458
211	Pius II	[Conclave 29]	1458-1464
212	Paul II	[Conclave 30]	1464-1471
213	Sixtus IV	[Conclave 31]	1471-1484
214	Innocent VIII	[Conclave 32]	1484-1492
215	Alexander VI	[Conclave 33]	1492-1503
216	Pius III	[Conclave 34]	1503
217	Julius II	[Conclave 35]	1503-1513
218	Leo X	[Conclave 36]	1513-1521

Number	Name		A.D.
219	Adrian VI	[Conclave 37]	1522-1523
220	Clement VII	[Conclave 38]	1523-1534
221	Paul III	[Conclave 39]	1534-1549
222	Julius III	[Conclave 40]	1550-1555
223	Marcellus II	[Conclave 41]	1555
224	Paul IV	[Conclave 42]	1555-1559
225	Pius IV	[Conclave 43]	1559-1565
226	Pius V	[Conclave 44]	1566-1572
227	Gregory XIII	[Conclave 45]	1572-1585
228	Sixtus V	[Conclave 46]	1585-1590
229	Urban VII	[Conclave 47]	1590
230	Gregory XIV	[Conclave 48]	1590-1591
231	Innocent IX	[Conclave 49]	1591
232	Clement VIII	[Conclave 50]	1592-1605
233	Leo XI	[Conclave 51]	1605
234	Paul V	[Conclave 52]	1605-1621
235	Gregory XV	[Gregory 53]	1621-1623
236	Urban VIII	[Conclave 54]	1623-1644
237	Innocent X	[Conclave 55]	1644-1655
238	Alexander VII	[Conclave 56]	1655-1667
239	Clement IX	[Conclave 57]	1667-1669
240	Clement X	[Conclave 58]	1670-1676
241	Innocent XI	[Conclave 59]	1676-1689
242	Alexander VIII	[Conclave 60]	1689-1691
243	Innocent XII	[Conclave 61]	1691-1700
244	Clement XI	[Conclave 62]	1700-1721
245	Innocent XIII	[Conclave 63]	1721-1724
246	Benedict XIII	[Conclave 64]	1724-1730
247	Clement XII	[Conclave 65]	1730-1740
248	Benedict XIV	[Conclave 66]	1740-1758
249	Clement XIII	[Conclave 67]	1758-1769
250	Clement XIV	[Conclave 68]	1769-1774
251	Pius VI	[Conclave 69]	1775-1799

Number	Name		A.D.
252	Pius VII	[Conclave 70]	1800-1823
253	Leo XII	[Conclave 71]	1823-1829
254	Pius VIII	[Conclave 72]	1829-1830
255	Gregory XVI	[Conclave 73]	1831-1846
256	Pius IX	[Conclave 74]	1846-1878
257	Leo XIII	[Conclave 75]	1878-1903
258	Pius X	[Conclave 76]	1903-1914
259	Benedict XV	[Conclave 77]	1914-1922
260	Pius XI	[Conclave 78]	1922-1939
261	Pius XII	[Conclave 79]	1939-1958
262	John XXIII	[Conclave 80]	1958-1963
263	Paul VI	[Conclave 81]	1963-1978
264	John Paul I	[Conclave 82]	1978
265	John Paul II	[Conclave 83]	1978-